OUR SACRED LAND

Voices of the Palestine–Israeli Conflict

RELATED TITLES

The Palestine–Israeli Conflict: A Beginner's Guide, Dan Cohn-Sherbok
and Dawoud El-Alami, ISBN 1-85168-332-1

OUR SACRED LAND

Voices of the Palestine–Israeli Conflict

Kenizé Mourad

ONEWORLD

OXFORD

OUR SACRED LAND

Oneworld Publications
(Sales and editorial)
185 Banbury Road
Oxford OX2 7AR
England
www.oneworld-publications.com

Originally published in French as
Le Parfum de Notre Terre: Voix de Palestine et d'Israël
© Editions Robert Laffont, S. A., Paris, 2003
English translation © Oneworld Publications 2004

Translated by Catherine Spencer

ISBN 1–85168–357–7

Typeset by Jayvee, India
Cover design by Mungo Designs
Hebron doves © J. D. Perkins
Landscape © Esaias (Shayke) Baitel / Israelimages
Printed and bound in India by Thomson Press Ltd

I have striven not to laugh at human actions, nor to hate them, but to understand them.

SPINOZA

CONTENTS

ACKNOWLEDGEMENTS

Other than the people whom I have acknowledged in the book, I would like to thank, for their information and assistance, my Israeli friends Amnon Kapeliouk, Avraham Havilio, Uri Davis, Naomi Weiner and my Palestinian friends Amina Hamchari, Camille and Sylvie Mansour, Yacub Odeh, Vera Tamari, Diala Husseini, Ghassan Abdallah, Issam, Leila, Samira, Etedel, as well as Farouk Mardam bey, Dominique Vidal and Benjamin Barthe.

My special thanks to the ex-consul-general of France in Jerusalem, Denis Pietton, for his incisive analysis as well as the marvellous hospitality that he and his wife Marla extended to me. Thanks are also due to all the members of the consulate for their kindness.

In Spain, I would like to thank my publishers Mario Muchnik and his wife Nicole for their support and valuable advice, as well as my brother Jean Roch, and Marie-Louise Naville for their hospitality in their sunny home.

In France, I thank my friends Jacques Blot, Janine Euvrard, Malika Berak, Rana Kabani and Ken Takasé for their encouragement and, for the welcome they gave me to their quiet havens, Jean-Michel and Frédérique Guéneau and Claude and Lisa Broussy.

All my thanks, also, to Thierry Bleuze for his frequent help in my computer struggles and to Colette Ledanois, who was always ready to decipher and type my scribbled texts.

Finally, acknowledgements are due to Sylvie Delassus of Éditions Robert Laffont, who reread my manuscript with much patience and skill.

INTRODUCTION

Although I have been a journalist specialising in the Middle East, particularly the Israeli–Palestinian conflict, for over 15 years, I decided long ago not to write a book on the subject. It is almost impossible to deal with an issue on which passions run so high without accusations of anti-Semitism from some quarters and anti-Arab racism from others.

Recent events in the region demand that this silence be broken. Great human tragedies concern everyone and this is also a struggle for justice and for rights: the right of the Israelis to live in peace and the right of the Palestinian people not only to exist but also to live in their country, at a time when Israeli leaders talk of forced exile.[1]

Shutting our eyes and remaining tightly enclosed in our own selfish viewpoint entails the risk of terrible consequences. The Palestinian situation is a time bomb, yet we allow it to grow ever more inflammatory. Not only the Middle East but the whole western world – accused of bias and hypocrisy – is in danger of exploding.

We are on the brink of a wave of unprecedented terrorism that no one and nothing will be able to stop, unless we act now. Whatever we are told, terrorism will never be contained by police or military action: the only solution is to address its causes. Distancing ourselves from acts of terrorism by calling them acts of madness or fanaticism is not an option. Many Israelis understand that the more Palestinians are killed by Sharon's soldiers, the more suicide bombers are created.

I wanted to avoid political analysis and interviews with the powers that be. I went into the region to give voices to 'ordinary people': men, women, children, Palestinians, Israelis. In setting down their stories and those of their parents, some of whom had survived the concentration camps and others who had been forcibly ejected from their villages in Palestine and taken in by refugee camps, I wanted to understand their needs, their concerns and their sense of the present situation.

I wanted to understand the narrowing of Israeli popular opinion. Israelis supported the Rabin–Arafat agreement, with its goal of peaceful coexistence, but have now embraced the Sharon-led extremists who reject the idea of an independent Palestinian state. The Israeli people have been persuaded that Palestinians want an end to the Israeli state. They live in the irrational terror of reliving the nightmare of the Holocaust – when in reality they possess one of the most powerful armies in the world and face an onslaught of nothing more than stones, a few rifles and the tragic human bombs.

I wanted to understand the bitterness and fear of the Palestinians, who are convinced that the Israeli government lied to them, never had any intention of giving them their own country and is simply waiting for an opportunity to destroy them so that it can finally realise its dream of a 'Greater Israel'. I wanted to understand their revolt in the face of the proliferation of new colonies and the misery of a population forced into poverty by a system of expropriation, curfews and checkpoints. I wanted to understand the despair that leads to extremism.

During my time there, I was filled with the sense that every encounter was weighed down by a terrible misunderstanding. Manipulated by extremists at either end, most of the people whom I interviewed were convinced that the other side wanted to annihilate them.

To understand what is going on, one has to have waited for hours behind a checkpoint, in the scorching heat, amid lorries of rotting vegetables and stalled ambulances, listening to mothers pleading with implacable, sometimes mocking, soldiers to let their sick child through; one has to have seen the father turning away to weep for his eight year old son, killed while running after an escaped chicken; or the little boy paralysed in a hospital bed, explaining that he was on his way back from school when three soldiers 'shot him for fun'. One has to have seen Orit, a young Israeli woman whose sister was killed in a suicide bombing, bravely holding back her tears and repeating implacably: 'You don't understand. They don't want peace; they want to destroy us'. Palestinians such as Samira, Etedel and Leila all said exactly the same.

I met also a minority on both sides who do not want peace, or who want it at the price of the other side's total defeat: the Israeli groups for whom the West Bank should be part of Israel, because it was given to them by Yahveh and the Palestinian groups who want all the refugees to return home – to areas that for the most part are what now constitutes Israel – which would upset the demographic balance of the country and its rationale as the 'Zionist' state, created for Jews.

Equally, I met people on both sides who are actively militating for peace. Most Palestinians realise that, given the balance of power, compromise is the only realistic choice. Above all, they refuse to equate extremist Israeli governments with a people with whom they feel they could live peaceably.

On the Israeli side, I particularly wanted to give a voice to a minority from which one rarely hears, yet which represents hope for the Middle East: those few men and women who, in the face of everything, continue to fight for the rights of the Palestinians. They do so to enable not only a victimised people, but also their own country, to survive since they know that the policies of Sharon and his ilk are, ultimately, suicidal. They are also fighting, with a rare moral courage, for universal human rights. Indeed, in their own words, they are fighting to be different from those who have persecuted them over the centuries.

In this conflict, victory will be won only if each side agrees to certain compromises. Violence and war are futile. Those who achieve their objectives through such means do not maintain the upper hand for long. This land is too deeply anchored in people's hearts for a military solution to be anything more than ephemeral. Each new generation will take up the struggle, and ever more ruthlessly. As the killings and the suffering accumulate, the hatred grows deeper. Solutions have been proposed but we need the willingness to implement them and, above all, the generosity and the courage to make them work.

Note: I have changed the names of most Palestinian people and places, to protect those who agreed to tell their story. I sometimes did so even when people told me that it was not necessary because their life was so unbearable that they no longer cared if they lived or died.

1

◆

Daily Life

A HOUSE DESTROYED
THREE TIMES

I arrived in Jerusalem one evening in May 2002. From the balcony of my room I had a view of the old city, bathed in golden twilight. Behind the high crenellated walls, dating from the Ottoman period, I could glimpse the roofs of churches and large mosques, next to which fluttered the blue and white Israeli flag, stamped with the Star of David.

In the flaming sky, great flocks of skylarks darted and weaved in the dying light while the muezzin's call to prayer reverberated in the distance. Then, everything fell silent and, as the heady scent of jasmine began drifting across from the surrounding greenery, I felt cradled in the atmosphere of serenity and began idly to dream of the eternal Jerusalem, the city of peace, forgetting for a moment the fratricidal war that has raged here for centuries.

The following morning I have a meeting with Salim Shawamreh in east Jerusalem, on the lush, bougainvillaea-bedecked terrace of the American Colony. This ancient Palestinian complex, with its magnificent verandas and high windows with pointed arches, was taken over by an American community at the end of the 19th century and turned into a hotel over 50 years ago.

I know nothing about Salim other than that he is a member of an organisation that militates against the destruction of Palestinian houses, his own house having been destroyed three times. He arrives – a small, stocky man, his black, tightly curled hair framing a smiling face – apologising profusely for his lateness.

"I live in Kufr Aqab," he explains, "a suburb of Jerusalem separated from the city by a military checkpoint. You often have to wait two or three hours to get through and sometimes, like today, it is completely closed. I had to drive across the hills, on small roads."

"Why was it closed?"

"They're frightened that something will happen; a child was killed this morning in Ramallah[1] during the curfew. Children have been killed every day for two years. The worst thing is that it has almost become normal ..."

Salim's parents were farmers from Oum Shawaf, a village that they had to flee in 1948 when it was bombed by the army of the *Haganah*, a Jewish paramilitary organisation, created in Palestine in 1920, that became the Israeli army in 1948.

"My family managed to take a little money and some jewellery with them and came to live in old Jerusalem, where I was born. I remember a quiet town, where everyone in the area knew each other: we played in the street and every Friday we went to the al-Aqsa mosque. My father owned a café; we lived well. But in 1967, when the Israeli army occupied East Jerusalem, our café was confiscated and we became refugees again. We were five brothers and five sisters; I was 11 years old.

"Like thousands of others, we had to escape – soldiers were threatening to destroy the houses on top of us. We went to the camp at Shufat, where there were hundreds of other families who had had to leave. We were given two small rooms, in which we lived for years. My mother cried a lot ... You know, the dream of Palestinians who have lost everything and who live in the miserable conditions of these camps is one day to have a house and a decent life. We work, we put aside the tiniest sums so that we can save the necessary money and when we finally manage to build our house ... the Israelis destroy it!"

"But why?"

"Supposedly because we don't have a permit. But they never give permits! I'll tell you my story – although it's only one of thousands ...

"Despite all the hardships, I spent my youth studying because I knew it was the only way out. In 1977, I got my qualification in construction engineering. After marrying a Palestinian cousin, also a refugee, I went to work in Saudi Arabia. Ten years later I came back with my wife and three children. I had money and I wanted a house for my family. I bought a piece of land in the village of Anata, three kilometres from the old city of Jerusalem.

1. Ramallah, 15 kilometres from Jerusalem, became one of the two Palestinian administrative centres (the other is in Gaza) after the return of the Palestinian Authority nine years ago. Situated at an altitude of 900m, it is a large town with a pleasant climate, attractive villas, blocks of flats and modern buildings that house the various ministries, including the Mouqata'a, where Arafat has his office.

"I first applied for a building permit in 1990 and paid $5000 to the Israeli civil administration[2] to register my application. Eighteen months later they rejected it, saying that my land was outside the building plan for the village. In fact, there is no land register for our villages, since there was none under the Ottomans but the Israeli government uses this so-called land registry as a pretext to prevent us from building. They have simply drawn boundaries around the outlying houses in the villages, so that there is no permissible building zone. When people build houses, the authorities destroy them, saying that they have to do so because the houses were built without permits. In the eyes of the world, they are acting legally but in fact they are making life impossible for us, to force us to leave the country.

"As soon as I got their decision, I went to the civil administration and said, 'I'm going to build. I have to house my family. You can come and knock it down if you want'. They replied, 'OK, we'll give you a permit but because the land is outside the village, make an application as if it were for agricultural land and you were building a farm'.

"Once again I paid $5000 and waited 18 months. At which point they told me that they couldn't give me a permit because the land was on too much of an incline. I said, 'No problem, I'll flatten it with a bulldozer!' They refused – when the whole of Jerusalem is built on the side of hills! They told me to apply again.

"And so once again I paid $5000. And once again they turned me down, saying that the house would be too close to an Israeli road. They were obviously just coming up with pretexts for not giving me a permit. I had made three applications, waited four years, and spent $15000 and all for nothing! Fifteen thousand dollars – how on earth can a Palestinian who earns $500 a month pay that kind of money just for a permit?

"My savings were disappearing and my family was getting bigger; I couldn't live in one room any more. And so in 1994 I decided to risk building a house. All Palestinians take this risk. We need to live somewhere. You say to yourself: maybe I'll be lucky, they can't control everything, thousands of houses are built without permits. Maybe they won't come for a year or two and maybe there'll be peace by then ... It was just after the Oslo agreement and I thought, maybe everything will be all right now, they won't be so strict, they won't knock everything down. How naïve I was!

---

2. The civil administration is in fact a military administration that issues permits regulating the residence and movement of Palestinians inside the occupied territories.

"We lived in our house for four years. They were good years! The children were happy: for the first time they had a place to study and to play. We even created a garden, which we planted with flowers and fruit trees – oranges, lemons, figs, olives. It was all possible because of my ten years of working in Saudi Arabia. We enjoyed it to the full.

"Until the 9th July 1998, the worst day of my life ... I was having dinner with my family when I heard a noise. I went out and saw dozens of soldiers surrounding the house. An officer in plain clothes asked me if it was my house. I said it was. 'Well, it isn't your house any more. You've got 15 minutes to get your belongings out.'

"I protested and they started beating me. Then they handcuffed me and threw me to the ground. My wife panicked and locked herself in the house with our six children, then called friends for help. The soldiers broke a window and threw in tear gas; then they broke down the door to bring out my wife, who had fainted, and my children, who were screaming in terror. They kept me down on the ground – I could see everything happening but could do nothing.

"Neighbours came running to help. The soldiers opened fire. Seven people were wounded and a fifteen-year-old boy lost a kidney. Israelis from the anti-demolition group came to the rescue and tried to stand in front of the bulldozer but they were also arrested and beaten.

"After having destroyed everything, even the trees, the army left, giving us a bill for $1500 to pay for the demolition of our house ...

"The next day, the Red Cross brought us a tent in which we lived with our six children, next to the ruins of the house. We felt numb, as though we were anaesthetised. The children cried all the time.

"The Israeli Committee against House Demolition came to see us and encouraged us to fight back. They said that they would help us rebuild, in the same place. They persuaded me and together we began rebuilding. We finished the external structure of the house on the 2nd August 1998; only the walls and the roof were in place and it wasn't yet habitable. But we were happy. We even held a little celebration.

"A week later, on the 10th August, at four o'clock in the morning, we woke up to machine guns pointing at us. The place was surrounded by soldiers and again a bulldozer was advancing on the house to knock it down. Our Israeli friends arrived. An American teacher tried to chain himself to a balcony but they threw him off. He had three broken ribs. They pulled up the rest of the trees and even took our tent, on the pretext that I had not applied for a permit to live in a tent ... "

"You're joking?"

"I don't have the heart to joke about it. They left us, my wife and six children, in the dust and the rubble, with nothing. That night, Jeff Halper, the co-ordinator of the organisation, who has since become a friend, stayed with us, as well as two other members of the NGO.

"It was too much for my wife. She went into a deep depression. She stopped talking and didn't seem to hear anything. I sent her with the little ones to stay with her family in Jordan. She had to go into hospital for several months and she still isn't completely well. For a long time the children were frightened to go from their bedroom to the bathroom at night and they would wet the bed. They couldn't concentrate at school."

As we talked, we could hear the sound of military helicopters passing overhead.

"On their way to Ramallah", Salim said, sombrely.

All conversation on the terrace of the American Colony had stopped.

"That second demolition caused a scandal", Salim continued. "Thanks to Jeff, the newspapers covered the story. The office of the civil administration wrote to the newspaper saying that the ownership of the land was in question and that two signatures were missing. They had never raised that as an issue before.

"For three months, our lawyer tried to find out the identity of the missing signatories but they could get no response. As Anata is a small village, I asked everyone to sign a document declaring that they had not objected to my ownership of the land or to my building on it. I took the 300 signatures to the lawyer.

"The authorities said that they did not recognise those names and refused to consider the petition. It was obvious that they were just playing games and that there was nothing more to be had from them.

"For the third time, Jeff Halper convinced me to rebuild. Hundreds of volunteers – Israelis, Palestinians and foreigners – helped. We finished on the 9th July 1999. We had completed only the outer shell: we weren't living there. Nobody came. After several months I started to paint, to do up the inside and the wiring. I finished on the 3rd April 2001. We lived there for one night. On the 4th April, at eight o'clock in the morning, the bulldozers came and destroyed our house for the third time ...

"The children were at school. When they got home, at first they didn't understand what had happened and started looking for the house. But when they realised that it had been knocked down again, their expressions were indescribable. The six year old went into convulsions. You know, it's even worse for children. The house is their security, their nest. If their nest is destroyed, they think their life is in danger.

"Last April, my eleven-year-old daughter saw helicopters dropping rockets onto the headquarters of the Palestinian police in Ramallah. In her terror, she lost the use of her legs and fell. She also got violent stomach cramps. I tried to reassure her, telling her that Daddy was there to protect her. She looked at me: 'How can you protect me? I saw the soldiers holding you down on the ground while they knocked down our house'."

He hides his head in his hands. "That destroyed me ... my children think their father can do nothing for them."

I try to change the subject.

"How do you earn your living?"

"I can't get work here as an engineer. I am a driver for a newspaper. But it isn't enough: my sixteen-year-old son had to leave school to help us. He works as a labourer and gives us all his wages. The rent of our house at Kufr Aqab is paid by the Israeli Committee against House Demolition."

"What do you intend to do now?"

"Continue to fight. Two months ago we started to rebuild. Two hundred volunteers came to help us. Soon we are going to put the roof on the new building."

Salim looks at me intently. "Anyone in this world who has his land occupied and does not fight back is an animal! We will continue to fight back, even if over the past 35 years the situation has just got worse. The other day, the soldiers picked up a man trying to get through the Qalandiya checkpoint to go to work. They blindfolded him and kept him tied to the barricade for hours. The man was thirsty and asked for a drink. I saw a soldier urinate into a bottle and say, 'Open your mouth'. The man began drinking but when he realised what he was drinking, he started throwing up and writhing on the ground with humiliation. The soldiers roared with laughter and then took him away. That is what goes on under the occupation. The international community knows about it and does nothing."[3]

---

3. This sort of incident happens every day. Israeli soldiers seem to enjoy total impunity: 'In Naplouse, under curfew for months, a 25-year-old man who went out to get food was arrested and forced at gunpoint to strip and cross the town on all fours, barking.' (Reported by Reuters.) 'In a new lottery game at the Hebron checkpoint, the soldiers make young men waiting to get through draw a piece of paper on which is written the part of their body that will be broken: an arm, a leg, a hand ... sometimes the men are given the choice. In December a 22-year-old man drew the forfeit of being hit on the head. He subsequently died of his injuries.' (Reported by al-Jazeera.)

JEFF HALPER

After my encounter with Salim Shawamreh, I wanted to meet his friend Jeff Halper. We fix a rendezvous outside the big post office in Jaffa Street, in the centre of Jerusalem's shopping district.

This Friday afternoon, everyone is buying for Shabbat. Outside the covered market and the department stores, green-uniformed police check bags. The passing buses are almost empty; since the bombings, people prefer to walk or, if they have the means, take a taxi. Behind some boarding, Israeli Arab labourers work on a construction site.[1] They look at no one and no one looks at them.

A motley crowd throngs the street. Young female soldiers in khaki uniform, with the matt complexion of easterners; slender gazelle-eyed Ethiopian girls from the Jewish tribe of 'Falashas'; pale women wearing hats; other women in jeans, their navels exposed; many young men in the *kippa*; an orthodox priest in a dusty black robe, his hair dishevelled; young Filipinos, immigrant workers who have for some years replaced 'Arabs'; and finally, standing out in the crowd, a Palestinian woman waiting for a bus, her hair covered with a white *hijab*,[2] her expression closed against the surrounding world.

A small man wearing shorts comes up to me. "I'm Jeff," he says, with a firm handshake. His large face, adorned with a grey beard, is open and lively.

We have a great deal of trouble finding a quiet café in this area, where bars and restaurants attract customers with the latest pop songs. We finally pick a spot near a building site, a place of relative calm.

Jeff Halper is the co-ordinator of the Israeli Committee against House Demolition. Nine thousand houses have been torn down in the occupied territories since 1967 and 2000 since the beginning of this intifada.[3]

"House demolition is part of a policy designed to confine Palestinians to small islands in the West Bank, Gaza and east Jerusalem,

---

1. There are a million Arabs with Israeli nationality in Israel, descendants of the Palestinians who stayed behind in 1948 and 200,000 Palestinians under Israeli authority in Jerusalem.
2. A scarf covering the hair, worn by traditional Muslim women.
3. Intifada: literally 'shaking off', usually used to mean 'uprising'.

in order to keep as much land as possible free of people", he explains.
"This has been the policy of every Israeli government since 1967:
they have all, whether of the left or the right, continued to expand the
settlements."

Jeff began campaigning on the issue seven years ago.

"After the Oslo agreement between Rabin and Arafat, the peace
movement died down. With the election of Netanyahu,[4] we woke up
and realised that while our movement supported the Palestinians, we
had made the big mistake of never having gone into the territories to
meet them or ask how we could help. In fact, the movement had for
years reflected Israeli society in the sense that we were sure we had all
the answers. We decided the agenda instead of listening to the
Palestinians.

"Perhaps because of my training as an anthropologist, I wanted
to use another method and we are now trying to establish a relationship
of partners. We have to watch ourselves because even though we
are men of peace, we often tend in meetings to act like overlords –
talking loudly, sure of ourselves. We ourselves have nothing to fear;
we think only of taking action. It's easy for us – we're not going to return
home to find our house destroyed! The Palestinians do not always tell
us everything because they're frightened that we might respond in ways
that will cause them trouble. Developing trust is therefore essential.

"The Palestinians tell us that their worst problem, the one that
affects the most people, is the demolition of their houses and the confiscation of their land and so that is where we should concentrate our
efforts. Since 1967, the Israeli authorities have demolished houses and
expropriated land for all sorts of reasons: security, to give land to the
army or because there is no permit. They use an ancient plan drawn up
under the British administration that categorised the West Bank as
agricultural land to prevent construction.[5] Curiously, that does not
seem to apply to buildings in the Israeli settlements!

"In reality, it's a form of 'soft' transfer, which has the appearance of
legality. When the Palestinians have no more houses or land left, where
can they go? Sharon has made no secret of his policy: when he came to
power, he declared; 'We need to build more and more settlements so

---

4. Benyamin Netanyahu, the Likud (Conservative party) candidate, was Israeli Prime
   Minister from May 1996 to May 1999; he was replaced by the Labour candidate, Ehud
   Barak.
5. The British ruled Palestine, previously part of the Ottoman empire, from 1922 to 1948,
   when the state of Israel was created.

that it will be impossible to give the territories back to Palestinian people'. Benny Allon, a minister in the present government, has said 'We must make their life so difficult that they will leave of their own accord'.

"We are trying, in opposition to that policy, to help Palestinians. They ask us, 'Can you get us a building licence? Can you prevent demolition by getting a lawyer involved? Will you be there to obstruct the bulldozer when it arrives? Can you help rehouse us or find money to rebuild?'"

Jeff is interrupted by his mobile phone. He talks for a long time, seeming agitated. When he hangs up, he says: "Sorry, I've got to go. I've just been told that 34 houses were destroyed this morning in a village near Ramallah; new houses, built for workers' families, that had never been lived in! You can imagine the despair of people who, after years of waiting, were finally going to get decent housing and no longer be squeezed into 15 square metres ... Last week, six houses were destroyed – and they didn't belong to families suspected of terrorism, as the Israelis always try to make out. It is a systematic policy, which we have to fight in practical ways. The Palestinians need our help, not our sympathy".

I return to old Jerusalem by the Damascus Gate. Beneath the high walls, built by Sultan Suleiman the Magnificent, is the daily 'Arab market', where peasant farmers from the surrounding areas come to sell their fruit and vegetables and where itinerant sellers tout drinks, postcards and every kind of trinket.

Soldiers, rifle on shoulder, walk around making various purchases, while green police jeeps, covered with wire netting, drive past, blasting their horns. On the grass verges, women sit picnicking in small, animated groups while men take a siesta in the background. The atmosphere is relaxed, easygoing.

Coming into the old city I pass crowds of holidaymakers, who have come for the feast of Sukkoth:[6] women wearing hats or wigs,[7] pushing heavy prams over the bumpy paving; young men wearing the *kippa*, their white fringes of the *tallith* – symbols of their religious vows – drumming against their thighs; orthodox Hassidim in black tunics and baggy trousers wearing, despite the September heat, enormous fur

6. Sukkoth is a week-long religious festival during which Jews are required to live very simply, in remembrance of their ancestors who spent 40 years in the desert before reaching the Promised Land.
7. Married Jewish women are not allowed to show their hair.

hats. Returning from their prayers at the Wailing Wall, some of them venture into the Christian quarter, patrolled by the police.

Several stalls are open: behind them, men sit on low stools, playing backgammon. Since the beginning of the intifada, business has been very poor, which seems to have given a certain incentive to greater ecumenism – ideological differences are no reason to turn away customers! In every shop one finds an assorted collection of seven-branched candlesticks, alongside statues of the Virgin, icons, wooden rosaries and Stars of David on top of a little statue of Jesus, embroidered Palestinian robes and kippas of every colour alongside T-shirts printed with 'Don't worry, be Jewish!' in golden letters.

A welcome cool descends on the narrow, twisting alleyways, under the magnificent stone arches. Children play with a ball or race their bicycles; they have the street to themselves. The multitudes of tourists who, until as recently as two years ago, thronged one of the most beautiful cities of the world, have disappeared.

I cross the Jewish quarter, deserted during this holiday period, through the streets of perfectly restored and meticulously maintained buildings, the golden stone façades lit by the soft light of wrought iron lamps. It has the air of a beautiful theatre set.

Further on, the Arab quarter provides a striking contrast. No more pretty tourist shops; we are once again in the Orient, with its crowds, noise, colours, spicy odours, piles of fruit and mouthwatering pyramids of sweetmeats. We stroll through the traditional bazaar, where the Arabs of Jerusalem do their shopping and buy their food, household goods and clothes – all the everyday items – but also beautiful copper and tin vessels, carpets and jewellery. Women in long black robes with coloured embroidery, their heads covered with light veils of white cotton, crowd round the stalls, examining the merchandise and discussing the prices but, most importantly, swapping the latest news. The Jerusalem market-place is, like every Middle Eastern bazaar, the greatest sounding board in the city.

Seeing me hesitate, a young man offers himself as guide. He leads me through a maze of alleyways to a narrow street lined with shops, its entire length covered by wire mesh.

"It's to stop the Jews who live above dropping their rubbish on to us", he explains.

I look doubtful and he explains that the overhanging houses were gradually taken over by militant Zionists – often recently arrived immigrants – from the previous Palestinian occupants. The new inhabitants tried to extend their territory by every means possible.

A shopkeeper, seated in front of his fabric shop, intervenes: "Ten years ago, this area was completely Arab but day after day the Jews nibble away at us, to get us out so that they can take over Jerusalem. They draw up false documents to prove that such and such a house belonged to Jews. It's easy – they've got money, the police and even the law on their side! Come, I'll show you the area above, which they've completely taken over".

Climbing a spiral staircase, we go up to a delightful little square, set out with lawns and surrounded by restored stone houses behind wrought iron railings. The blue and white Star of David flag flies at every window. The names of the inhabitants are marked on the doorplates: Pamela Nash, John Irving, Michael Ford ... The final result is successful, if a little overdone; no expense has been spared in the restoration.

"Most of these houses belonged to Palestinians who left in 1967 and then rented them to other Palestinians", explains my guide. "Now they are inhabited by immigrants, principally Americans."

He nods his head at the young men in black robes and side curls and the young women pushing prams, who pass by without seeming to see us.

"The most fanatical Jews come to live here, in the heart of the Arab quarter. They know nothing about this country but they are convinced of their right to the whole of Jerusalem and to all of Palestine. They use every method they can think of, however trivial, to get us out. They are trying to get me to leave my shop, for example. I'll show you how!"

He leads me over to a flourishing flowerbed in the middle of the square.

"They water it heavily every day and the water leaks into my shop just below. I have asked them several times to let me fix it, if they don't want to do it themselves, but they refuse. I tell them that my merchandise is being ruined. They couldn't care less, because their policy is to get us to leave!"

Opposite the Jewish quarter, separated only by a high gate and a rubbish-filled ditch, stand greying, dilapidated Palestinian houses, several of which look like they are on the verge of collapse. Two worlds face each other, 50 metres apart; two worlds that are entirely ignorant of each other.

"Why is all this rubbish here?" I ask, pointing to the ditch bordering the Palestinian houses.

"The Jews throw their rubbish there and the town council doesn't pick it up. It's the same throughout the old Arab quarter, as well as in all the Arab villages in Israel. We pay the same local taxes but while dust-men collect from the Jewish areas every day, they come to us at most once a week."

We climb back down to the old city and I take leave of my compan-ions, rejoining the route to the Damascus Gate, through side streets strewn with litter and broken objects. Men in galabiehs, the traditional long cotton robe, smoke hookahs in front of their stalls, while loud-speakers play songs by Fairuz[8] and young men wearing T-shirts bearing the images of Marwan Barghouti[9] or Che Guevera walk arm in arm.

In just a few minutes, I have passed from one continent to another ...

8. Fairuz is, after Oum Koulsoum, the most famous singer in the Arab world.
9. Palestinian political activist, one of the principal actors of the intifada, imprisoned by the Israelis.

A DIFFICULT MARRIAGE

Christine Koury is a young Palestinian woman who was born in Jerusalem, where her Catholic family has always lived. Two years ago she married a Palestinian from Ramallah. She told me the ensuing saga.

"Since our marriage, the application for my husband's blue card has been held up because the Israelis have blocked all permits since the intifada.[1] That means that my husband does not have the right to set foot inside Jerusalem, even though he has never had any political involvement. For five years he was chief accountant for an American NGO and is now director of an NGO in Ramallah. Three months after applying for residency in Jerusalem, I was summoned by Israeli intelligence in the military colony of Bet El, to provide information about him. I was eight months pregnant and they left me waiting outside, in front of a gate, for five and a half hours; I was freezing to death. In the end, I never saw anyone!

"When you marry a Palestinian from the occupied territories, you risk losing your blue card because the Israeli authorities think that you should no longer live in Jerusalem. And so you no longer have the right to social security, to a pension, to health insurance, to anything. The Israelis do everything they can to get Palestinians to leave Jerusalem.

"At first I didn't notify the authorities of my marriage for fear of losing my card. But in the end I had to because the Israelis wouldn't accept that I was a single mother. It's acceptable for Israelis but not for Arabs. They say: 'It doesn't happen.'"

"So where did you live?"

"Just after we were married I naturally went to stay with my husband in Ramallah, which is only 15 kilometres from my work. But driving can take four or five hours because of the checkpoints, so people mostly get around in shared taxis and on foot – even then, the 15 kilometres takes at least two hours. I had to leave home at a quarter to seven to be at the office for nine o'clock. And then going from Ramallah to Jerusalem every day while I was pregnant was risky. The soldiers can shoot at any

---

1. Only Palestinians who hold the blue card that proves that they are residents of Jerusalem have the right to enter the town. There are around 200,000 such residents.

moment or let off toxic gas at the checkpoints if people get impatient. Many pregnant women have had miscarriages because of that.

"But it was the first occupation of Ramallah, from the 12th to the 18th March 2002, that decided me. We were under a total curfew and snipers were on the roofs, shooting at anyone who risked going out. Because our building had been taken over by the Israeli army, we were forbidden even to leave the apartment. I was in the last stages of pregnancy and I was very frightened of being imprisoned there and not being able to get to hospital to give birth. To avoid that, I left for Jerusalem in the middle of the ninth month. Too many women have lost their baby during a siege. Husbands try to deliver the baby with a doctor helping on the end of a phone – but what can they do if there is the slightest complication? Women lose their babies trying to get between the village and the town. The barricades around the villages near the colonies are very tight, particularly those established by Israeli settlers, who are usually deaf to all pleas.

"In Jerusalem, I had to give birth in a private clinic. When I tried to book into a hospital in Jerusalem, they refused. I queued at the social security office for three days, where thousands of people were standing waiting outside. In the end, they said they could not take me in for the delivery because my husband was from the occupied territories. Even though I had been paying social security contributions for 12 years, I was forced to pay all the costs myself! I was lucky enough to have the necessary money, but what about those who don't?"

"Could you not have given birth in Ramallah?"

"Of course not! My child would not have had right of residence in Jerusalem and I would not have been able to keep him with me. I would have had either to part with my new-born baby or lose my work, with all my rights to insurance and a pension. I would no longer have had the right to visit Jerusalem, the city where I was born and where all my family live.

"My husband was absolutely determined to be with me for the birth but to get to Jerusalem he had to take a roundabout route, risking being shot at. When he got here, he had to stay inside the house for a week. If he had been stopped and asked for his papers, he would have been sent to prison.

"After the delivery you have to go to the Department of the Interior within ten days with the child, to register the birth, queuing up with hundreds of other people. But at that time Sharon had frozen for four years all measures relating to couples in which one of the partners was from the terri-tories. We were very worried: we could not declare our child, he had no identity documents and in the eyes of the law he did not exist. Luckily, at the end of May the government lifted the ban for new-born babies and my son finally got a birth certificate."

"During the curfew of April 2002, which lasted almost a month, you were in Ramallah with your baby. What was that like?"

"We lived in terror because our building was near a military camp and every night the tanks stopped very near us to shoot. The building next to us was hit. We prepared somewhere in the flat where we could shelter with the little one but it had no heating, electricity or water. Water is always a problem here. Even when things are normal, the Israelis cut off the water in all the territories two or three times a week. They need it for their lawns and swimming pools in the settlements! It's worse for my grandmother who lives at Beit Jala, near Bethlehem: she usually has a water supply just one day a week.

"During the curfew, they cut off the water every day. We saved some in the bath for the baby, but we had no way of heating it. They also cut off the electricity and it became very difficult to feed ourselves. We had set aside provisions for the curfew but when they cut off the electricity, everything in the freezer rotted and we had to throw it all out; after that, we had nothing left to eat. In our building there were 17 kids, aged from four to 12 years old. They were hungry. During the 25 days of the curfew, when no-one could go out, we shared everything out between us: bread, milk, flour. When I had no more milk for the baby, I had to appeal to the Red Cross who negotiated with the Israelis and managed to bring us what we needed in an ambulance."

"Where do you live now?"

"I split my time between Jerusalem and Ramallah. I realised that it was impossible, and above all too dangerous, to make the journey every day with the baby. So I rent a small apartment in Jerusalem and spend the three days of the weekend with my husband in Ramallah. But when I go back to Ramallah, I am always scared of being held up: if my baby gets sick, how will I get him to hospital? Moreover it's no life for my husband! He can make his own meals, but he needs to talk to someone. He has to stay shut up in the flat without seeing anyone, especially when the curfew is on and he can't get to work. Apart from which, it's dangerous: in April 2002, during the long curfew of Ramallah, soldiers arrested people in their own houses. To the Israelis, a young man alone in an apartment is probably a terrorist. They would have arrested him as a matter of course.

"Our child is very disturbed by the separation. When he sees his father, he throws himself at him. It's also difficult for me: we are a newly married couple and we celebrated our first wedding anniversary apart ... We didn't imagine our life together like this!"

She smiles with resignation.

"For eight years we wanted to be together but our families did not agree: his mother wanted to choose a wife for her son. It dragged on like that – and now we're finally married, we have to live apart! I am expecting a second child; I don't know how I'm going to go back and forth to Ramallah at the end of every week! It's already difficult enough walking through the checkpoint with a pushchair, bags and my son. Imagine what it will be like when I've got two!"

Her shoulders sink at the thought, but she quickly recovers herself.

"I hope that Sharon will lift the ban on permits and that we'll get authorisation for my husband to live in Jerusalem. If that happens, he will be the one to visit us here."

I stop myself from asking why, in such circumstances, she is expecting a second child ... After all, she is in her early thirties: if she wants children, now is the time. And then, like all Palestinians, she refuses to stop living because of the Israeli occupation. Refusing to be intimidated or disheartened is a form of passive resistance: to keep going, despite everything!

I admire her optimism, but then, in such difficult conditions, a certain lack of realism is perhaps the wisest attitude.

Christine continues: "At the moment the curfew is not as heavy and there aren't any snipers on the roof shooting at everything that moves. But the hard thing is that it's completely unpredictable: it changes from one hour to the next and we can't make any plans. What often happens is that they announce in the evening that the curfew will be lifted the following morning and then at the last minute they reimpose it. If people are outside during that time, soldiers arrest them or confiscate their car keys, or else break off the key inside the lock ... or they make them strip, beat them and force them to go home naked. Despite everything we are trying to lead a more or less normal life and see friends; we fight not to let ourselves be reduced to animals, content just to eat and sleep. The occupiers want to break our spirit and our hope, and they use every means of doing so. But we find all sorts of ways to resist.

"If, for example, the shops are closed because of the curfew, the small shopkeepers take their goods home and sell from there. We spread the word and the support network goes into operation. Later on, if there isn't a school, I will educate my son at home. Teaching groups have been set up in every building. That was already happening during the first intifada. Even if life is difficult, even if I am separated from my husband, we resist! Believe me, we Palestinians are strong. We will not give up!"

TO BE EIGHTEEN IN PALESTINE

It is Maha's eighteenth birthday today.

To celebrate the occasion, she has invited her friends, twenty or so young men and women, and has chosen her favourite music; they will dance until dawn. Her mother has spent the night baking cakes and has set out a magnificent spread, getting out the white damask tablecloth and the porcelain set that belonged to her grandparents.

Maha stares at the table with vacant eyes. Her friends will not be coming. This morning the radio announced that the Israeli army was imposing a curfew for an entire week. Why? No explanation was given. There have been no terrorist attacks for some time. Doubtless it is simply because the Jewish feast of Sukkoth is beginning and the Israelis feel more secure with the three and a half million Palestinians locked up at home. It is the same for every Jewish holiday.

"It doesn't matter", says Maha, with a shaky little smile, "we'll give the cakes to the children next door ..."

Having come to visit her parents for the day, I too risk being stuck for a week, unless I try to use my journalist's card to get out. This, however, they do not advise: "It's dangerous; sometimes the soldiers fire without warning".

I will therefore have plenty of time to get to know Maha, a tall, intriguing girl with delicate features and slanting eyes, beneath whose apparent softness I sense a core of steel.

"After all we went through to sit our matriculation exams, this is nothing!" she says, in response to my clumsy attempt to comfort her.

"Tell me how you managed to sit your exams when Ramallah was under curfew."

"It was a nightmare. From the end of March, everything was closed, night and day, with a few hours a week to run and buy provisions. There were tanks in every street and armed men on the roofs, shooting at anyone who set foot outside. Schools were closed of course – there were no teachers – and we had to get by as best we could ourselves. For the whole of May we were shut inside revising, but we didn't have the heart for it. We telephoned each other all day: 'X has been arrested, they've imprisoned Y, our friend Z has been beaten up by the soldiers and taken away, M has been wounded ...'. We were completely stressed. It was the first time that we had gone through something like that: every five minutes, something happened.

"Finally, on the 23rd April, the army withdrew but the tanks stayed outside the city. We could go back to school; we had eight days left to make up the whole of the month. Our first exams were at the beginning of June. I worked like crazy to make up the lost time. I think I got about two hours sleep a night. I felt like a zombie.

"When the exams began, the Israeli army was no longer in Ramallah. But in the middle of the exams, they started to take over the town again. We couldn't go out any more. They imposed or lifted the curfew whenever they fancied. We never knew what day or hour it would be lifted or whether we would be able to sit an exam. We had absolutely no idea what would happen; we would revise a whole book for an exam the next day, only to find out at the last minute that there was a curfew and everything had been cancelled. It was terribly stressful.

"On top of that, the orders were often contradictory. Orders given by the Israeli military headquarters were not always relayed to all the military posts. Sometimes the radio would announce that the curfew was lifted, people would go out and soldiers who had not yet received the order shot at them. Many people were killed like that. I had two friends who heard that the curfew had been lifted and who went out one morning to sit their exams. They were arrested by soldiers, who beat them up badly. They kept shouting, 'We're students! We're going to our exams!' The soldiers carried on beating them up. Finally they let them go. They went back home in a terrible state, completely traumatised. They had exams over the next few days; they failed everything.

"Once, before one of my last exams, the radio announced a curfew. So I didn't revise – I was completely exhausted and I just went to sleep. In the morning, the curfew was suddenly lifted. I woke up with a jolt, ran to school, unwashed and really panicking: if I didn't arrive in time I was going to waste the whole year. I remember it was a maths exam. I did it in a trance and went home in tears, convinced I'd failed.

"They sometimes announced a curfew in the middle of an exam. We finished the exam but then had to go home – we walked back through empty streets, really frightened. One time we saw jeeps coming at us and we rushed into a building; the people opened the door and took us in. We couldn't go home until the following morning. Luckily the phones were working and we could let our parents know."

"Despite all that you passed your exams, and with distinction!"

"Yes, I manage to keep calm. Last year, for example, I nearly died. I was in our apartment, studying, when I felt like going to get a Coke from the fridge. I kept on working for a bit: finally, I got up. I had just got into the kitchen when a bullet came through the window and embedded itself behind the desk where I had been studying, just where my head would have been. I was shaken up, of course, but I quickly got back to normal. I don't panic easily, maybe because I've been used to difficult situations since my childhood. We were exiled from Beirut to Tunisia and then came back here, where it was really hard at the outset. And then I'm lucky enough to have the example of my parents, who are very courageous people. They have been through the worst events in the history of Palestine. My mother is always laughing; she jokes about problems. My father is more reserved. He is a stoic; he never complains.

"On the other hand, a lot of my friends haven't been able to sleep for two years, because of the bombings and the gunfire from the nearby settlements. My neighbour, for example, who has always lived a quiet life in Ramallah, was so frightened that she slept in her parents' bed.

"I have another friend, a brilliant girl, who should have got a distinction in her matriculation exams. In May, soldiers broke into her house, destroyed everything and arrested her father, who is a doctor. She was completely traumatised, of course. She managed to sit the exams but she didn't get enough marks for a distinction, which means that she can't get a grant. It's very difficult for her to pay for university.

"But it was worst for the students who live in the villages. They were waiting for exam papers when the roads were closed. Teachers got the papers to them by foot or on donkeys over the mountains and brought their exam answers back in the same way, stuffed into bags carried by donkeys. But they were never sure that they would arrive at their destination!

"Then there were those people who live outside but are affiliated to the exam centre at Ramallah, like one of my friends who lives in Betunia. That's only a few kilometres from Ramallah but separated by a barricade. To sit the exams, she had to go round the barricade and walk across the mountains, which is very risky because sometimes the soldiers shoot without warning. She left home at four or five o'clock in the morning to be sure, or to try to be sure, that she would be on time. She risked her life to sit the exams, in a way ... Because studying, for us Palestinians, is really vital. It's the way to build not only our own future, but also the future of our country."

"Some people say that the Israelis deliberately reimposed the curfew during the matriculation exams."

"We all think that. They knew very well that tens of thousands of students were sitting those exams and they must have thought that we would never manage to do them in those conditions. They want to stop Palestinians from developing, like when they confiscate our land or demolish our houses. They want to make us into pathetic creatures, incapable of demanding our rights. Sitting our exams in spite of everything was an act of resistance for us."

"But how did you manage to concentrate on your studies in those conditions?"

"We had no choice. We're not going to shut ourselves away in fear. The occupation, bombings and arrests have gone on for two years – we have to get on with our lives. The other day I was coming back from school with a friend when we heard shots really close by: we carried on walking calmly as if nothing was happening. We have got tougher, and sometimes it's not good. At the beginning of the occupation, every time we heard someone had died it was a tragedy. Nowadays, it still causes large demonstrations but there are so many deaths that if we don't know the family it almost seems normal ... The other day, for example, a friend telephoned to say that she couldn't come the next day. She said there was a curfew because someone had died in Ramallah. I said, 'Oh, there's been a killing? Oh, so we won't be able to meet. Good night!'"

Maha looks at me, tears glistening in her eyes.

"When I realised how I had reacted, I felt like a monster, but we have to harden ourselves."

"Tell me what you'd like to do later."

"Everything is so uncertain here. We have hopes, lots of hopes, but we prefer not to dream too much. For the moment, my main desire is to be able to study. I've rented a room near the university at Bir Zeit. That is a big sacrifice for my parents but it's the only way to be able to study – otherwise it's impossible, because even if the Surda checkpoint is open, the soldiers can keep you there for one hour, two hours, whatever they want and you miss your lectures or your exams. I'm living there now, but the university still isn't open – it should have started two weeks ago – because the checkpoint is closed and the lecturers can't get in ... I am not sure how I am going to continue in my studies: I feel like it will take eight years to complete four years of university."

"What subject have you chosen?"

"Management studies. In fact, I want to work in the arts. I would like to create an arts centre in Palestine one day, bringing together theatre, ballet, painting and literature. But it's a dream and I doubt whether I'll be able to do any of it ..."

"But why?"

"Because the situation is getting worse every day. We are all very pessimistic. When the repression began, we said it was going to last for a month; then they took over the towns and started shooting at us. That went on for a year. We said, 'A year, and hundreds of civilians killed, our towns occupied: it can't last, the world will intervene!' Two years have gone by without the world doing anything. Now we are beginning the third year ..."

I try to lighten the atmosphere by asking her what she likes doing in her leisure time. What can a Palestinian of her age do in this situation?

Maha bursts out laughing.

"Things to do? There's hardly anything! Before, of course, we had basketball and football clubs, we swam, we went to the cinema, the theatre. I even took drama classes for two years – not professionally, just for fun. Now, everything is closed. So I read, I listen to music: it's a good way of relaxing, forgetting. Or else I go for a drive with friends. We take the smallest opportunity to have fun and we have learnt to enjoy the present. If there is no curfew, we all go to the café. Actually we're all so sick of it that sometimes we go out even if there is a curfew. Now there are no snipers on the rooftops, we take the risk."

"But isn't that rather foolish? There are jeeps and tanks everywhere – you could get yourselves killed!"

She shrugs.

"Palestinians take risks every day, to study, to go out, simply to live. When I look objectively at the life we lead, I ask myself how we can put up with it. And yet we find ways to keep on living. For more than 50 years our people have proved that they are survival experts. Whatever happens, we stand firm."

"Standing firm is what Palestinians call *Sumud*?"

"Exactly. *Sumud* is never giving up, resisting against all odds – passive resistance if nothing else is possible. *Sumud* is patience: if we are weak and under the enemy's thumb, it means staying still, not moving. *Sumud* means keeping a free spirit, the spirit of revolt, when we are oppressed or even tortured; it means continuing to believe in your ideals, your country ... *Sumud* ... [the girl's voice breaks] ... means continuing to believe in Palestine, against all the odds."

I leave Maha, deeply moved. In the course of an hour she has told me far more than most politicians. If Sharon and his kind could hear what these youngsters – the future of Palestinian society – think and feel, they would know that continuing to kill thousands of civilians or planning the expulsion of an entire people is futile. They would know that in the long term they cannot win.

2

◆

In the Name of God

AN ISRAELI SETTLER

I had been warned. "You'll never get a taxi to Pisgot. You have to change several times because Israeli taxi drivers are frightened to go into the occupied territories and Palestinian taxi drivers aren't allowed to take you into a settlement."

I therefore prepared myself for a three or four-hour journey, with car changes, to travel the 20 kilometres that separate west Jerusalem (the Jewish side) from Pisgot, an Israeli settlement on a hillside overlooking Ramallah, which was established in 1981 on land belonging to the neighbouring town of Al Bireh. But in Israel/Palestine there are no rules and you must always be ready to take your chance. Small miracles are a daily occurrence.

I chanced upon a Sephardic driver who, to my great surprise, agreed to drive me to the settlement. I later found out, whilst I was held up outside the town, that he had a secret service card that opened all doors.

We took the excellent road from Jerusalem to Naplouse, reserved for Israelis and almost empty. It was a circuitous route and it took almost an hour, travelling at high speed, to get to Pisgot.

"Before, we went by the main road", explained the driver, who had taken a liking to me, "but now people are frightened".

We arrive at the entrance to the settlement, patrolled by police armed with machine guns. I give them my passport, cursing myself yet again for the Pakistani visa spread insolently across the first two pages; it is so huge that it could be interpreted as some kind of provocation but I really don't have the heart for such tactics. It was ridiculously difficult to get this interview. I had telephoned the settlement's central office twenty times, spoken to various people who promised to get back to me straight away and left messages on an answerphone that spoke to me in Hebrew. All in vain.

I had begun to despair when I got a call from one of the settlement leaders, giving me details of a Dr Tubiana. I immediately felt reassured, on familiar ground – in France, Tubiana is the name of an eminent professor, who had treated some of my friends. Totally irrationally, I felt less apprehensive about meeting him? I had been warned that settlers do not like journalists, particularly French ones, who are portrayed as anti-Semitic by government propaganda. I therefore needed to avoid contention. Settlers could be violent and some journalists had been insulted and unceremoniously thrown out.

I give the soldier on duty Dr. Tubiana's name, but he has failed to leave my name, as required. They try to phone him but none of his numbers respond. They get in touch with the settlement office, which says that it will try to help. We wait for half an hour, sitting in the taxi in the scorching heat while I watch the comings and goings of jeeps, protected with wire mesh and equipped with enormous aerials, in and out of the settlement.

In front of me, less than a kilometre away, the town of Ramallah is visible. I recognise the road on which, three days earlier, I had walked with Liana Badr, one of the great Palestinian novelists.[1] She had pointed out the settlement to me, with a shudder of anger and fear.

"We are totally vulnerable", she said. "We are under constant surveillance; they shoot whenever they want. We have had several deaths, including a boy who was playing football on that pitch down there and another, recently, a man who was jogging on this road that we're walking on."

There is still no news of Dr Tubiana. I am worried that I will have to go back empty-handed but finally, thanks to my driver's insistence – and his card – they let us through.

We drive through the settlement. It is composed of pretty stone houses, each with its own little garden and red-tiled roof, from which flies the Israeli flag. Few people are about. Many are doubtless at work, but some houses seem deserted; my driver tells me that many families left after the start of the intifada because it got dangerous in the area. None the less, security measures seem in place everywhere and we pass many tanks, armoured jeeps and soldiers milling about. But the greatest concentration of forces is positioned on the side facing Ramallah, around an impressive electronic radar system and behind high concrete walls, erected to defend against gunfire, stones or possible suicide bombs.

---

1. Liana Badr has written several books, of which *A Compass for the Sunflower* (Women's Press, London, 1989), *Balcony over the Fakahini* (Interlink, NY, 1993) and *The Eye of the Mirror* (Garnet, Reading, 1996) have been translated into English.

We finally arrive at Dr Tubiana's. He opens the door to a house decorated very much in the style of the French middle classes, apart from the numerous Hebrew scriptures on the walls and the menorah – the seven-branched candlestick representing spiritual light and the divine presence that will ultimately overcome violence – in pride of place on top of the television. Embarrassed, he apologises: he had forgotten our appointment. Forgotten? I had had to twist his arm to get this meeting. He had claimed to be preparing for an exam but the truth was that he, like all settlers, is wary of journalists.

Dr Tubiana is 47 years old. Small, chubby, light skinned, with lively eyes shining behind steel-rimmed glasses, he sports a fine goatee and, of course, the kippa of every practising Jew. His speciality is acupuncture – or, he specifies, 'auriculotherapy'. He begins his story.

"I am from a *pied-noir* Tunisian family and my wife is from Algeria. We arrived in France as children, during the events of 1962. In 1985 my wife and I decided to come to Israel with our three children, first to Jerusalem and then to Pisgot in 1991."

"Why did you come to Israel – weren't you happy in France?"

"It was becoming difficult to fit my religious practice – even though I am not a fundamentalist – into daily life: respecting the Jewish feast days, not working on a Saturday, not sending children to school on the Shabbat ... For me, as a doctor in private practice, it was relatively easy but it was difficult for my wife, who worked in the state education sector, to obtain a post that would give her Friday afternoons and Saturdays free. My family had gone to France because of the language, although some of my relatives had already come to Israel, but when one is a practising Jew it is a natural step to make one's 'aliyah' – to go back to Israel to assert one's Zionism.

"When we first arrived it took some time to adapt. I knew the literary Hebrew of prayers but I had to learn the everyday language. In 1986 I became a self-employed doctor but we gradually realised that it was very difficult to live in Jerusalem and practise our religion and our Zionist ideals because we were weighed down with mundane problems; our ideals were threatening to get lost in everyday life. So we came to Pisgot to establish our right to return to our land and our history. The real aliyah is not living in Tel Aviv or Haifa but here, in Judea Samaria, a land that has belonged to us for three thousand years."

"Are there many settlers in Pisgot?"

"There are 250 families, around two thousand people. People leave but others take their place. Pisgot attracts people because the standard of living is much higher than in Jerusalem or in other *yishuv*.[2] We also have a very good school here and, since 1995, a road that allows us to bypass Ramallah. All these things, as well as our proximity to Jerusalem, attract families."

"Despite the lack of security?"

"The claim that those problems make people leave is false! Of course we have been forced to arm ourselves since the intifada began. Our inhabitants have learnt to shoot and we have set up voluntary watches. We also have a very effective body of reservists. And then the soldiers came to help us build a huge wall, five metres high, to protect the houses on the Ramallah side. But we are a religious and community yishuv, not a military one, even though Pisgot was created in 1981 as a military base to protect the communications centre that covers the entire north of the country as far as Jerusalem. Bit by bit people came to live here. There were no problems: they established good relations with the 'mukhtars', the mayors of the surrounding villages. But the 'commanders of Tunis', Arafat's people, began to put pressure on them and the first intifada started in 1987."

"But it is common knowledge that the first intifada arose out of the frustration of an occupied people who had seen their living conditions worsen and settlements springing up all over their land. It was only afterwards that Palestinians from outside the country began to take matters into their own hands."

"That's not true! The people here had no problem with us! In any case, I don't see what harm I am doing Mr Mohammed by living on this land, it was state land that belonged to no one. And then, don't forget the war in 1967 against the Jordanians, which we won and which gave us the right to the conquered territory. Any discussion on the subject has to begin from that basis!"

"Do you know that there are around forty United Nations' resolutions declaring that Israel should give back those occupied territories?"

"Forty?" He laughs. "There are a lot more than that! Three-quarters of United Nations' resolutions are against Israel but that does not change our position one iota: Judea Samaria is an integral part of Israel, no other peoples have lived on this land and it has had no other capital. Those are indisputable facts!"

"But the Palestinian people also lived here, and for a very long time!"

---

2. *Yishuv*: originally, Jewish community in Palestine; now used by settlers to mean the settlements.

"The Palestinian people have never existed; you invented them. They have never existed!"

"So who were the people who lived here?"

"Read Chateaubriand, read Napoleon. There were several thousand nomads who went between Egypt and Syria, stopping here and there. To talk about the Palestinian people is an aberration, a theoretical concept. Where is its capital? Its flag? They have had one for only the past fifty years. Do you know any such thing as a people without a country? I don't. The British talked about Palestine because they wanted to break the Jewish link with this land. They coined the word Palestine, which comes from the root 'Philistine'."[3]

I refrain from pointing out that there was indeed another people who existed for two thousand years without country or flag: the Jews. As for his allegation that the British wanted to break the Jewish connection to the land, it is at the very least eccentric, given that the Zionist aspiration got off the ground in practical terms in 1917, with Lord Balfour's declaration promising the Jews a homeland in Palestine.

In the fervour of his argument, Dr Tubiana has got up and is now pacing up and down his sitting room.

"We have reached this impasse because Begin accepted a reference to the rights of Palestinian people in the agreement with Egypt. That was a very grave mistake because the Palestinian people do not exist. We are still paying for that mistake."

"There was, however, a very developed society in Palestine, with a middle class, artistic life, a particular culture and large towns such as Haifa, Jerusalem, Nazareth and so on."

"As I said, they were nomads. As for the towns, they were ancient Jewish towns, with different names, like Jerusalem or Hebron."

"Supposing that is so, what is your solution? Because, whatever the case, there are now two and a half million Palestinians in the West Bank. What are you going to do with those people?"

"It is a problem. We would need to go right back to the beginning; I can't explain it all in an hour. We would have to go back into the causes ..."

He goes over to the terrace and points to the view.

"That hill opposite, that's Ahai, the second town that Joshua liberated when he came from Jericho. Archaeologists recovered an old olive

3. The Philistines, who probably came from Crete, settled between Gaza and Mount Carmel on the Canaan coast, around 1220 BC. Around 1095 BC they were conquered by King Saul, who established the kingdom of the Hebrews on their land.

press there, a bread oven and basket-making materials. There is no doubt that there was a town there. Life is a cycle. Coming back to Pisgot completes the cycle – it is the return to my land, my history and my religion."

He is so sincere, so convinced that I am almost moved. But he quickly resumes his pet theme.

"Don't forget that it was the Arabs who asked the Palestinians to leave. Even at Deir Yassin people left because of Arab propaganda!"[4]

That was going too far. The Palestinian village of Deir Yassin was the site of a terrible massacre ...

"At Deir Yassin, Palestinian civilians, women and children, were killed by Irgun troops!"[5]

"Two hundred people, not everyone!"

"Two hundred is enough for those who were there to feel terrorised and to run for their lives. Hearing about the massacre of Deir Yassin also incited the people of the neighbouring villages to escape before Jewish troops arrived."

"No, they left because of Arab propaganda."

"OK. Let's go back to the United Nations resolutions, to Rabin, who agreed to give back the territories."

"Not 'the' territories; just 'territories!'", corrected the doctor. "The French added 'the' in their document. There's no 'the' in the English version. If we agree to give something back, it is up to us to decide what we do and don't want to give back."

"At the moment, Palestine is not a viable country. It is a collection of Bantustans separated from each other by the settlements and minor roads."

"They are not separated in Gaza."

"But Gaza is only a minute part of Palestine ..."

He makes no comment. Perhaps he thinks, like some Israeli extremists, that the Gaza Strip – already over-populated and impoverished – should constitute the whole of Palestine.

"The hatred stirred up against us by Europe and the Israeli press", he goes on, "claiming that the whole problem comes from the *yishuv*, and connecting our presence in the territories with terrorism, is shameful! It sanctions our murder! Supposing that, as they say, I have conquered

4. 120 to 150 civilians were killed in April 1948 by Jewish Irgun militia, led by Menahem Begin. It was one of several tragedies that led to 800,000 Palestinians fleeing the country, according to the Israeli 'new historians'.
5. Irgun: Jewish militia active in Palestine until 1948.

a territory that does not belong to me. I have to enlarge it because I have children. So I build other houses. How does that cause existential problems for the Arab opposite me? Why would he come to kill us and commit terrorist acts in Netanya, Galilee and elsewhere? Where is the logic? How can you compare the actions of our soldiers, our army, to the actions of the terrorists? That is pure propaganda, an incitement to kill Jews because they are Jews! What percentage of the West Bank should or should not be given back does not interest me. In fact, Israel should extend much further!"

"The question of how much territory is given back is, none the less, what will allow Palestinians to have a country or not. Do you recognise that Palestinians have that right?"

"No, I do not! Understand this: the Palestinian people do not exist. How can they have a country?"

"But the millions of Palestinians ..."

He shrugs his shoulders, exasperated.

"Look in the Jordanian telephone book: seventy percent are Palestinians. The start of the solution is for them to be reattached to Jordan. These two peoples, Jordanians and Palestinians, are the same. The Palestinians who are here should be administered by Jordan and vote in Jordan. The Israeli army will have control over security, pending a solution with the Arab countries. And then, the new generations of Palestinians need to be educated and distanced from the propaganda of European books."

"What propaganda?"

"Europe has spent ten million Euros on anti-Semitic books, money given to Palestinian national education, without right of inspection. Books that teach that four Jews minus two Jews equals two Jews left to kill. Yes, that is written in all the books![6] They are teaching hatred of Jews; they tell them that Jews have taken their land and they have to get it back. The problem is that the Arabs do not accept that the Jewish people have come back to a land that entirely belongs to us. So the negotiations about forty per cent, sixty per cent or one hundred per cent do not mean anything. In any case, a Palestinian state would be a castrated state, without an army, with borders that we control and with a water problem, because the water comes from us. Do you think an Arab is going to accept that? I don't think that there will ever be a Palestine. That goes against the reasoning that made me settle here in

6. These allegations are obviously false.

the first place. They have no legal or historic right to be here. No more than the Basques!"

He laughs. "Hang on, that's an idea. Do you think the Basques should come and live here? Why not? That would resolve the Basque problem between Spain and France!"

He goes on.

"In my view we mustn't rush things. All Palestinians need to be re-educated, so that they understand that the Jews are in their own home. We can live together if they understand that the Israelis are the dominant party and they the tolerated party. Let's be serious. They cannot have an independent country. Do you see their planes flying over us, do you see us letting them make agreements with other countries such as Iraq, or pumping water from us? No Israeli, left-wing or right-wing, with or without the kippa, could accept that! And if we give them forty or sixty per cent of the territories, they will always want more. That's the Arab mentality!"

I am certainly not going to get into a debate with him on the 'Arab mentality', any more than the 'Jewish mentality'. I tackle a less explosive subject.

"Are you a member of a political party?"

"No. I am deeply Zionist and I don't want to adulterate that by getting involved in politics."

"The Zionist ideal is for all Jews to return to Israel, but how is that possible? There isn't room!"

"That is why the mountains exist! The Psalms state that 'When the people come back, the mountains will stretch out.'"

I think that I must have misheard him. Helpfully, he enlightens me: "We can cut into the mountains and build on that land. That is what we have begun to do. That is what has happened for the *yishuv* around Jerusalem. This country is a country of hills. If we raze them, there will be enough room to build houses for all the Jews in the world, who will one day be able to return here. There is no problem. The country can get larger by itself."

He smiles at this idyllic vision.

"Real Zionism asks all Jews to return to Israel to practise their faith, not because of anti-Semitism. That is bargain basement Zionism! Although", he concludes, "that is better than nothing!"

"So, was it interesting?" asked my driver when I got back to the car.

Interesting, yes ... but above all moving and terrifying. Dr Tubiana is the kind of rare man who can send shivers down your spine. But, as always, one can understand – without sharing – his rigid views and his visceral attachment to the myths for which he is ready, like thousands of settlers, to give his life.

A life that has been marked by trauma. First, the Holocaust, which neither he nor his family in north Africa experienced personally but which he had gone over in his mind again and again, reliving its worst details as though it were a relentless nightmare. And even if those responsible for it were not Arabs – with whom Jews had lived on good terms for centuries – the blame had been passed, with the help of the West, on to the evil Arab, the bloodthirsty Muslim.

But I also imagine that Dr Tubiana has been marked more deeply by a personal trauma: being torn away, as a child, from Tunisia, his sunny home where, as a French Jew, he had been a privileged being among the Arabs; to arrive in a cold France where his family were confronted with all sorts of difficulties. And it was the Arabs who had pushed him out of that paradise – the same people who today challenged his presence here!

He had been told that Tunisia was not his country when he had known, in all the childish fibre of his being, that it was. The land of *Eretz Israel* would never be taken from him; it had been given him, not by some colonial power, but by God! God had chosen the Jews to live in Israel, to prepare for the glorious coming of the Messiah. No power on earth could eject them.

The car braked suddenly, jolting me out of my thoughts. Outside a kibbutz, a young girl was signalling to us. Could we take her to Jerusalem?

She was stunningly pretty and the awed driver made room for her beside him. Naomi was at art school, studying painting. Thin, with cropped hair, hatless and wearing a long skirt, I imagined that she was not a practising Jew. I was wrong. She didn't wear a hat because she was not married but she was a firm believer, she told me. Had she done her military service? Yes, but in peaceful surroundings, looking after children.

I try to get into deeper conversation with her. She is so young, she must be more open-minded than Dr Tubiana.

"You live near Ramallah; have you ever been there?"

"Yes, before the intifada I sometimes went shopping there."

"Did you ever speak to Arab girls?"

"What for? I've got nothing to say to them; why should I speak to them?"

"But to achieve peace, don't we need to speak?"

She made no reply. I sensed that she regretted having got into our car but I persist. At her age, she must have asked herself questions.

"Do you think that the territories should remain Israeli?"

"Of course. It's *Eretz Israel*. It is ours because God gave it to us thousands of years ago."

"And what are you going to do with the Arabs who live there?"

"They have to accept that it is our land, even if they have been there for hundreds of years. God gave it to us."

Despite her angelic face and her gentle smile, one senses that nothing will make her budge. For this land that 'God gave us' she would fight to the very end. Like Dr Tubiana.

FATHER BERNARD

The cypress trees form a guard of honour along the steps going up to the old city. Leaving behind the gardens planted with laurels and purple bougainvillaea bushes, I make my way towards the crenellated walls and Jaffa Gate.

An imposing stone arch forms the entrance to Jerusalem's Christian quarter, where I am instantly surrounded by souvenir-sellers, desperate for a client: scared off by the troubles that began two years ago, tourists are now almost non-existent. I make my escape and take refuge in Latin Patriarchate Road, a quiet little street lined with restaurants. In their gardens, shaded by centuries-old trees, sit potbellied orthodox priests, sipping Turkish coffee and savouring sweetmeats.

The street climbs up to a large building with high, arched windows, its entrance protected by a beautiful wrought iron gate. The internal courtyard is a cool oasis of silence after the stifling heat of the city, the stone arches supported by columns giving a rough imitation of a cloister or cathedral nave.

I am welcomed by an attractive man, of fifty or so, wearing a black suit topped off by a white ecclesiastical collar. Underneath the large forehead, serious eyes are leavened by an almost child-like smile: Father Bernard Betran, a son of this soil.

"I was born in the village of Beit Sahour, a kilometre east of Bethlehem, a village which, according to tradition, is the site of the field of the Gospel shepherds. The Holy Scriptures relate that at the time of Jesus' birth, angels appeared to shepherds and told them, 'A child is born to you at Bethlehem, wrapped in swaddling clothes. Go there and you will find him'. And the angels sang, 'Glory to God in the highest and peace on Earth to men of goodwill'. Well, my village is there and my house is the same distance from the Church of the Nativity as from the Chapel of the Shepherds' Field."

"Has your family lived there a long time?"

"For centuries. My father was a teacher of English, French and Arabic. He was one of the most learned men of the village. He studied at the seminary of Beit Jala,[1] where he did two years of philosophy. He also learned Italian. When I was born, in 1950, he was an English teacher in Hebron."

"Did your parents talk to you about the events of 1948?"

"Of course – particularly my mother, who was from Jaffa, near Tel Aviv. In 1948 she was already living in Beit Sahour because she had married my father in 1946, even though she was Orthodox and he was a Catholic. It was a love match. But she missed Jaffa. She went there often until 1948, when all her family were forced to leave by Israeli guns. After 1967, when Palestinians had the right to return to Israel, the first thing my mother thought of was going to see her house in Jaffa again. A family of Bulgarian Jews now lived there. She often told me the story: 'I went back to my house and those people didn't even offer me a coffee. They let me go in and out as if I was a stranger there ...'. She always cried at that. You know, it's hard to be a refugee. Millions of Palestinians dream of returning one day to the town of their birth."

"Is that possible?"

"There are, alas, certain events and injustices in history that are irreversible, one of which is this question of the Palestinian refugees. After fifty years, another people have taken their place. It is difficult to imagine returning all those refugees to their home towns because there are now millions of them. It would completely change the demography of Israel. But one can at least give them back their dignity and give them compensation; a house. We must also allow some to return to Israel so that families can be reunited. If the will is there, there are feasible solutions to the problem. Believe me, not many Palestinians are going to want to live under Israeli authority!"

"Were you aware of the Palestinian problem from a young age?"

"As a kid, I remember my grandmother going to collect the rations allocated to refugees by UNWRA.[2] I would go with her and we would queue up to bring back flour, butter and rice. I would ask her why we were queuing and why we had to have rations, when our neighbours didn't have them. She explained that the family had been forced to escape and that she had lost her house, but that she hoped to return one day. She told us that she had hidden the key carefully, under a paving stone ..."

"In 1967, when you were 17, there was another catastrophe: the Six-Day War and the occupation of the West Bank, where you were living. What were you doing at that time?"

1. A town next to Bethlehem.
2. United Nations Relief and Works Agency.

"I was studying philosophy at Beit Jala seminary. I wanted to become a priest. I remember when, on the 4th or 5th June 1967, the Israelis entered Bethlehem. We could hear the sound of gunfire in the town from the seminary. It didn't last long. A few hours later, we learned that the town officials had gone to the Israelis with a white flag."

"The Jordanians didn't fight for long!"[3]

"There wasn't really any resistance, apart from a bit in Jerusalem. In fact the two sides were hugely unbalanced in terms of arms, technical know-how and preparation. We were being told on the news that the Egyptians had shot down one or two hundred aeroplanes and we stopped counting how many came down – but in the end we found out that it had been Egyptian planes that were shot down, from day one. So many lies were told at the time. 1967 revealed not only Israeli's military strength but also the extent to which the Arabs were caught unprepared. After the defeat, Jordan, Syria and Lebanon took in a certain number of Palestinians. A few of them got rich working in the Emirates but the majority remained in poverty, living in terrible conditions. The refugee camps, which were supposed to be temporary, still exist after thirty-five years!"

"Are Arab governments indifferent to the situation?"

"Unfortunately, yes. We counted a lot on our Arab brothers, on the petrol countries, but we were living in Utopia. Our illusions were terribly shattered."

"What was your personal experience of the occupation?"

"The first few years were peaceful. Palestinians found work in Jerusalem, set up small factories and family businesses. Workers brought money back to the villages and towns and in the beginning there was even an economic boom. The Palestinians had not yet organised themselves into a resistance and the Israelis were happy to have occupied the whole of Palestine. It was almost a honeymoon period between them, which lasted more or less until the first intifada."

"But resistance organisations still existed?'

"There were some acts of resistance and demonstrations against the occupation, but they were a lot less violent than today. There wasn't a climate of war. We could drive from Bethlehem to Tel Aviv."

"If life was so easy, why did the Intifada begin?"

"There were many reasons: the unresolved refugee problem; the issue of Jerusalem; the growing number of people arrested simply on suspicion and held in prison for renewable periods of six months,

3. The West Bank was under Jordanian authority until its defeat in 1967.

without sentence and without even a clear accusation![4] Above all there was the expropriation of land and the uninterrupted building of settlements. We felt that our homeland was disappearing.

"And then, permits to travel or to build a house were almost always refused. The slightest protest incurred severe repression. Political parties were of course banned and even the word 'Palestinian' was forbidden; we were Arabs, with Israeli identity cards! And people were imprisoned on the smallest suspicion."

He pauses, clenches his long white hands and then, after a prolonged silence, speaks again.

"I will give you a personal example. My elder brother was imprisoned twice. The first time, he was 20 years old. It was in summer and he had come back from an Arab country from which he had got a grant to study chemical engineering. He was a quiet boy who had never wanted to join a political party. The Israelis presumed that because he was a Palestinian studying in an enemy Arab country he must belong to an organisation.

"At two o'clock in the morning they came to arrest him. We didn't know what prison he was being held in. We looked for him everywhere, getting sent from office to office, not being given the smallest clue. Finally, thanks to the Red Cross, we learnt that he was in Jerusalem, in Moscobyia prison, in the centre of town. After 12 days, we were given permission to visit him. My mother spent the night making his favourite dishes.

"We waited from ten o'clock in the morning until four in the afternoon. And at four o'clock, when our turn came, a soldier said to us in Hebrew, '*Gamarnou*' – 'That's it'. It was the first time I had seen my mother in a raging temper. She slammed the door, shouting in fury. We had to wait until the following week to see him. We were entitled to just one visit a month. He was freed after four or five weeks."

"Was he tortured?"

"Yes. The Israelis put a foul-smelling bag over his head to smother him, beat him and prevented him from sleeping for days and nights on end to try to break him. At the time, my father was being operated on for cancer: I wrote to the military governor of Bethlehem to appeal for my brother's release since no firm accusation had been made against him. The secret police intercepted the letter and used it as blackmail: 'Your father is going to die. If you don't confess, you will never see him again'. He didn't give in. But when he got out – they had found nothing

---

4. This 'administrative detention' is still widely used against Palestinians.

against him – he was furious. 'What did you write? I almost confessed to things I hadn't done.'

"He left again and the following year, thinking that the danger was over, he came back on holiday. He was arrested again and tortured. When he got out of prison, after 40 days, he had lost so much weight that he was unrecognisable. He had two years of university left but he was forbidden from leaving the country. At the time I was a priest in Bethlehem. I wrote to the president of the Republic, asking him to enforce the law, since no evidence had been found against my brother. Six months later we got a letter declaring that he could leave Israel and go to whatever country he wished. He left to finish his studies and then came back because, despite everything, he wanted to live here. But he was never able to find work."

"Why not?"

"There was a lot of manual work for Palestinians in Israel, but very little for those with qualifications. He was offered a good job in Canada and went to live there. Unfortunately, many qualified Palestinians are forced to go abroad."

"They say that more Christians leave because they have more opportunities."

"Yes, they fit into life in the West more easily. It's a temptation to which numerous Palestinian Christians succumb every year."

"What proportion of Palestinians are Christian?"

"Around three percent of the occupied territories – 70,000 people. Before 1948 we were almost ten percent, which is still the case in Israel, where of the one million Palestinians, 100,000 are Christian."

"Are there problems between the two communities?"

The priest, until now extremely affable, suppresses an obvious irritation.

"There aren't problems between the communities – there are problems between people! When there is a conflict between two Muslims, we say, 'It's a problem between them'. When there is a conflict between two Christians, we say, 'It's a problem between them.' But when there is a conflict between a Muslim and a Christian, it becomes a so-called 'national problem'. It's a tribal mentality; everyone supports their co-religionists. For the Christians, it's a problem of feeling the weakness of their minority status; the Muslims react along the lines of, 'the Christians are always complaining'. Neither attitude helps the dialogue.

Apart from these small incidents, in general we get on well with each other. The Latin Patriarch of Jerusalem, for example, is highly thought of by the Muslims because he is a courageous man who dares to tell the truth. The Muslims know that our presence here helps Europeans and Americans understand the situation better. We act as a bridge with the West."

"What was your experience of the first intifada?"

"I was in Rome. I followed the demonstrations on the radio, longing to be here with my people. When I came back, after the Oslo agreements, I was present when the Palestinian Authority entered Bethlehem and during the early days of self-government. That was when Palestinians got a Palestinian passport instead of an Israeli identity card!"

His eyes moisten at the memory.

"I felt an immense pride and a lot of hope. We had passports, control of our systems of education, health, communications – radio, television, the post – and every month two more towns became self-governing. We thought that we had won, that we would soon have an independent country. We were proud of what we had achieved. We were blissfully optimistic. But after the assassination of Rabin, as time went on it became more and more obvious that the Israeli government did not want to honour his signing of the agreement. They had done nothing other than give autonomy to the big towns. They had not freed the majority of political prisoners, as they had promised, and they refused to allow east Jerusalem to become the Palestinian capital. They refused to dismantle the settlements, in fact were building more and more, and also refused to give back all the occupied territories, as the United Nations resolutions demanded."

"So did you foresee the second intifada?"

"I didn't foresee the situation we now have. But the failure of Camp David showed that no further dialogue was possible."

"Palestinians say that Sharon's visit to the Esplanade of the Mosques was a deliberate provocation to obstruct the peace process. What is your opinion?"

"Sharon clearly wanted to say to Israelis, Palestinians and the world that the Esplanade of the al-Aqsa mosque was the site of the Temple Mount. It was the assertion of an Israeli claim. For Palestinians it was a provocation. Arafat had in fact urgently requested Barak to prevent the visit but Barak was not able nor willing to do that."

"How do you think the conflict can be resolved?"

"There is a profound lack of understanding between the two communities. Each has a different vision of the past, the present and the future. What the Israelis call the Temple Mount, the Palestinians call the Esplanade of the Mosques. What the Israelis call the city of David, the Palestinians call al-Qods al-Sharif, the Arab name for Jerusalem. What the Palestinians call occupied territories, the Israelis call liberated territories. The notion of rights and even the vocabulary used by each of them demonstrate a total lack of mutual understanding.

"As an Arab, I understand the Palestinian position and as a Christian who knows the Old Testament, I understand why the Jews speak as they do. Each side relies on a different notion of rights. The Israelis speak of divine right, based on the book of Genesis and on having lived in this land for a thousand years, from David to the Maccabeans in the first century. I also understand the position of the Palestinians, who have been here since the seventh century and who assert an historical claim to Palestine. Each demands their due.

"The other big difference between them is that the Israelis want the problem of security resolved first and the Palestinians want the problem of the 1967 occupation resolved first. They say: 'It's simple: acknowledge the occupation and give back the occupied territories, and all the problems will be solved', while the Israelis declare: 'We are threatened by the Palestinians. As long as we have no security, we are not ready to begin negotiating'. Each side has its own vocabulary, language and demands."

"Do you believe that if the Israelis agreed to withdraw from the occupied territories, there would be peace?"

"Absolutely! The United Nations resolutions would be enforced, which is what everyone is asking for – the Palestinians, the Arabs and even the Americans! The problem is that the Israelis do not believe there would be peace if they gave up the territories. Or rather, their government makes out that it does not believe that, so as not to have to give them up ... Sharon wants to discredit the Palestinians by saying they are all terrorists and one cannot negotiate with terrorists. The Palestinians respond by saying that it is not terrorism but resistance and that they will resist as long as the Israelis will not leave."

"As a Palestinian, but also as a priest, what is your view?"

"I think that the Palestinians have the right to live on their territory but that resistance should be non-violent."

"Can non-violent resistance work?"

"Yes, look at Gandhi's movement in India!"

"It is the one and only example, and it succeeded because the British colonists wanted to leave, for economic reasons."

"The Palestinians have tried violent action and it has not succeeded. They were stronger when they used stones rather than bombs; the world was with them. We have to prove that we are not terrorists but resistance fighters. But we are totally incapable of exploiting the media ... ten million Jews have more world influence than three hundred million Arabs. If the Western media are in the Israeli camp, it is because the Israelis are eloquent. Whereas we, who have obvious right on our side, are unable to get it recognised.

"A suicide bombing in Jerusalem or Netanya loses Palestinians all the sympathy that they had in the past. Killing innocent people goes against all ethics. Whether it's Palestinians against Israelis or Israelis acting in inhuman ways in our territories – as they often do – both are unacceptable and both breed a never-ending cycle of violence."

"The soldiers justify their actions by saying that most of these people are terrorists and that they are merely defending themselves."

Father Bernard goes red with anger.

"I say, and I repeat, that the Israelis committed the original sin of occupying territory that did not belong to them. If there had not been an occupation, there would have been neither resistance nor terrorism. On the other hand, if the Palestinians refused to sign a peace treaty or if they did not honour it, the Israelis would of course have the right to defend themselves."

"Most Palestinians have no more faith in the negotiations and they support the suicide bombings because they are convinced that the Israelis will not withdraw until they are forced to do so."

"Doubtless that is so, but there is also economic force. The Arabs could use the weapon of petrol. They don't do so because they are disunited. That lack of unity is one of the main ills of the Middle East. It led in particular to the Gulf War."

Father Bernard seems suddenly very weary and I cannot stop myself from asking, "Do you feel abandoned?"

He recovers himself.

"No. Many journalists, many European countries, have demonstrated their solidarity and sympathy with us. It's simply that there are things that neither the Europeans nor the Americans can ever understand, such as the suicide bombings. They attribute it to fanaticism, whereas the reality is a lot more complex."

"Do you understand them?"

"I understand them, but without condoning them. And I would also like Europe to understand them. There is a logical relationship between the Palestinians' despair and these bombings. But they have harmed our image terribly. After September 11, the Americans and Sharon tried to establish a link between the Palestinian Authority and al-Qaida. For the Americans, Afghanistan equals Palestine and Osama

Bin Laden equals Arafat. The blindness of the greatest power in the world is terrifying."

"In your opinion, when Sharon and Bush reproach Arafat for not trying to control the suicide bombers, is that a completely unfounded allegation?"

"Obviously! How could Arafat, imprisoned in Ramallah, control the streets of Jerusalem? Accusing him of responsibility for all the Israelis' ills hardly makes sense plausible. Sharon is trying to eliminate him from the political scene but he has no peace strategy and does not realise what disasters would ensue from getting rid of Arafat. Because, even though he is criticised, Arafat remains the symbol of Palestinian power. If he were not there, I fear that there would be anarchy."

3

◆

Army Abuses and
Conscientious Objectors

THE ARTIST

I arrive at the small artist's studio on the Ramallah heights just as the sun is setting on the town. The reddening sky is streaked with birds flying overhead, mating a deafening cacophony that is, none the less, welcome after the constant rumbling of F-16s of the past few days.

Yussef comes to open the door. He is small, frail looking, with a black beard; twenty-five or so. Complete chaos reigns in his room: canvasses piled up against the walls, overflowing ashtrays and paint-stained rags strewn across a floor covered with multicoloured stains. It resembles any artist's studio anywhere.

Yussef has just come out of prison – or, rather, he came out six weeks ago but is still traumatised, he tells me.

"I am an artist; I have never been involved in politics. Perhaps I became a painter in the first place to escape from a daily life that was too painful. I wasn't really destined to be an artist, as I am from a poor family. My father is a construction worker – or rather, he was, because there's no more work. I loved to draw when I was little and my teachers and my parents encouraged me."

"Where were you brought up?"

"In Gaza. My family still live there, although we are originally refugees from the region of Ramleh, which is now in Israel. In 1994, I left to study fine art in Naplouse. I went back to Gaza in 2000 to spend some time with my family. I haven't seen them since. You can't get in any more. I only get news by phone."

As he talks, Yussef gets out several of his paintings for me. Semi-figurative but very dreamlike, with vivid colours. One depicts a kind of narrowing labyrinth.

"That is Palestine, where land is confiscated and which is getting smaller and smaller."

"And this painting, with the footprints?"

"That one is very important to me; it's like a magic pass. It represents the route between Ramallah, where I live, and Gaza, where my family live. It is a trip I have often made. With all the difficulties, it used to take 17 hours to get to Gaza; normally it should take an hour and a quarter. They have closed the road now, but I can still travel back home, to Gaza, by looking at the picture. I paint Gaza a lot; the sea, the birds, my family. Gaza is a very different world from here – more rural, more authentic, I think. At any rate, it moves me more and I miss it terribly."

"How do you see your paintings? As an expression of the Palestinians' problems?"

"No, they represent the difficulty of being human in general, but in their form they are influenced by Palestinian society."

"You said that you are not a political activist. So how do you explain your arrest and the way in which you were treated?"

"On the first day of the invasion of Ramallah, on the 28th March, soldiers knocked on my door at two o'clock in the afternoon. There were five of us living here, all friends. They told us to get out of the apartment and then they went through everything, from top to bottom. They did the same to all the apartments in the building. After they had finished ransacking the place, they took us away, our hands tied behind our backs and hoods over our heads, and put us into an armoured vehicle. I was really frightened. I thought that they might stop somewhere and execute us. Finally we arrived at a place that they said was Ofar military camp. We got out, they took off the hoods and there we were facing Israelis in civilian clothes.

"They had barely taken my hood off me when an Israeli asked: 'Do you belong to Hamas?'

"'No, I am an artist.'

"'An artist?'"

"Another Israeli said, 'Leave him to me. I'll take care of him'.

"He took me up into a room. That's when the interrogation began: 'What's your name? The names of your family?' Routine questions. Then the Israeli started going into more detail. 'What are your sister's children called?' I hadn't seen my family for a long time and I couldn't remember the names of my nephews and nieces. The Israeli said, 'I'll tell you what they're called', and he began to reel off their names. He knew everything!

"Then he said, 'It's eight years since you left Gaza. I want you to tell me everything you've done during those eight years'.

"I told him that I had studied, worked here and there ... everything I could remember. I had nothing to hide.

"After the interrogation I was transferred to an area of tents surrounded by barbed wire. It was the detention centre. There were around fifty prisoners to a tent, in inhuman conditions. There was almost nothing to eat, just unleavened bread and yoghurt. We were hungry, we felt dirty; there was just a bit of cold water to wash, no soap, and the toilets were disgusting.

"I stayed there for 43 days, during which I was interrogated four times. I was not tortured, but I was hit. All the prisoners were hit. Every time we were taken from one place to another, every time we were in contact with soldiers, they hit us. Without fail.

"Finally they brought me before the military tribunal. The judge said to me: 'You have done nothing wrong. You are not a member of Hamas or Islamic Jihad. You have told the truth. You are free to go'. But the public prosecutor objected. 'He must stay in prison. There is a secret file on him'. The judge replied: 'You have 48 hours to show me this file. Otherwise he will be released'.

"I was taken back to the camp. That afternoon, I was brought before the intelligence services officer. He offered to send me to Tel Aviv for a month, as a tourist, all expenses paid, and to arrange meetings with Israeli artists. All on one condition, of course: he wanted me to pass on information about the artists and about Palestinian intellectuals who are opposed to the occupation and who hold extremist views. Obviously I refused. So the officer asked me: 'Which hand do you use to draw?'

"I had a premonition. I replied that I drew with my left hand. 'Very well. Draw my portrait', he said.

"Luckily, at one time I used to practice drawing with both hands and I was able to draw a more or less convincing portrait. When it was done, he said, 'OK, you can go'. When I put my hands on the table to get up, he slammed his rifle butt down on my left wrist and broke it.

"Then I was pushed on to a bus with other men who, like me, had been freed. They threw us off the bus in the middle of the night, near the Ramallah checkpoint – a very dangerous thing to do because it was during the curfew and the soldiers shoot without warning. We managed to get through the checkpoint; I was holding my wrist with my right hand, in terrible pain. With a friend's help, I was able to get back home. The next day I went to the hospital to get treatment. Today it is almost healed but I don't have the same mobility as before."

"Has that experience changed how you view things? Are you more frightened than before? Are you very angry with the Israelis?"

"I'm frightened and I don't want contact with them any more. Before, I accepted the concept of living with the Israelis and I was ready to discuss their point of view. I was very open. I cannot be any more. The harm done to me was much more psychological than physical. I am still traumatised and I have constant nightmares. I am obsessed by a feeling of powerlessness before a totally arbitrary system, with its violence and contempt – they can do what they want with us, according to their whim. Like that soldier who was furious that I was being released and that I refused to collaborate and who broke my wrist so as to destroy my career.

"I would never have believed that was possible. I had heard many terrible stories, but as long as it happens to other people and not you, you can't understand."

He pointed out a picture, painted in blues and yellows, that portrayed children running.

"I call this picture *Waking from a Dream*. I show people who are still dreaming; I, for one, have woken up now!"

THE THREE KHALILS

Today, the 20th May 2002, my friend Leila and I have been invited to a house in the old town of Ramallah for the birthday of little Khalil, the youngest son of Oum Khalil,[1] who is celebrating his ninth birthday. At the entrance to the tiny house we are greeted by a dozen or so laughing children, little girls in their best dresses of heavy lace with neat white collars, and boisterous boys with lively eyes and grazed knees. The family and their friends are gathered in the main room, in front of a low table covered with cakes and sweets.

We are in luck: today the curfew has been lifted and we can all meet here. I feel a little guilty about disturbing these rare moments of relaxation but Oum Khalil had insisted. She points out a poster on the wall, between the lithographs of snowscapes, depicting a dark-skinned teenager with curly hair: her eldest son, Khalil, killed on the 10th March, 1990,[2] at the age of sixteen, the brother of the little boy whose birthday we are celebrating.

"It was a Monday; he had come back from school and had offered to go and do some shopping for me. He was a very helpful boy ..."

Oum Khalil must be forty or so. Dressed in a dark *abbaya*, the long, enveloping black cape worn by traditional women, her hair covered with a white veil, she is small and thin; her dimpled face is lit by large black eyes. We seat ourselves in the narrow area outside the house.

"This is the only quiet place. We can enjoy the cool of the evening", she says. "We've only got two rooms and there are nine of us; the children suffocate inside ... How can I stop them going out and getting into mischief?"

"Khalil got up every day at five o'clock to go and sell newspapers", she goes on "and then he went to school. In the afternoon he left to go and work in a supermarket. He gave me all the money he earned because we didn't have enough just with the wages of his father, who worked in a restaurant near Lod airport. In the evening he went out with his friends. He didn't talk to me about it but I know that he took

---

1. In Arabic countries, parents are designated by being given the name of their eldest son: Oum Khalil is the mother of Khalil, Abu Khalil the father of Khalil.
2. During the first intifada, the 'war of stones', from December 1987 to September 1993.

part in demonstrations against the occupation and that he threw stones. During that first intifada, the Palestinians didn't use arms against the guns, just stones.

"My son was arrested twice. The first time I had to pay 500 shekels to have him released.[3] The second time he had climbed a tree to attach a Palestinian flag when an Israeli patrol had passed by; he just had time to hide in a dustbin. They found him and took him to the military camp at Mouqata'a, which is now Arafat's headquarters. That time the fine was 2,000 shekels. I couldn't pay such a big amount. I waited for my son all night behind the barbed wire surrounding the camp. The soldiers let him go in the early morning, with a fractured knee and a swollen face. They had tied him up and hit him with their rifle butts, mainly on his knees. That was the order given to Israeli soldiers at that time: don't kill but break stone throwers' limbs. Thousands of young people were mutilated, some of them handicapped for life.

"I cried and I begged Khalil to stop: 'Next time we won't be able to get you out. We're poor, your father can't pay'. He promised me he would but I knew that as soon as he could, he would begin again."

"Did he belong to a political organisation?"

"He was in the student branch of the Democratic Front for the Liberation of Palestine, but we didn't know. Neither I nor my husband had ever been involved in politics. We are refugees from 1948, from a village near Jerusalem that is now in Israel. My father worked for the post office and my husband's parents were farmers who lost everything. When he was very small, Khalil had seen his father wounded by an Israeli bomb. A shell fell right in the centre of Ramallah, killing two men and wounding my husband. We carried him to the house bleeding.

"You know, we don't need to talk politics to our children: they see what is happening, the curfews, the mistreatment, the humiliation and all kinds of deprivation, and they are outraged. Caution comes with age, and sometimes the resignation that we call wisdom. But for Khalil and for young people generally, not to fight against injustice is cowardice."

Oum Khalil goes over her son's last day, replaying the film, minute by minute, like all mothers who have lost a child, as if trying to pinpoint the exact moment at which they could have intervened or events could have taken a different turn ...

"That Monday I had the flu and he wanted to take me to hospital but I refused. I can't stop telling myself that if I had accepted, he

3. 1 shekel = 0.18 Euros (at time of printing).

wouldn't have gone out on the streets and he wouldn't have died ... Then he wanted to know when his father was coming back because he wanted to go out. I knew he was going to throw stones again. I telephoned my husband, who tried to reason with him: 'You're the oldest, you should look after your brothers and sisters'. He said that he would, took a shower and then, just as he was going out, at three o'clock, he said to me: 'By the way, mother, we owe the grocer 70 shekels. We mustn't forget to pay'. Did he have a premonition? I myself had had a heavy heart for two days, as if I knew something was going to happen.

"Half an hour later, as I was doing the washing up, a plate broke in two in my hands. At that moment, someone rang at the door. It was friends of Khalil. They said, 'He has fallen down a staircase, his leg is broken, come quickly'. They took me in a car, all rallying round. At the hospital I saw members of my family walking towards me and I understood. I shouted, 'Khalil is dead!' and fainted.

"When I came to, the nurses refused to let me see him and because I struggled they gave me an injection to calm me down, promising me they would bring him to me at the house. They didn't. I only saw my son again at the cemetery – or, rather, I saw a shape under a blood-stained sheet."

She stops, huddled up into herself, her shoulders shaking with sobs. I reproach myself for having made her relive these moments, 12 years later, particularly when I hear the rest of her story.

"His friends told me what happened. After throwing stones, he ran away from the soldiers who were chasing him and tried to run up into a building to hide. They shot him in the leg but he still managed to get to the top. They got him on the top floor. It was a building under construction. The soldiers got hold of him and threw him into the lift shaft and then ... they threw a slab of cement on to him."

We say nothing, petrified with horror. Oum Khalil's husband, a small, taciturn man, has joined us. Diffidently, he evokes the image that I can see only too clearly.

"If they had shot him with a bullet", he murmurs, "But that ... I will never forgive them."

Since then, both of them have joined their son's political party, the DFLP, which supports the peace negotiations.

"But the situation has got worse and worse and the Israelis don't want to give anything up in exchange for peace", said the father. "They accept Palestinians as long as we are a cheap labour force who keep quiet, work and eat. But if we want a state, we have to pay a high price for it."

"What do you think of the suicide bombers?"

"All my life I have been against violence towards civilians, but since the death of my son I have changed my mind. The Israelis come and kill our women and children – why should we have any scruples? Why is the life of an Israeli child more sacred than the life of a Palestinian child?"

His daughter Iman's husband, Bassel, joins the conversation. Like the great majority of Palestinians, he approves of the suicide bombings against soldiers and settlers: "That is resistance to the occupation", but he is opposed to suicide bombings of civilians in Israel. When he was 18, at the time of the first intifada, he spent four years in prison for throwing stones. His brother Issa, who organised demonstrations in front of the military barricades at Ramallah, was shot dead.

Iman and Bassel had a child nine days after the birth of little Khalil. In memory of the beloved brother, they too named their baby Khalil.

Today the two boys, one all dark curls, the other blond, are insep-arable. They have joined our group, hiding behind their parents, laughing and making faces. These young children sometimes manage to escape their parents' surveillance to go and throw stones – like many children all over the world. Except that, for them, death lies in wait at the end of the stones. When questioned, Israeli soldiers say that they have been ordered not to shoot children under 12 – one wonders how a soldier can determine the age of his target from a distance – in fact, many young children are among the dead and wounded.

"Why don't you stop them going to throw stones?" I ask Oum Khalil a little brusquely. "Do you know that some people in Europe say that the Palestinians use their children to fight their cause?"

Oum Khalil gives me a look so full of pain that I feel ashamed of myself.

"Only someone who has never been a mother could dare say such a terrible thing! Look at my house: 25 square metres in all. Punishing him, even beating him, does no good. How could I keep him prisoner? He has to go to school and I can't always go to get him; it's coming home from school that they go to the barricades. There are no playgrounds here; there is only the street. Challenging the soldiers is like a game for them. They don't realise that it's fatal; they think they can run faster than the bullets and that they're going to liberate Palestine with stones. We try to reason with them but it doesn't work. If we lock the door, they jump out of the window!"

I tell her she's right and that I understand how impossible the situ-ation is and she once again bestows her beautiful smile on me. I don't say that calling these two children Khalil can only bind them to the older boy, the martyr and hero, with whom they will inevitably identify. Did we not in Europe, before the age of popular psychology, often name children after siblings who had died an untimely death? It was a way of making them live again, of denying their irrevocable disappearance.

Changing the subject, I ask the boys what they want to do when they are older.

The little dark, curly-haired Khalil, the picture of his mother and of his dead brother, says he wants to be a doctor.

"That's good, but for that you need to study and not spend all your time demonstrating on the streets!" I say, knowing that my words are falling on deaf ears. He laughs and tells me proudly that he has just made a new catapult.

The other Khalil, blond with light eyes, does not accompany him on his escapades. He is the intellectual of the family. He follows all the political debates on television and wants to become a journalist.

Two small boys, brimming with life and fun, the hope and joy of Oum Khalil. Two adorable youngsters whom I leave with a heavy heart ...

On the way back, Leila senses my unease and tries to explain.

"You know, victims will inevitably be glorified. It's the only way that people can grieve. Something that cannot be accepted – the violent death of a young son – has to be placed into the context of the struggle for the homeland, so that it is no longer just total loss but has a meaning. Otherwise, one would go mad. But of course this glorification of 'martyrs' means that youngsters are not afraid to die. Their death gives meaning to their life, which in the current situation has none. They are willing to take any risk and even to become a suicide bomber. Because for most of them their existence is nothing more than a series of humiliations, frustrations and deprivation."

I leave Leila to return to Jerusalem where I have a rendezvous with a conscientious objector, one of the Israeli soldiers who refuse to participate in the repression of the Palestinian people.

However, when I get to Qalandiya, I see a crowd of people waiting. The checkpoint has been closed since the beginning of the afternoon and no one knows why. Accompanied by a young woman, I approach the barrier, the soldiers threatening us with their machine guns. The young woman implores, tears in her eyes: "I'm from Jerusalem, I have to get back; my children are waiting for me."

At the sight of her pleading, a soldier begins to laugh.

The solution? To make a large detour around 'al Kassarat', the quarry, to the checkpoint at Ram, which might be open.

Next to me a small group are discussing what to do. Finally they decide to try to get to Ram by taxi, across country roads. I join them. We make slow progress, a passenger in the first vehicle occasionally getting out and walking ahead a little to see if the way is clear. At one point he signals us to stop while we hold our breath; after several minutes, he indicates that we can go on, the soldiers having departed.

Finally the taxis set us down in the middle of the country. A dozen of us walk down the hillside in single file. There is no path and the stones slide beneath our feet; I thank my stars that I have not brought a bag. This is athletic enough. The men walk quickly, without waiting to see if we can keep up. With my French mentality, I find their behaviour somewhat boorish, until I realise that here women have to be, and are, as strong as men: sometimes stronger. They are not weak creatures but mothers, sisters, wives and fighters.

We cross through fields. Below, we can see the motorway reserved for Israeli cars and those with the yellow licence plate of Jerusalem.[4] There may not be any soldiers around, but if settlers see us from the road, might they not shoot at us? We have the look of real terrorists, a small group of grimy men and women coming down the mountain to the barbed wire fence, almost three metres high, bordering the road. I think my companions are completely mad but what can I do? I continue following. We get to the fence and start walking along it, sweating heavily under the midday sun. Suddenly I see the leader of our little group weaving his way through the barbed wire: it has been cut. We all slip through. One of my companions explains that Palestinians regularly cut the wire and the army regularly replaces it, until it is cut again.

On the road we wait while the Israeli vehicles passby. It is a surreal situation. They know who we are and that we have no right to be here, but fortunately not all Israelis are keen to enforce the law ...

We do not wait long. A small van with a yellow number plate stops. "It's a Palestinian from Jerusalem", one of my travelling companions, a cheerful young girl who has learnt French through a correspondence course, tells me. We all pile into the back. Our driver asks no questions and makes no request for payment. He knows that he has taken us out of a dangerous situation and that he runs the risk of being arrested or

4. The yellow plate is for Israelis, and Palestinians who live in Jerusalem. The blue plate is for Palestinians in the occupied territories.

denounced on by an Israeli driver. But like all Palestinians he feels a clear duty to help his compatriots.

An Israeli military jeep is just behind. With the incredible self-control these people have, no one turns a hair. The jeep overtakes us and a soldier leans out of the window to stare at us, my companions continuing to look straight ahead. Palestinians never look at soldiers or Israeli settlers and prefer not to see them. Their expressions could reveal too much and be too dangerous.

We pass Atarot, a small Israeli airport, and then approach the Ram checkpoint. Just before we get there, our driver stops and, still silent, opens the door. We walk the last few hundred metres to the barrier. There, to my surprise, instead of queuing in front of the sentry box to be checked, my companion signals to me and we calmly cross the road, without anyone asking us anything!

In a war-torn country that is entirely sealed off, such crazy contra-dictions are rife: at times military control reigns, at others oriental mayhem! Palestinians take advantage of this paradoxical situation – in which civilians are killed without reason while gaping holes exist in the Israeli security system – to live, to work, to visit family in Jerusalem ... There aren't really any rules. You stay at home, which is actually no guarantee of safety, or take your chance and risk your life outside.

Palestinians seem ready to run this risk to fulfil not only their vital but also their frivolous needs. They have had enough of all these restric-tions and need to get out, to breathe freely!

I hail a taxi and get to the King David Hotel just in time to meet Itaï.

A CONSCIENTIOUS OBJECTOR

He is like a breath of fresh air blowing across the starchy entrance of the King David Hotel. I know immediately that this tall young man with an open expression, athletic movements, bright eyes and wide childlike smile, is Itaï. I had been told: "You'll see, he's an exceptional chap".

We begin by discussing the bomb attack in Jerusalem the night before, which had killed nine people. He talks calmly, without the passion usual in Palestinians and Israelis when such a sensitive subject is raised.

"I am against the occupation but I am also against the suicide bombings. The Palestinians are weakening their cause and losing the sympathy that they won at the beginning of the intifada. I know a great deal of the responsibility is ours, having occupied and mistreated them for 35 years, but I don't think the suicide bombings are a good strategy. I could perhaps understand someone from Jenin waking up one morning and, in an act of despair, going to blow himself up in the middle of a group of Israelis, but these acts are planned and encouraged. That is what I cannot accept. Even if they believe that it is the only way of ending the occupation, of being heard, they do not have the right to do that. It really disappoints me that more Palestinians do not take a firm stand against these attacks but just condemn them half-heartedly. People here are more and more convinced that they are hell-bent on killing us, driving us out of the country into the sea.

"Even if you convince me that it is a good means of advancing their cause, I would still say that it is harmful for them. They are destroying their society. You can't educate young people by telling them it's accept-able to kill women and children to achieve your goals, that the end makes all means legitimate ... An individual needs to draw a 'red line' that he will never cross, for the simple reason that he is a human being and to cross the line is to become less than human. That is the line that we conscientious objectors have drawn for ourselves."

"How did you come to take that decision?"

"I've just turned 30. I've served in the army for 12 years, four full years as a captain and then for periods of about a month every year. From 1991 to 1994, during the first intifada, I did my military service in the occupied territories. It took me 12 years to realise that what we were doing there is unjustifiable and goes against all morality and all humanity. Even if you tried to convince me that it is the only solution, I would say that we still should do all we can to find another one."

"When Palestinians say: 'We condemn the suicide bombings of civilians but not of soldiers or settlers because we don't have any weapons and the Israelis refuse to negotiate', how do you respond?"

"They are perfectly entitled to do what they want against soldiers. I have often tried to put myself in the place of Palestinians and I have no doubt that I would act in the same way, but I also know that I would never put a bomb in a discotheque."

"And against settlers, who are occupiers?"

"I'm not sure I know the answer to that. It's complicated. There are children, women; and most of them go there for economic, not ideological reasons, because the Israeli government is mad enough to give them all sorts of material aid as incentives to settle. Most of them would be happy to leave if they were given financial compensation."

"To come back to you, where are you and your family from?"

"I was born in Jerusalem in 1971. My father's side of the family come from Turkey; my father made his aliyah in 1954, not because the family had problems in Turkey but for ideological reasons. My mother's side of the family are Sephardic Jews who have lived in Jerusalem for generations. When I was young I didn't have much to do with Arabs. When I went to Bethlehem or to east Jerusalem, I spoke to Arab traders, but just on a superficial level. At university, where I am still studying geology, there are no Arabs in my class and just a few in the entire university, though we have little contact with them. But I spent two years in Jordan, doing fieldwork. There, I made many Palestinian friends and we had many discussions.

"At the time of the first intifada, I was 18 and had served as a soldier everywhere – in Hebron, in Gaza. From the beginning I tried to stand back and look objectively at what we were doing there, in even the smallest daily situations. I felt that it was wrong.

"I always tried to be polite and to persuade others to be, to do their duty as humanely and as honestly as possible. I told myself that it was the only way to defend the state of Israel, and I believed it. You feel better if you smooth the rough edges, prevent gratuitous brutality – but in the end you realise that just by being there you are part of the operation and whether you do it with more or less consideration, at the end of the day, you are arresting and humiliating people, carrying out searches. So whether you say hello or not, it ultimately comes to the same thing.

When all is said and done, we are doing what every army of occupation does and doing things by the book when you arrest people at checkpoints doesn't make the inhumanity of what you are doing disappear.

"Sometimes soldiers cry after they have shot someone. That is pure hypocrisy, a way of absolving yourself, of persuading yourself that you have a beautiful soul. What do the Palestinians that we are occupying care about our guilt?"

Itaï fiddles with his glass.

"The most terrible experience is the way people look at you when you go into a house at night and wake them up; you have entered their private space, walking around their tiny rooms and stepping on their blankets with your huge boots. Then you start going through their things. Small children cry, cling on to their mother, who protects them from the giants that we must seem like to them. Almost all Israeli soldiers will tell you it's wrong to do that but that there is no other way ..."

Shuddering, he stares at a point high above our heads.

"That haunts me, the way people look at you ..."

"What led you to decide to give it up?"

"It wasn't a particular incident. It was two years of a series of events and discussions with my military friends. Many of them thought that what we were putting the Palestinians through was unacceptable. They thought that we should avoid the abuses and the brutality but that we had to continue despite everything to protect Israel. Some even said, 'We live in a democracy and we have no choice; we have to do what the democratically elected government is asking us to do'. I tried to explain to them that it was precisely because we lived in a democracy that we had the right and the duty to speak out when we thought that we had gone beyond the limit. That debate still goes on between us. I say to them, 'This conflict has gone on for 35 years. Thirty-five years should be long enough to understand that we cannot conquer by force and that that the only solution is real negotiation: we must agree to give Palestinians an independent country and not, as we propose, autonomous Bantustans under army surveillance'.

"But, you know, the decision to refuse to serve in the occupied territories has been a difficult one. I had 50 soldiers under my command. I felt responsible. Now they will go in without me and things could go badly; one of them could be killed and I feel guilty about not being with them. It's not easy. That is why many carry on, even if they know this is no solution. They go out of loyalty to their soldiers. As officers we are taught to give an example and always be first in the pack. But when I was in the occupied territories, I couldn't simply shout out to my men, 'Follow me!' I knew that if one of my soldiers had been killed there, I couldn't look his mother in the eye and say, 'He didn't die in vain'.

"On the other hand, I think I have the right to say 'Follow me!' in terms of what I am doing now. Today I could look the mother of a soldier in the eye and say, 'I have done all I can to try to prevent these totally futile deaths'.

"Before I took my decision, I thought about it for two years. I talked a lot with my commanding officer and then, one day, I said to him: 'I won't be coming for the next tour of duty. I am willing to serve absolutely anywhere else and I'm very happy to do a longer period, but not there'. He agreed to transfer me elsewhere.

"I was lucky. I only got 21 days in prison; the average is 28 days. The maximum is 35. You have the right to a very brief military trial but the result is a foregone conclusion. The judge was one of my superiors. Before the trial we talked for three hours but what counted most for me was that at the end he said, 'I do not agree with you but I totally understand the reasons for your decision and I respect it'.

"The conscientious objectors movement began with two officers who came back from Gaza and said, 'It's over, we're not going back!' At the moment[1], there are 460 of us who have said that we are ready to serve anywhere except the occupied territories. We have formed a group and issued a public statement saying that what soldiers are doing in the territories has nothing to do with the defence of Israel. Some people have accused us of being traitors, but the media have increasingly tried to understand what has led to young patriots saying, 'We've had enough!'

"It's obvious to everyone that we're not trying to get out of serving; we are officers of élite regiments and no one can question our devotion to our country. That is why our position is so strong and why it makes people think. We are very active and we hold little meetings at which we talk about our experiences and our activism, about what it is actually possible to do to stop the occupation as soon as possible."

"What is your family's reaction?"

"It has not been easy for them. They understand me but I'm not sure that they really agree. My sister, for example, is in total disagreement. The situation is so complex in Israel that there are differences of opinion even within families.

1. Summer 2002.

"The problem is that all these suicide bombers don't make it easier for conscientious objectors to be understood. It is difficult for me to talk about morality when we are seeing civilians massacred. When you see bodies blown to pieces in the street, the natural reaction is to want revenge. But one mustn't forget that that is also how Palestinians react when the army kills their children.

"We have to stop this infernal cycle of violence that feeds on itself. One man is like another; he wants to live in peace. We don't know the Palestinians, we don't see them, we make them out to be very different from us, create an image of them as fanatics who love death; we cannot believe that they want to live normal lives, in their own country, like all people who have the right to a country.

"Of course I want to fight terrorism. But how do we fight it? Is it by occupying a city, arresting families, destroying houses, humiliating people and torturing suspects? It's true that we sometimes find guns or catch a perpetrator but at the same time we are inciting thousands of young people to become the next generation of terrorists."

"There are very few conscientious objectors. Do you think that they can have a real influence?"

"We know that we will never be a mass movement. What counts is the discussions we organise, the street activities. We are ready to pay the price for the stand we are taking. In fact, many people approve of what we are doing but don't want to do so publicly. Very few, for example, will agree to put a sticker saying 'Stop the occupation now!' on their cars.

"There is only one solution to this conflict: two states living side by side. The proposal of a single state is unrealistic. Everyone will be happier with two separate states."

He hesitates slightly.

"I would like to be sure that the Palestinians will agree to a country within the limits of the occupied territories and will no longer look towards Israel but, unfortunately, I am not certain they will. Even so, I support the creation of an independent, thriving Palestine that will do business with us. Those who still dream of taking Israel back would be increasingly marginalised by the majority that want to live in peace. The minority are desperadoes who will eventually cease to exist.

"But a lot of money is needed for the refugees, who cannot return home, and who should be given what they need to make a new life elsewhere. A lot of money also needs to be given to help set up the new Palestinian state and to ensure that poverty doesn't force a frustrated people to listen to extremists. All that is possible but it will take time. It will take a long time to establish peace between the two countries. You cannot expect, the day a Palestinian state is created, all the Palestinian attacks to stop or Israeli extremists not to fire another shot. It will take perhaps a generation for those who oppose a compromise solution to accept it.

"Israel should remain vigilant but the issue of security doesn't bother me because we will be able to defend our country much more effectively, both morally and practically. In terms of the international arena, we will have clear, recognised borders, whereas at the moment we are fighting for a country that isn't ours. At the moment there are no borders – there are settlements. Everything is confused. What am I fighting for? To defend my country or as a colonist, trying to keep something that doesn't belong to me?

"What frustrates me is that I am sure that most people in Israel would be willing to give back most of the occupied territories, if not all of them, and I also believe that most Palestinians will want peace if we give them back the occupied territories.

"Both sides will need leaders who have a vision and who are courageous enough to take tough decisions. It isn't easy for Arafat to say, 'OK, I'll sign a peace treaty but the refugees – apart from several thousand who can go to join their families – will not be able to go home'. And it isn't easy for an Israeli leader to say, 'Let's give back the Temple Mount to Palestinians, because their mosques are there and they need to be able to look after their sacred sites'.

"All that will be difficult. But I remain optimistic. I know that the great majority on both sides are willing to make sacrifices to obtain peace."

4

◆

Suicide Bombings

WAFA, THE FIRST FEMALE
SUICIDE BOMBER

On the 27th January 2002, a 28-year-old woman blew herself up in the centre of Jerusalem, killing one man and wounding forty others.

For the first time since the beginning of the intifada, the suicide bomber was a woman and the shock was as great among Palestinians as among Israelis. The Israeli and Western media rushed – as they had done since the suicide bombings began – to point to the fanaticism of religiously indoctrinated, perhaps even drug-crazed, young people promised the delights of a Muslim paradise, with its seventy virgins. For men, that is; Islam is less specific about heaven for women ...

But once the facts were revealed, it became embarrassingly clear that Wafa could not be put into the category of fanatic or crank – categories that allow us to label without need to explain. She had studied, had a profession and, if she was undoubtedly a good Muslim, she was not particularly religious because – an unmistakeable sign in her community – she refused to wear the veil.

Accompanied by a neighbour, I go to visit her family in the al-Amari camp, just outside Ramallah. Like all Palestinian camps, this has not for many years been made up of tents but is an accumulation of small houses built of daub or breeze block with corrugated iron roofs: boiling in the summer and freezing in the winter. In the maze of narrow alleyways, mostly dirt tracks with an open drain running down the centre, swarms of children are playing. The air is thick with a suffocating white dust – a minor inconvenience compared with the problem of the winter months, when the camp is engulfed by torrents of mud.

Wafa's mother, Wasfiyah, a robust, white-haired woman dressed in the long embroidered traditional robe, sits waiting for me on the mattress covered with bright-coloured material which, in Middle Eastern families of modest means, serves as a sofa. To either side are other mattresses, covered with cushions, for guests. In the middle of the room stands a low table. The rug, gold-coloured trinkets and artificial flowers that usually adorn Palestinian homes are absent. The only decorations are on the wall: a map of Palestine in cross-stitch embroidery and the sons' wedding photos, showing men with scant moustaches and brides dressed, European-style, in white organza. In the centre, in a golden frame, a young woman with red hair tumbling on to her shoulders, dressed in the black gown and mortar board peculiar to British students, receives a parchment scroll.

"That's Wafa", her mother says proudly, "at the graduation ceremony for her nursing diploma."

I approach the picture and examine the rounded face, with its peach complexion, light eyes and carefully made up smiling lips. I try to understand ...

The family came from a village outside Ramleh, near Jaffa. Her mother's parents, who were farmers, fled in July 1948, terrified, like tens of thousands of other Palestinians, by the oncoming Israeli troops and the tales of massacred populations in Deir Yassin, Al Doueimeh, Abu Shusheh, Kafr Kassem and dozens of other villages.[1] At the time, Wasfiyah was just 10 years old.

"We walked and walked for days", the old lady recalled. "The heat was overwhelming. People let us take shelter in their orchards and gave us food. We were frightened and we wanted to get as far away from the Israelis as possible. Finally we stopped here, at Ramallah. The Red Cross had put up a camp of tents. We stayed and in time the tents became houses."

Wasfiyah married a boy from the camp, who had also come from Ramleh. They had four children: Wafa being the only girl and her father's favourite. He died when she was eight.

"She went to primary school in the camp and then to secondary school in Ramallah. She got interested in politics very early on. At the time of the first intifada, the 'war of stones', she was barely 14. Her teachers came to see me, asking me to control her because she was going to all the demonstrations and they thought it was dangerous for her. At 15 she was already a leader. Look!"

She pointed out a photo that I hadn't noticed, showing a teenager with sparkling eyes, the black and white band of the Fatah fighters wound round her head.

---

1. In 1948, Jewish militia such as Irgun, but sometimes also the *Haganah*, which would become the Israeli army, destroyed entire villages and massacred the inhabitants, to terrorise the Palestinians and force them to leave. These facts were denied for many years but were confirmed by research carried out by Israeli 'new historians' 15 or so years ago.

"She was outraged by all the injustice – the injustice done to Palestinians but also here in the camp, the little, everyday wrongs. She was always trying to be of service, to help people who had problems."

Thronging the entrance to the house was a group of neighbours come to see the foreign journalist; at this, they registered their agreement. Everyone in the camp had loved Wafa; she was so helpful and cheerful. They could not understand how a young woman like that had brought herself to do such a thing. They could imagine it of anyone but her!

In a corner of the room, surrounded by her children, her sister-in-law sits silently. She looks as though she knows something more, but I sense that she will not talk in front of the others.

"We married her at 17", her mother continues. "A good age for girls." And doubtless also a way of getting her to settle down. There would be no question of her going out on to the streets. And then things were also beginning to sort themselves out politically. The Oslo agreements were a light at the end of the tunnel and Palestinians were full of hope; they had begun to establish a framework for their future country.

"But the marriage failed. Wafa could not have children. Her husband loved her but in the Middle East a man is not a man if he doesn't have offspring. After ten years, he asked for a divorce."

"That must have been a shock. Was she depressed?"

Depression after the divorce was the reason that some people had offered as explanation for the young woman's actions. To be divorced and without children is not an enviable position in Middle Eastern society.

Her mother did not reply, no doubt split between the traditional sentiment that a young woman who has been divorced must be unhappy and a refusal to reduce the reasons for her daughter's actions to psychological problems, as the Israeli papers had immediately done.

Her sister-in-law, Mervet, indicated that she wished to speak to me. I went to sit next to her.

"You know, I was Wafa's best friend. We lived here together for three years. We were more or less the same age and she told me things that she could not have told her mother. It's true that she was sad just after her divorce but she got back on to her feet very soon and was enjoying her new freedom. She began by removing her veil. I reproached her for that but she just laughed and said that faith wasn't measured by a veil; she said that it was better to be an honest woman without a veil than a hypocrite with one. The truth is, I think her divorce liberated her. When she was with her husband she felt guilty about not being able to give him children, but afterwards she forgot all about her problems. She seemed much happier than before. Her horizon had broadened from her family to the whole community. As a nurse she just didn't stop, what with visiting old people and giving injections to the sick. She was like a ray of sunlight for everyone!"

"So how do you explain what she did?"

"She had been deeply upset for months by what she was seeing. She had joined the Red Cross as a nurse and there she saw the worst. She had witnessed atrocious things in Naplouse, Jenin, Ramallah – women and children killed when they broke the curfew to go and buy food, wounded people dying without her being able to help. Three times when she had tried to go to people, she had been shot with rubber bullets.[2] She had seen women give birth in front of checkpoints and lose their baby and sick people dying because they couldn't get to hospital. She told me how she had pleaded in vain with the soldiers to let ambulances through ... Every night she would come home exhausted and stressed and tell us everything she had seen. She was more and more outraged by what the Israelis were doing to civilians and by the world's indifference. But she never talked to me about the suicide bombings. I even remember that she would say nothing when the subject came up."

"Do you think she had been thinking about it for a long time or did she do it in a moment of despair?"

"Well, it's something you need time to prepare for. You have to get hold of a belt of explosives and to do that you have to be in touch with certain groups. They have to accept you and be sure that you are reliable enough not to panic at the last minute and, under pressure from the Israelis, give information that would lead back to them. And then you have to choose the place where you are going to carry out the attack and work out how to get into it – which, given the surveillance, must be very difficult. All that must take days, if not weeks."

Mervet shakes her head, her eyes filling with tears.

"When I think that Wafa was carrying that terrible decision alone all that time and that I suspected nothing ... If I had known ... perhaps I could have dissuaded her."

"Yet you didn't notice anything the night before?" I persisted. "She wasn't anxious, tense?"

"No. We all had dinner together and she told us about what she had done during the day, as usual. In the morning she left for the Red Cross

2. So-called rubber bullets are in fact bullets made of steel but covered with rubber; shot from close range they can break limbs and even kill.

at 8.30. When she didn't come back at six in the evening, we began to worry, because she was usually very punctual. We contacted the Red Cross, family, friends, but no one had seen her. So we began looking in all the hospitals, thinking that maybe she had been wounded. It was only three days later that we heard on television that the suicide bomber who had blown themselves up in Jaffa Street, in the middle of Jerusalem, was she. We just couldn't believe it and we still cannot understand how she had got to that point. She loved life so much."

I rejoin Wafa's mother, thinking that perhaps she can give me an explanation, but I can get nothing from her other than the usual pronouncement made by the mother of a 'martyr'. In Palestinian terminology, anyone killed by the Israelis is deemed a martyr, particularly if they die fighting.

"I am proud of my daughter", she declares firmly, "because she served a noble cause and sacrificed herself for Palestine."

"But didn't she also serve it by looking after the wounded?"

She doesn't reply, doesn't look at me, sitting as motionless as a statue. Finally she speaks.

"Nothing could dissuade Wafa when she was convinced that something was right."

I could not be so cruel as to ask her if she too believed that it was right to kill civilians.

After Wafa, other young women have followed her example in becoming suicide bombers. On the 27th February 2002, Darine Abu Aisha, 21, who was studying English at Naplouse University, blew herself up at a military checkpoint in the West Bank. Three Israeli policemen were wounded. Darine had said that she could no longer bear to see so many Palestinian women and children being killed and she wanted to avenge their deaths. On the 29th March, Ayat al Akhrass, 18, from Deheish near Bethlehem, blew herself up in a shopping centre in west Jerusalem, killing two people. On the 12th April, a young Palestinian woman, pretending to be pregnant, blew herself up in west Jerusalem, killing six people. During the three months of interviews, I met many young men and women who replied in the affirmative to the direct question, "Would you be willing to carry out a suicide bombing?" Organisations say that they receive so many applications, they cannot deal with them all.

ORIT'S SORROW

On the 9th March 2002, at ten o'clock in the evening, a Palestinian went into *Moment*, a Jerusalem café very popular with young people, and blew himself up, killing 11 people and wounding dozens of others.

One of the victims was Limor ben Shoham. In Hebrew, 'Limor' means the delicate perfume of a flower. She was 27 years old.

Three months later I meet her sister, Orit, through the intermediary of an Israeli friend. Her mother had refused to see me, as she had refused to see any journalists – in her eyes, vultures feeding off her suffering. Orit, however, had accepted, saying that she wanted to talk, to explain ...

I meet her in the foyer of the King David Hotel, one of the few places where my Israeli interlocutors said they felt safe. Why? The security service there seemed no more nor less effective than anywhere else but it is one of the grand places in Jerusalem, an oasis of luxury that houses eminent guests, and doubtless that is why people feel particularly protected.

I see a tiny figure coming towards me, wearing a simple linen dress. I am immediately struck by the large, cat-like eyes that engulf a small, pallid face framed by red hair, cut short like a boy's as though to offset a feminine fragility. She emanates an extreme sensitivity alongside a kind of rebelliousness. There is an indefinable sadness about her.

She sits straight down on the edge of an armchair and struggles to compose her voice, to seem natural, objective – though who would demand, dear Orit, that you be objective about the series of assassinations that tear apart your nation and which have torn apart your family? Bravely, she begins speaking calmly about the conflict and the need for a 'democratic', negotiated solution, not based on hatred ... but it is too much, and she breaks down.

"Arafat is no different from Hitler – you can't negotiate with him! Why doesn't the world understand that? How can the world not see that we have nothing but this country? Where can we go? It is the only place we Jews have! The Palestinians want to force us to leave. Recently they placed another bomb underneath a truck carrying gas bottles in Afpula, right in the town centre; if it hadn't been defused, hundreds of people would have been killed!"

I let her talk. She needs to pour out her pain. When, after a while, I venture that Sharon is himself no choirboy and that, since the beginning of the military operation, many Palestinian children have been killed, she is clearly startled.

"How can you compare Sharon and Arafat? And those burials of children are usually fake. Spy planes have taken photos that show that as soon as the funeral procession is out of camera shot, the corpse gets up and walks."

I look at her, stunned. She persists.

"You think I'm lying? I have seen it on television!"

No, I don't think you're lying. I only know that hundreds of journalists covering the conflict have seen Palestinian children killed and have attended funerals – of which, unfortunately, there are enough not to have to stage macabre pantomimes. I also know that with digital technology one can 'show' whatever one wants.

She seems so frail, with her bare shoulders above her white dress, in the midst of the golds and the fake marble of the King David: an image of purity, foiled justice and wounded innocence.

"We live with fear and anxiety every day; I don't dare go out any more, hardly go to work, I don't dare take public transport or go into a shop, I'm frightened to go to the bank, to walk in the park, I am constantly terrified ... How would you cope if you couldn't go out into the street without fear of being killed?

Orit is even frightened to tell me her story. "Perhaps I shouldn't tell you my name; the terrorists might try and get revenge, come to kill me as well."

I struggle to convince her that if they can put a bomb in a café, they are not interested in her personally; she is not a political leader. Gradually I manage to reassure her and in the end she acknowledges that speaking to me will not put her in any danger.

Orit is 38 but has the air of a tragic little girl. She has lost a lot of weight since her sister's death.

"I can't eat", she confides. "I think about her all the time. If only you had known her! She loved life so much; she adored dancing, had so many friends – most of them artists, like her. Her hobby was theatrical make-up and she was really good at it. She wanted to make a career of it ... Oh, I hate that monster!"

Her lovely smile cracks and she is on the verge of tears. I feel almost guilty about daring to say that Sharon might not be doing all he can to put an end to these killings. She defends him, seeing Arafat as the personification of Evil and Palestinians as heartless creatures prepared to send their children to their deaths to advance their cause. How could she see things any other way? It is what the majority of the mainstream Israeli media dole out to their audiences all day.

"Perhaps you think I hate Arabs?" she parries. "Not at all. There are two Arab women in the firm where I work. I don't have any problem with them, even since my sister died. I have nothing against Palestinians or Israeli Arabs. I will never hate them. It's Arafat that I hate; he exploits his people and doesn't give them any means of educating themselves. All he can do is teach them how to kill."

I don't try to tell her that Palestinians place so much importance on education that they are the most qualified people in the Arab world. She repeats, through tensed lips, "Arafat is like Hitler. There is no comparison with Sharon – he doesn't send children or terrorists to kill themselves".

What can one say to that, Orit? Tell you about the camps of Sabra and Shatila in Lebanon, where, in 1982, around two thousand people – civilians, women and children – were massacred over a period of 40 hours, the camp having been sealed off by Sharon's soldiers? Describe what the soldiers of this same Sharon are doing today? It would be cruel and futile ... My attitude, being other than one of unreserved approval, is already hurtful to you, an insult to your suffering.

Orit is reluctant to leave now. Having tried to convince me of her arguments, without real success, she feels wounded, and that she should not have come. But even though I feel a real empathy for and understanding of her, I cannot agree with her conclusions.

She silently reproaches me, her eyes thunderous and her smile tinged with bitterness.

"You think the Israelis are just as much to blame. You don't understand, you put us on the same level but it's false. We are not the same! Our soldiers are not there to kill. It's a war and they are defending themselves; sometimes there's an accident, that's all. The Palestinians want a bloodbath. They don't care if they die or if they see their children dying. You can't compare us and you don't have the right to do that!"

Her voice cracks with indignation. The despair of not making herself understood makes her aggressive and I am suddenly worried that she will have some kind of nervous attack or that she will jump up, sweep the table of its contents and leave. But she controls herself, swallows her anger and, courageously, smiles again ...

How can I describe to you, dear Orit, the pain of Palestinian mothers whose sons of eight or ten have been killed or of the parents weeping for their children, shot or crushed under the rubble of their house? How can I tell you about the honour of certain Israeli soldiers but the dishonour of others; the inhuman attitude that many of them have – such as those who targeted a 10 year old child coming back from school and shot him five times, leaving him paralysed for life?

I cannot tell you all that, Orit; it would be cruel even to try because at the moment you cannot hear anything.

I talk to her very gently, as one talks to a sick child, but my conscience does not allow me to agree with her perspective, despite my desire to help her and to comfort her in her pain. I cannot lie to that degree. Sometimes one lies to the dying, who cannot face their inevitable demise, but you have your life before you, Orit and one day you will have to understand, even if only to be able to live.

"The world does not react", she repeats, half-angry, half-despairing. "They try to blame everybody and they try and say everyone is the same. The Palestinians are killing us and no one says anything."

Her lips fold into an expression of disgust.

"More than anything, I hate those Israeli intellectuals who blame us and say everything is our fault."

Her pretty face suddenly twists into an expression of hatred.

"Because of them, it is going to happen again!"

"What?"

"The Holocaust! The Palestinians don't want us here, they don't want Israel. I am certain of that – certain! There is going to be another Holocaust, created by the Palestinians! But the world does not want to accept that. The world hates us!"

She gets up, biting back her tears. I take her hands. I want to stop her going, console her, but what can I say? I cannot enter her nightmare.

On the pavement outside the King David, I watch her leave, alone and helpless. I too feel like crying for the distress of this fragile young woman, so lost and so disgusted with a world that does not understand her and that she does not understand, who is taking with her the bitter sense that her efforts to convince me have been in vain …

No, dear Orit, your effort has not been in vain. You have taken me into the depths of your people's suffering and, above all, into the ocean of incomprehension that exists between two nations manipulated by certain politicians and extremists.

The words of Leila Shahid, the PLO representative in France, come back to me: "The conflict is less between Palestinians and Israelis than between those who want peace and those who want war".

5

◆

Freedom of Expression

ITINERARY OF A PALESTINIAN JOURNALIST

Jawdat Mannar has been held up in Ramallah, where he works, for four months, since the Israeli invasion in March 2002. His family live in Bethlehem, half an hour way. In normal times he commutes every day but since the start of the curfew and the reinforced checkpoints, he hasn't seen his wife and four children. As soon as he can, he will try to bring them here – if he can find accommodation and can afford to pay for what he hopes will be a temporary arrangement.

"If it isn't very comfortable, too bad", he laughs. "We're used to it; we're children of the camps!"

Jawdat's family came from the village of Zakariya, near Lod airport. They were forced out in 1948 and went to a village near Hebron, which again, they had to leave, finally settling in Bethlehem, in the refugee camp of Deheishe, where Jawdat was born. He is a dark-skinned, big man in his early fifties.

"Before 1948, my father fought with the Palestinian movement against Zionism and Jewish immigration. Afterwards, under Jordanian rule, he continued the struggle for an independent Palestine. The Jordanians imprisoned him for three years, because although they let us live how we wanted, all political activity was forbidden. I remember going with my mother to visit my father in prison when I was five years old. It was an old prison in Jerusalem, dark and dirty. As I was a child, I was the only one allowed into his cell; my mother would give me little bits of paper scrunched into balls – messages – to give him. So, I quickly learnt to keep quiet about things. My father came back when I was eight. One day the teacher came into the class and told me, 'You can go home; there's a surprise for you'. When I arrived, lots of people from the camp had come to welcome my father. That was the most wonderful day of my life!"

His eyes fill with tears at the memory.

"I think of all those children whose fathers are in prison today – five thousand men since the last Israeli invasion. A house without a father is a terrible thing …

"At first, we lived in tents in the camp. The school was also a tent and there was no health centre. More than anything, we were always hungry. One time, a teacher brought some bread into the classroom and went out for five minutes, leaving the bread on his desk. There were 40 of us; we took the bread and shared it out. When I think of it now, I am certain that he did it on purpose but he didn't want to wound our pride by handing out the bread himself. He pretended not to have noticed anything.

"Every child in the camp whose father was absent – dead or in prison – was entitled to one meal a day, distributed by UNWRA. But you had to have a card to get it, the same card they gave malnourished children. I queued up at the doctor's, along with hundreds of other children, to get that wretched card. I remember appearing in front of the doctor three times. Each time he said, 'You're fine; you don't need a card', but I was hungry!

"When I left the camp school, I went to secondary school in Bethlehem. I didn't go to university. At that time, there wasn't one in the West Bank and I didn't have the money to go abroad."

"When did you begin to be politically aware?"

"As a child. At home I listened to Radio Cairo – under the blankets, because it was forbidden. Nasser was my hero, with his talk about liberating Palestine. My father's imprisonment and the situation of people in the camp influenced us politically. We would ask each other: 'Where do you come from? Which village? How were you evicted? How many died?'.

"When Nasser passed away in 1971, I and a group of friends organised a peaceful demonstration in Bethlehem. There were 25,000 of us. The Israeli security forces arrested me and threatened me. They kept me in prison for two weeks. I was 16. From then on, I began to be really active. As I had no contact with the PLO, which was based outside the country, I worked on the ground. I campaigned in defence committees against settlers who shot at people in the camps; later, I was their spokesman and met various delegations. But I never had any military involvement. It's not in my nature and I feel I can be more useful in the political arena, by speaking and writing. That is why I became a journalist, which has earned me quite a few stints in prison!"

"For expressing your opinion? In Israel?"

He is surprised at my surprise.

"The Israeli press is free, but not the Palestinian press. The truth is dangerous for Israel, which has to give the world the image of a democratic country so that it can continue oppressing us in peace. These days, the battle for public opinion is vital: it is what precedes and justifies wars.

"During the first intifada, I spent several months in prison. They surrounded the building where I worked and ransacked my office. They wanted to bring me to a court martial because they had found 'dangerous literature' in my house. When they showed it to me, I pointed out that it was the copy of an article from a big Israeli daily, *Ha'aretz*. 'Do *they* have the right to publish that but not *me*?' I asked them. 'It's against the state of Israel', they said. 'So what about freedom of speech? I thought Israel was a democracy!'

"I spent several days in prison and then they let me out, with a huge fine. The Israeli soldier who accompanied me said, 'I'm sorry about all this – I'm also a journalist'.

"I was free but I couldn't work any more. They closed my office for six months, confiscated my press card and my driving licence and cut my phone line abroad for two years.

"The third time, in 1990, they closed my office for two years. I had uncovered and published a story, backed up by evidence, implicating the security service. A Christian cemetery in Bethlehem had been desecrated and, according to the Israelis, it was clearly the work of Muslims. They are constantly trying to divide us. I found out, through a soldier who was overcome with remorse, that the Israeli security service had taken Palestinian prisoners during the curfew – it was at the time of the Gulf War – and forced them to desecrate the graves. To protect myself, I had used an Israeli witness who had heard the story direct from the soldier's mouth. But of course I was still put in prison, where they tortured me."

He turned his head away. It was obvious that he did not want to say more about it. I changed the subject.

"Have you ever been back to your family's village near Lod?"

"Yes, in 1967, when the borders were opened. I was 12. I knew the village like the back of my hand because my grandfather had told me about it every night. He had described the farm, the fields, the peace, the contentment ...

"When we went there, there were still a few houses standing, but the cemetery where our ancestors were buried had been destroyed and only the cellar of our house was left. My grandfather sat in it for a very long time ... Finally, I went up to him. His eyes were full of tears and he said, 'I remember our life here and I think of our life now in the camp ...'. We went home and he died two days later."

The smile that Jawdat had had throughout our interview suddenly disappeared.

"The Israelis continue to take our land and on top of that they want security! They will never have it as long as they act in that way. This generation feels more hatred than mine or my parents'. They have suffered even more and they have seen what was done to their parents and grandparents. The Israelis will never be able to impose peace through force.

Why does the West refuse to understand? Why does it let Israel do what it wants? Don't you see what we are going through? The Israelis are waging a clever and ruthless war against us. Is the West also at war with the Palestinian people?"

CHARLES ENDERLIN, ISRAELI JOURNALIST

Charles Enderlin, an Israeli of French origin, has, for over 22 years, been the well-known Jerusalem correspondent for the TV channel *France 2*. The author of a widely respected book on the conflict – *Shattered Dreams: the failure of the peace process in the Middle East, 1995–2002*[1] – he says that his work has become more and more difficult in the current climate of intolerance.

I had met Charles Enderlin often in various theatres of war in the Middle East, but had never before gone to his office on Jaffa Street. I went to see him on the 19th September 2002. It was a beautiful morning, but just as I got there, we learned that, in the centre of Tel Aviv that morning, a suicide bomber had blown himself up in a bus, killing five people and wounding over fifty others, of whom half a dozen were in a critical condition.

Between telephone calls and interviews for foreign radio and television, Charles still took the time to invite me to lunch at a corner of his desk and to speak to me about the problems of press freedom in Israel.

"Would you believe they have just awarded me the Goebbels prize!", he thundered. "I'm sick of these Jewish extremists trying to intimidate me! Since my report about little Muhammad al Durra,[2] who was killed in his father's arms in front of an Israeli post – a report that went round the world – they have been pursuing me with their hatred, trying to scare me out of doing my job as a journalist.[3] I received death threats and, on the advice of the police, had to hire the services of a security guard to watch my house at night. In the end we moved, because we were on the ground floor, we took a flat on the seventh floor with an entry phone.

---

1. Other Press, NY, 2003 (translated by Susan Fairfield).
2. Killed on 29th September 2000.
3. In its 2002 report, the Committee to Protect Journalists, based in New York, declared that the territories occupied by Israel had one of the worst records in the world in terms of the number of violations of press freedom and violence against journalists. Its findings were also corroborated by the report of the organisation Reporters sans Frontières.

"My wife and children, aged eight and ten, were physically attacked in the street by a Jew of French origin. My e-mail has been flooded with threatening and insulting messages – all fairly similar, which indicates an orchestrated campaign by an extremist group. And now they are awarding me the Goebbels prize! Mind you, I am in good company, alongside *Le Monde* and *Le Nouvel Observateur*, which one cannot really suspect of anti-Semitism!"

"How was your book *Shattered Dreams*, which deals with the real history of the Camp David negotiations, received in Israel?"

"No Israeli publisher wanted to buy the rights to publish it in Hebrew. On the other hand, my film on the negotiations will doubtless be shown in the autumn. It proves that Israel, and above all Ehud Barak, shared responsibility for the failure that has led to the current situation. This film, which has been shown in France, has also come out in the United States, but there they edited it in such a way that almost all the blame fell on Arafat.

"The atmosphere here has become oppressive. More and more, you are supposed to toe the party line. They tell you: 'We have no choice – we have to defend ourselves'. That blindness is dangerous for Israel and that is what really concerns me.

"A correspondent who specialises in military affairs reported that during a three-week period at the beginning of the intifada, when the Palestinians were using nothing but stones, the army shot 300,000 bullets in Gaza and 700,000 in the West Bank. He wrote two long articles severely criticising the army. Those allegations have not been taken up anywhere and there has been no response to them. This correspondent commented that all intelligence services analyses contradicting the official position are dismissed. That is very serious, because since 1973 and the phenomenal failure of our military intelligence at that time, all analysis is meant to be followed by counter-analysis. We need thinking, strategies and tactics, which do not exist now. We smash the Palestinians but the government has no serious long-term policy. They don't know where they're going.

"Do we really believe that we can suppress all the Palestinians? The persecution is creating thousand of suicide bombers, against whom no one can do anything much. We mustn't forget that in Gaza, the poorest region and the one in which the extremists hold greatest sway, fifty per cent of the population is under 15. Where does Sharon think he is going with his policy of repression, persecution and refusal of all negotiation?

"I believe we are heading for a catastrophe."

RAM LOEWY, ACTIVIST
FILM-MAKER

In Tel Aviv, I very much wanted to meet Ram Loewy, the Israeli film-maker. His films show, without militancy but also without ambiguity, the reality of Palestinian oppression; and destroy certain Israeli myths. I was impressed by them, particularly his documentaries on the eviction of Palestinian families in 1948, which demolish the official theory that the Palestinians left of their own free will; his film on the different treatment that Jewish and Arab delinquents receive; and that on torture testimonies, by Israeli soldiers themselves.

And not forgetting his short film about Mohammed, the little Gazan boy whose legs had to be amputated because soldiers had not let him through the checkpoints in time to get treatment. Thanks to Ram, I was able to meet Mohammed (see pages 167–74).

"I've had to fight like a demon to get every one of my films out", laughs this man, in whose open face enthusiasm and a certain idealism override the wrinkles and receding hair. "The censors did everything to try and get them banned, but the more obstacles they put in my way, the more publicity I got. There were big demonstrations outside the television station where I work, in which even the Right participated, in defence of free speech."

Despite the difficulties and the defamation that he experienced, Ram Loewy never gave up. He acknowledges, however, that he was able to make his films because he is Jewish.

"The Israelis would not have accepted a fraction of these criticisms from a non-Jew, who would immediately be accused of anti-Semitism, which has become the sledgehammer argument to refute all blame."

Where do his clarity and his courage come from?

"I was lucky enough to have an exceptional family. I was born, here in 1940, to parents who, Polish immigrants to France, had taken the last boat from Marseille to Haifa in 1940. My father published a Jewish newspaper – *Dantzig* – the only anti-Nazi newspaper. He was imprisoned in 1938 but as soon as he got out, he started publishing his newspaper again in Gdansk. The Germans were furious and forced the Poles to deport him – which saved his life, because he left Poland a month before the beginning of the war!

"My paternal grandparents, on the other hand, died in the Lod ghetto. And on my mother's side, all my uncles, aunts and cousins were killed in the Warsaw ghetto, apart from an uncle who was a poet and an aunt who was able to escape thanks to a Christian family.

"When my father found out about the death camps, it was a personal as well as a Jewish tragedy; he had received a German education and the Nazis' actions made him re-evaluate his entire culture, of which he had been so proud. Born in 1905, he had his youth before the coming of Hitler. He wrote in German, had been a student and a reporter in Berlin – in fact, he was much more German than Polish. He had met my mother when he went to interview her in Gdansk, after she won a beauty contest ..."

"Did your parents often speak about the persecution of the Jews?"

"No. When I was young, we never spoke about the Shoah, either in the family or with neighbours. And I have never wanted to make a film about the Holocaust. One does not have the right to use it for political ends, although that is constantly done these days. I find that contemptible and I agree totally with Finkelstein about the 'Holocaust industry' that allows us to justify the unjustifiable.[1]

"My father came to Israel because of the war, not because he believed in a Jewish state. He was a sceptic, with a keen sense of humour, while my mother was an enthusiastic Zionist and had been active in the Zionist movement in Poland. I was a member of the Scout movement and somewhat socialistic.

"But above and beyond Zionism, the Holocaust remains a question mark, on a personal level, in the life of every Jew: what exactly happened, and why? When I was very young – 16 or 17 – I asked myself those questions. In a context in which such atrocities had been perpetrated, what could one do to resist? Personally, I think that we should be even more mindful of the atrocities that we inflict than of those inflicted on us."

I listened, impressed. I have found, in certain Israelis and Palestinians, a moral grandeur that has almost ceased to exist in our spoilt western countries. Those who are embroiled in this tragedy have doubtless had to reflect deeply to understand what has happened to them and come up with possible alternatives. Most react from their

1. American philosopher who wrote *The Holocaust Industry: reflections on the exploitation of Jewish suffering* (Verso Books, 2001).

guts, superficially, and do nothing but add to the hatred; others – because they realise that it is vital to find a real solution rather than an escape route – attain an admirable breadth of vision.

"We use the evil inflicted on us, like a banner, to justify our actions", Ram continued. "I think that what Germans or non-Jews did during the war to help us is very important and that what we are doing individually to denounce the horrors that are now being perpetrated is equally vital. Since the age of 16, I have thought like that. Everything I do is more or less directly linked to the Holocaust.

"You ask how I developed this consciousness. Dinner at home was a constant battlefield. There was my mother, a proponent of Zionist slogans, and my father, the sceptic, asking me Socratic questions that forced me to re-examine my beliefs. I was constantly referring back to Zionist and socialistic Scout ideologies – Zionism being the Jewish way of achieving justice on earth. The idea behind Zionism is to make the Jewish nation an example to the world. The Bible says that we are the chosen people and that at the end of time, everyone will come to Jerusalem, which will be the light for all nations.

"At the time, we interpreted those words in socialist terms. We were in solidarity with the Black struggle in South Africa, with peoples' liberation groups and with all those altruistic movements. We had very elevated moral standards, while being totally unaware of what we were doing to the Palestinians!"

Listening to him, I begin to understand better how unbearable it is for Israelis brought up with these ideas to have to acknowledge the injustices perpetrated in their name. They cannot accept a picture of themselves as torturers.

"I had never met Palestinians inside Israel (Israeli Arabs, as we call them) before going to university. There were no Arabs in Tel Aviv. Before the 1948 war I remember some coming on their donkeys to sell fruit and sweets, but nothing afterwards ... But I knew very well, from discussions with my father, that Palestine was not a land without people.

"Filled with Zionist socialist idealism, I decided to spend my military service in a kibbutz and to become a farmer. We were convinced that we had to build a new nation. From a people expert in money matters, we should become a people who worked the land and produced food. But I very soon realised that most people used the kibbutz as a soft option for their military service, before returning to civilian life. I rebelled, accused them of hypocrisy and we fell out.

"I left the kibbutz, with a guilty conscience. I needed to do something useful for society. I went to university at the age of 22 to study economics and political science, whilst also earning a living working for the radio in Jerusalem. That is where I made my first Arab friends. It was the period when Israeli Arabs were under military occupation.[2] They were subject to all sorts of restrictions and the government used village leaders, 'yes men', to control everything. There were many land confiscations and the Secret Service was all-powerful.

"Nowadays there are still land confiscations and all sorts of controls, but the difference is that Palestinians in Israel have become aware of their rights. At that time they were much more docile and fatalistic, taking things as they came, as though they were beyond their control, like the weather. In times gone by, they had been ruled by the Turks, then the English, then the Jordanians and finally the Israelis – whoever *Allah* sent. Today, they fight.

"My political activism began with a radio programme for young people about the conflict between Jews and Arabs. I deliberately wanted to show positive aspects of the Arab world. One day I went to a pro-Arab demonstration, knowing that it would cause me problems at work. Most demonstrators were Israeli Arabs. I was holding a banner and some hooligans attacked me; a news cameraman filmed it. I expected to be sacked but the woman who ran the department rang me and said, 'Hello Ram, I saw you on television; what you did was great!'.

"Contrary to what a lot of Palestinians think, Israeli society is not composed of a single body of opinion. Throughout my career, in radio and then television, I have had to face very severe criticism and censorship but I have also had a lot of praise. I even received the Israel Prize for communication, which is like the French 'Légion d'honneur'.

"But whilst I defend the rights of Palestinians, I remain very patriotic. In 1973, for example, when I was abroad, I took the first plane home to come back and fight."

"Have you served in the occupied territories?"

"Yes, I was a reservist in Gaza between 1967 and 1973. That was the period when there was the illusion of peace. Everything was calm. We were occupiers but the majority of the Palestinian population accepted the occupation and benefited from it economically. We dined in restaurants, like tourists, and used the shops; we were well received, despite occasional terrorist activity.

"I have never been in a position where I had to kill or be killed but I remember, for example, going into refugee camps, getting people out of their homes and making them gather outside while we searched their

2. From 1948 to 1965.

houses. There were soldiers who took the savings, or the radio, of very poor families: I would get angry and go and see the commanding officer. Sometimes he would ask them to return what they had stolen. Other times, soldiers would take sheep, goats, chickens, rabbits; everything that people needed to survive. I tried to stop them, but in vain.

"I was completely caught up in my contradictions, between wanting to protect my country and the constant immoral and counter-productive harassment of civilians."

"How do you see the future of that confrontation now?"

"The main solution is to understand two things: first, that Palestinians are people like us and second, that the current balance of power in the Middle East will not last for ever. We don't have much time to find a solution with the Palestinians and the Arab world. If we don't do it soon, we will disappear."

"You are pessimistic! The balance of power will be weighted in Israel's favour for a long time. America totally supports you."

"I disagree. What happened on 11 September in America is an example of what could happen here: a situation of permanent hatred and total incomprehension and of weapons of mass destruction in the hands of small terrorist groups – if they don't have them now, they soon will. That is a terrifying prospect.

"A bomb was recently found in a gas-producing region north of Tel Aviv, which, if it had gone off, would have caused thousands of deaths. All the Palestinians would doubtless have been expelled to Jordan – which is what I think will happen soon, whilst a conflict is distracting the world's attention, with Iraq or another country. The Arab world will respond and the whole power balance of the region will be upset.

"Our society is strong in one sense, but it is very fragile in another. Because of the trauma of the Holocaust, we have an irrational fear of our neighbours and instead of negotiating, we barricade ourselves in.

"We still have the possibility of reaching an agreement, but not for much longer. When everyone is armed with biological and chemical weapons, and if hatred continues to escalate at the present rate, we will be in great danger. Rabin understood that and that is why he tried to solve the problem by giving the Palestinians a country. He was killed by short-sighted people who did not want to give anything up."

"Israelis as lucid as you are in a tiny minority. Why?"

"The truth is, that deep down, Israelis know what they have done – they know their country is based on the theft of another people's land and on their violent eviction. But they don't want to think or talk about it, just as they didn't want to talk about the Holocaust at the time. Which accounts for their terrible inability to negotiate with the Palestinians. Because the suicide bomber who blows himself up as well as other people is not doing anything worse than what we are doing in Palestinian towns and camps. That is very hard for the Israelis to admit. They need to think of suicide bombers as non-people. And as soon as you see the other as non-human, you have the right to do anything to them."

"Tell me about your films. Do they all deal with political subjects?"

"No, I have made all sorts of films – a straightforward thriller, for example – although the detective in it was an Arab. Just putting an Arab detective in a Jewish context is in itself a shock for Israelis and makes them think. We artists know that we do not have much influence, but the little that we can do is important.

"At any rate, I am incapable of accepting things and shutting up. For me, that would be death."

6

◆

Palestinian and Israeli Children

A SCHOOL IN PALESTINE

It is a big, two-storeyed building, from which the Palestinian flag is flying. The classrooms look out on to balconies surrounding a large internal courtyard where, in a deafening tumult, hundreds of children are playing football or volleyball.

During a month of occupation, in April 2002, the school had been temporarily transformed into a detention centre, into which hundreds of prisoners were packed. This building, which had – like all public buildings occupied by Israeli soldiers – been ransacked, fouled with human excrement and deprived of its files and computers had now, in June, been restored to its original function. Seven hundred pupils, aged six to 16, had returned to their classes – except on the many days when the army imposed a curfew.

We are greeted by the principal, Yasser al-Qasrawi, a dynamic man in his forties, happy to have his school back, after having himself been imprisoned for two weeks.

"Why did they arrest you?"

"For no reason. They didn't even interrogate me. I was one of thousands; the soldiers systematically arrested any man between 15 and 70. One day, without any explanation, they released me."

Among the school trophies, displayed on the shelves behind him, are cartridges of various sizes, from the large cartridges of explosive bullets fired from helicopters to the small ones of machine guns.

"The children who live near the settlement of Pisgot bring me some almost every day", he says. "They tell me that they can't sleep, that they have been shot at, that they had to hide in the kitchen all night. It's not surprising that their school work is so bad. These poor kids can't concentrate any more. They jump at the slightest sound of a car or a plane; they are frightened, agitated, aggressive. Most of them have seen soldiers coming into their house, or a neighbour's house, humiliating or manhandling their parents, ransacking everything and often taking a

father or brother to prison. For the first time, they are encountering
tanks, aeroplanes and helicopters that shoot at them. Some of them
have even had parents or friends who have been killed. In our school
alone, three children died last year. Look ..."

He points out three photos of very young boys on the wall opposite.

"Obeid Darraj, who was nine years old, was shot at night, while he
was asleep. His house is near the Pisgot settlement. The day before he
had been helping his parents prepare for the feast of Aïd, at the end of
Ramadan.

"Mohammed Kuwaik was killed with his two sisters, in a car driven
by his mother, by a missile fired from an Apache helicopter – they're
equipped with guided missiles and machine guns. They were targeting
his father, an activist.

"The third boy, Amir Farouk, ten years old, was shot on his way back
from school. He was in the seventh year, the best student in his class, a
cheerful lad who was loved by everyone. Shot in the head, he spent 20
days in a coma at the hospital, where his friends went to visit him. After
he died, they put his photo on a desk in the classroom, with some
flowers. The following year they took the photo with them into their
new classroom. The teachers and I weren't happy about it; we don't
want to glorify the martyrs, for fear the children will copy their example.
But his friends insisted. Otherwise, they would have felt they were
abandoning him.

"Amir was killed when he was quietly making his way home. He did
not even throw stones. Children only throw stones at barricades and
there aren't any around here. It was the soldiers who mount guard near
the settlement who shot him, or it might have been a settler. The children are very frightened of the settlers – some of them are extremists
who even attack schools."

Seeing my look of incredulity – we never see that reported in the
international press – he insists.

"On the 18th September 2002, five children, aged around eight,
were wounded in an explosion in a school south of Hebron. The Israeli
police and Shin Beth[1] say that it was undoubtedly Jewish extremists. At
9.45 in the morning a bomb exploded near a fountain in the play-
ground. A few minutes later, 380 children would have been playing
there. The police and firemen who were called to the scene discovered a
second bomb which should have gone off two minutes afterwards,
when everyone would have gathered to attend to the first lot of

1. The Israeli Secret Service.

wounded. By chance, the first bomb exploded before the break and the only victims were several pupils wounded by bits of shattered glass flying into the classrooms. Otherwise, there would have been real carnage.

"That attack resembled two previous ones. In one, eight children were wounded in a school and in another, a group of settlers from Bat Ayin were stopped very early one morning near a girls' school in east Jerusalem. They had put a car filled with explosives in front of the entrance. In March 2002, a bomb exploded in another east Jerusalem school, wounding a teacher and four students. A clandestine Jewish group claimed responsibility for the attack, but no arrests were made ... as usual."

I took my leave of the principal and went to Amir's classroom. On a bench behind a desk in the front row was a photo of a small boy with bright eyes, with the date 14 January 2001 written on it in red letters. On the desk lay a bunch of flowers, replaced regularly by his friends. On the wall was a coloured print of the al-Aqsa mosque, where everyone dreams that they will pray one day. Jerusalem is only 12 kilometres from Ramallah but, forbidden entry by the Israelis, it is more inaccessible to them than China.[2] Next to the mosque is a picture of the Fatah leader Marwan Barghouti, hero of the younger generation, who is currently in prison. There are also several photos of 'martyrs'; the father of one boy in the class, and the brother of another ...

I ask to speak with Amir's closest friends. Half a dozen children aged between 11 and 12 come into the classroom. One is Imad, Amir's cousin, a thin, pale boy with sombre eyes.

"I was with him when it happened", he tells me. "We were collecting cartridges on the way back from school. Everything was quiet – there was no demonstration that day, nothing. There were some soldiers near the settlement and they called us. We ran away but there were also soldiers in front. They shot at us. One bullet went into Amir's head, another one into his mouth. I shouted as loudly as I could and people came running; they picked him up, while the soldiers just stood there in front of their checkpoint. Amir was taken to hospital. He was in a coma. He died a few days later ... I don't know how they dare call them rubber bullets!"

2. Under United Nations resolutions, east Jerusalem forms part of the occupied Palestinian territory that Israel should give back.

"After your friend died, did you stop throwing stones?" I ask the little group that surrounds me.

"It doesn't matter whether you throw them or not, the soldiers still beat us or shoot at us", replies a chubby lad named Abdel Rahman. "The other day I was going to school when a soldier called me. I went over and he hit me, just like that, for no reason ..."

Voices spring up in confirmation:

"That's happened to me too; one time they threw tear gas at me when I hadn't thrown anything!"

"Me too! I was with my friends, the soldiers called us and started punching us. That often happens, but you never know when – sometimes the soldiers don't do anything ..."

Their elderly teacher explains:

"When the soldiers can't catch the stone throwers, they take revenge on any child."

"OK, but don't try and tell me that you yourselves never go and throw stones at the barricades?" I ask the group.

They elbow each other, giggling, and finally admit that they throw stones and then run away. Ali, a curly-haired boy, does not join in the general hilarity. In response to my questioning, he eventually says, without looking at me:

"On a Friday a few weeks ago, I was with a group of kids who were throwing stones. An older boy passed close by us. The soldiers shot him, right in the forehead, and he fell down and began bleeding. People took him in a car but he died before they got to the hospital. He wasn't throwing stones, he was just walking past ..." he muttered, his voice choking.

"And what did you do after that?" I ask him very gently, afraid that he will start to cry.

"I went home. I was very unhappy; I told myself it was my fault. I stopped throwing stones for a few days ... and then I began again."

"But listen, what good do your stones do against soldiers with machine guns?"

"We also throw Molotov cocktails", they protest in consternation. "We know how to make really good ones – older children have taught us!"

A tiny blond boy, named Bassel, draws himself up.

"We throw stones to defend our country!"

"And what do you want to do later on?" I ask.

"Defend my country with weapons," replies the cherub.

Everyone signals their agreement.

"Us too. At the moment we throw stones so as to learn how to fight and how not to be frightened. Later we will fight for real."

"I want to avenge my cousin", says Imad, darkly. "When I am big, I will get a gun."

"But Palestine needs you all if it is to develop. What jobs do you want to do?"

Ali wants to be a primary school teacher, Abdel Rahman will take over his father's furniture shop, while Bassel wants to be a journalist. He explains why:

"I want to tell people what is happening here, about all the injustice, and the cruelty of the soldiers. I saw my neighbour being arrested. They made the whole family get out of the house and they hit the father and the two sons really brutally. They took the youngest son away. We haven't seen him since. His mother cries all the time."

"My father was arrested", says Salim, a thin boy, whose face is marked with the white blotches of malnutrition. "They released him after 20 days; they had nothing on him. It was in April. The soldiers imposed a curfew and said that all men between 15 and 70 had to go and wait in the square; then they went to search all the houses. They didn't find anything. As the eldest – I'm 11 – I am head of the family when my father isn't there. So I followed the soldiers everywhere to make sure they didn't take anything. They stole all our neighbours' savings: 7,000 shekels."

"In our house", says Ali, "they stole my mother's gold bracelets and 2,000 shekels".

"The soldiers steal from you?"

"Of course, they do it all the time. Israeli newspapers have even written about it."[3]

"The Israelis are very strong. How can you make them leave with stones?" I repeat for the umpteenth time.

Bassel, the little blond boy, eyes me reproachfully.

"There aren't only stones and Molotov cocktails. There are suicide bombings as well. At least with that you kill Israelis before you die."

"Do you agree with him?" I ask his friends.

They all do.

"But if you have to fight, isn't it best to fight with a gun?" I venture.

"A gun can work but it's more difficult – a suicide operation is guaranteed to work! And it scares them: people leave the settlements because of those operations."

3. Notably in the big daily newspaper *Ha'aretz*.

"But don't you think the only way to reach an agreement is by negotiation?"

To a man, they reply:

"No! With everything that's happened, with all the martyrs, it isn't
possible. We don't believe in negotiations any more – the Israelis do
nothing but lie!"

"But before the intifada did you think there was going to be a peace
agreement and that you could be friends with the Israelis?"

"Before, we didn't know what they were capable of. Now we know
them: they act like animals, even towards women and children. Even if
there was peace, we could never be friends with them."

The elderly teacher takes me to one side.

"You know, these are normal reactions. These children have suffered too much: they live with fear daily and also with hunger. When the
father is in prison, or simply unemployed, as most of them have been
here for two years, there is almost nothing to eat in the house. But these
kids – and much less their elders – will never admit that they are hungry. No, they tell us about the good meal they had at home the night
before. It's a matter of pride. Only the mothers talk about it. And the
problem has been getting worse over the past few months."

Indeed. According to figures from USAID, an American aid organisation for international development, in August 2002, thirty per cent of
Palestinian children suffered from chronic malnutrition and twenty
one per cent from acute malnutrition – a massive increase from the figures for 2000, which were 7.5 per cent and 2.5 per cent respectively.

Two recent reports by the United Nations and the World Bank
reveal that a large majority of Palestinians are now unemployed and
that sixty per cent survive on less than two dollars a day – when life in
Palestine is just as expensive as in any Western European country. These
reports conclude that the devastation of the Palestinian economy is due
to measures imposed by the Israeli army: curfews, checkpoints, all the
restrictions on farming and the transport of goods as well as general
work restrictions.

The humanitarian organisations that offer aid to the people of
Gaza and the West Bank have issued a warning cry: a disaster is in the
making and food supplies need to be replenished urgently. People also
need to be able to distribute them ...

The WFP, the UNO world food programme agency, recently
filed an official complaint against the Israeli army for its deliberate

destruction of more than five hundred tonnes of food aid donated by the European Commission. This food, stored in Gaza, was meant to be distributed to 42,000 needy people. On 3 December 2002, soldiers surrounded the building with armoured vehicles, put down sticks of dynamite and, despite the protests of the people in charge, who asked to be allowed to remove the food first, blew it up. During the operation, two Palestinian civilians who tried to intervene were killed and 20 others wounded.

These are not isolated or accidental acts. On 30 January 2003, two tanks and two bulldozers razed the al Menara food market in Hebron – a city under curfew in which a large proportion of the population are going hungry.

The white-bearded teacher who speaks to me in private is in fact only 55: as with many Palestinians, hardship has aged him prematurely. He has been a maths teacher for 35 years.

"We are scared too", he confides. "For the sake of the children we try to appear calm but we are constantly frightened that the soldiers will come in and behave violently and every evening we take important school documents home with us, for fear that they will burn them again, like they did in April. Why on earth do they destroy school books and pupils' desks? Does the education of the Palestinian people pose a danger to them? There are nine teachers in this school who live in the villages around Ramallah. Often we can't go out because a patrol will suddenly arrive, put up a road-block and keep us shut inside the village. It only lasts a few hours – generally, long enough to make arrests. To surround all the villages would demand too many men and armoured vehicles so they block us in by closing the checkpoint at Surda, which is the only way into Ramallah. For the country people, that is economic strangulation. They cannot go to buy food or to sell their produce in the town."

"How long does it normally take you to get to school?"

"I live in the village of Beit Safaf, which is just 16 kilometres away. But to get to school for eight o'clock, I leave at six, because I have to get through two checkpoints. Sometimes the soldiers close them completely and you have to turn around and remain stuck in the village, while the children are waiting for us at school ..."

He shakes his head: "You know, the situation in the villages is worse than in the towns. The country people are simple folk and the Israelis regard them as animals – they can be extremely brutal.

"Three days ago, the army went into my village and imposed a curfew. Then settlers from the nearby settlements of Halamich and Atarot came and, protected by the soldiers, tore up two hundred fruit trees. This is a frequent practice: they arrive, wreak havoc and then leave. They want to force people in the small villages to leave so that they can take our land and extend their settlements. Some villagers, who have family and means, have left to live in Ramallah.

"To get us to leave they also try to terrorise us, as they did with our parents in 1948. At the start of the intifada, they would come and get a youngster, take him back to the settlement and beat him up. They kept a military post in the centre of the village, for over a year, so as to control our smallest movements.

"They do all that because our village still owns quite a lot of land, even though the Israelis have already confiscated some to create a military zone. We don't have the right to go into most of our fields; they shoot at people who risk it. And then they use the old British law that gives the state the right to seize land that has been abandoned! I myself have a large piece of land that is now incorporated into the settlement. I own the title deeds. But what use is that, with them?

"In my village, as in all others, we are not allowed to build beyond the outlying houses. There is not enough room for families and young people cannot establish a home so they have to move away. We also don't have the right to dig a well in our own garden because the water table belongs to the Israelis. Infringements are severely punished. We try to manage by building pools to collect rain water but life is very hard in the summertime."

"I have heard that if there were a war against Iraq, the Israeli army would use it as an opportunity to force the transfer of people from the villages into the towns? Do you believe that?"

"Oh, transferring us is a very old plan! That is why they cut off our water three or four times a week. They try everything to get us to leave. But we will stay. We have nowhere to go."

Two days later, I read in the Israeli papers that Palestinians had shot at a car and wounded two settlers from Atarot. And once again I realised that these attacks, which are called random, are in fact not random at all: this one was clearly a response to the destruction of the orchards at Beit Safafa.

Three months later, in mid-September, when the schools were reopening, I went to visit the children again. The school had moved to another district of al Bireh and had become the *Amin al-Husseini* school, named after the Palestinian leader who led the revolt against the British and the Jews in the 1930s and 40s.

Astonishingly, the new buildings, smelling unmistakeably of fresh paint, had been built just below the Pisgot settlement. It would be impossible to get any closer to it, Pisgot being on top of the hill and the school two hundred metres below. The school entrance was within firing range of the settlement.

"How could you take such a risk?" I asked the elderly teacher who came to greet me.

"The land belongs to the town council – which is why we could afford it."

"But it is a clear challenge to the settlers!"

"The Palestinian Authority has taken the decision to occupy all land that belongs to us, even if it is close to the settlements. Otherwise, the Israelis will confiscate it and Ramallah will gradually be prevented from any development, as is already the case in most of our villages. We have to resist or very soon Palestine will not exist any more. As we can't force individuals to buy there, we are putting up government institutions in these places."

I go to meet Farouk's cousin Imad, little blond Bassel, frizzy-haired Ali, Salim – now even thinner than before the holidays – and Abdel Rahman, the son of the furniture seller.

They had moved into their new classroom the day before. They show me a desk in the front row, covered with flowers: Amir's desk. They will put flowers there throughout the year, they tell me, as well as on Obeid's and Mohammed's desks.

Bassel tells me that during the summer his neighbour was killed, at home. He was helping his father repaint the window when he was shot full in the chest.

"He was called Oubaiy and he was ten years old. We used to play together."

I ask whether they are scared to go to school so close to the settlement.

"No", they say, toughing it out. "We used to go past here anyway, to get to the other building. We're used to the tanks, the armoured cars, and the soldiers. A settlement doesn't scare us!"

The new principal calls the children: the inauguration ceremony is about to begin. The school has been open for a week but because of the curfew this is the first day that the pupils could get in. In the courtyard, some five hundred boys aged 11 to 16 are lined up. The principal picks up a microphone and begins his speech:

"The Israelis are destroying your schools and your books. They want to stop you studying and to keep you in ignorance so that you become poor, hopeless people. You must resist. In spite of everything, you must study so that you can build your country, Palestine. Long live Palestine and glory to our martyrs."

I am concerned that his voice will carry as far as the settlement ... but then I realise that they have nothing to hide. The settlers can have little doubt about the Palestinians' feelings towards them.

"Those children who have had deaths in their family will speak to you", the principal went on.

Imad came forward, his face even paler than usual.

"Amir, you're not with us any more. We cry for you but your death isn't in vain – we swear to you that we will continue the fight for the liberation of Palestine."

There follows a minute of heavy silence; some children have tears in their eyes.

Finally the principal gives the sign, the rows slowly disperse and the children return to their classrooms. I say goodbye to Bassel, Ali, Salem, Imad and Abdel Rahman. Watching them leave with a feeling of sadness, I am surprised to find myself praying to the one God of the Christians, the Muslims and the Jews to protect them.

CAIRO, CHILD PSYCHOLOGIST

Cairo is an elegant and distinguished woman in her fifties, a member of the Palestinian upper middle class. Her parents emigrated to the United States, where she was born, but she chose to return to work in her country after finishing her studies. A child psychologist, she works mainly at the Mughtanabeen boys' school in al Bireh, where she accompanied me on a visit.

In the taxi on the way back, Cairo tells me something of her concerns.

"This generation, which is exposed to constant bombardments, shootings and curfews, will have many problems as adults. In my work

I meet a lot of children who are so traumatised that they don't want to leave the house. They behave like toddlers, clinging to their mother and becoming very aggressive. They interpret every sound as a danger – a tank, an explosion, a bomb. They can't bear the dark and, when they hear an ambulance, some of them have anxiety attacks and hide under the bed, panicking. Children growing up in extreme poverty can also be as traumatised as children who have have been exposed to bombardment because they have, for two years, lived in constant anxiety about the future, with parents who are irritable.

"We carried out a study of 1200 of the poorest children or those who live in the most exposed areas. We asked them, 'If you could go home now, do what you want and have what you want, what would you choose?' A lot of them replied, 'I'd like to eat fruit' or 'I want the soldiers not to come into my house'. They don't have any dreams; they can no longer see beyond the immediate future. This situation has gone on so long that they have lost hope. They don't ask for anything any more – toys, sweets, television. They have given up, as though they have died on the inside.

"Even the parents don't have ambitions for their children any more and don't dare speak to them about the future. They live from day to day. And the children, who see the situation only getting worse, have become very pessimistic. A lot of the mothers say to me, 'I don't have any more money, or authority. I am exhausted, my children don't obey me any more and no longer want to go to school'. But it's difficult for children to go to school hungry. How can you concentrate when your stomach is almost empty and your main concern is knowing whether you are going to eat the next day? The effects of malnutrition do not show immediately but children lose weight and their ability to focus and to learn diminishes. And then they say to themselves: 'What's the point of studying?'. There isn't any work and their fathers have been unemployed for years ..."

"Do people in the countryside at least have enough to eat?"

"Not necessarily. Sometimes it's even worse for them because the villages are completely surrounded by the settlements and most of them have lost all their agricultural land. For those who do still have fields, the settlers often wait until the harvest and then come with their bulldozers to flatten everything – so often that many farmers don't even bother to sow anything any more. Since the beginning of the intifada, the Israelis have ruined thousands of *dunums* in that way."[1]

1. Dunum – a tenth of a hectare (10,000 square metres).

Arriving in the centre of Ramallah, we stop in a café and, under a climbing vine, drink a glass of very strong, sugary tea. I cannot help asking my companion why she was named Cairo. She laughs.

"My father was a nationalist and a great admirer of Nasser. When the treaty between Egypt and Syria was signed – it didn't last – he was so pleased that he called me Cairo, my sister Damascus and my young brother Abdel Nasser!"

"Tell me a bit about yourself. Why did you leave America, where you were born, to come and live here?"

"When I was 15, my parents decided to send me and my sister to Palestine for a time, so that we could discover our culture. We were completely Americanised. They are Muslim and although they never talked about religion or politics, their roots were important to them. They sent us here so that we could discover another way of life – not so that we would stay. But I fell in love with my country and I stayed here to study psychology at university from 1974 to 1979, then returned to the United States to do my thesis. That's where I met my husband, who also came from al-Bireh. We came back here in 1987 and we got married during the first intifada."

"In the difficult moments, do you sometimes miss your life in the United States?"

"Never! Here there is a humanity and a sense of community that no longer exists in the West. Our people are incredible survivors. They have lived under occupation for more than 35 years and have had to learn to survive under the worst conditions. The Israelis want to dehumanise us and make us despair so that we give up. But we know that if we keep our hope alive, they can never win. Unless they kill us all, that is! Which is impossible, not only because of the world's reaction but because they want to have an image of themselves as moral. They may be able to cover up certain things, but they can't cover up genocide.

"Another vital thing is that we don't have the feeling of inferiority that colonised people often have. We have never wanted to be like the Israelis. They are who they are, we are who we are, with our own values. They are perhaps in a better situation, but that does not mean they are better people. We like who we are. That is very important. Our people live in the worst conditions but we have doctors, engineers and lawyers.

"The children see everything that the adults manage to do, despite terrible circumstances. There is a pride in being Palestinian and, as long as that exists, the Israelis will not be able to finish us off. We see families who find it very hard to survive but we don't see people collapsing. They are not ready to give up."

She looks at me, her eyes shining. Her earlier tiredness has disappeared.

"We tell our children that no occupation anywhere in the world has lasted and that people always achieve independence in the end. We tell them: 'As long as you believe that you and your country have a future, you will survive. Yes, people have been wounded but people are wounded and die everywhere. As long as you believe, and you act to improve your life, they cannot destroy you. They can defeat you only if you accept defeat'.

"We repeat all that and try to help our children live it out. Which is why, for example, we organise summer camps in a school, with very young teachers, aged between 18 and 25, accompanying them. The children are with their friends and they can paint, dance, do drama. We teach them to choose what they want to do. Indeed, we insist on their right to choose and to decide for themselves. We also teach them how to find out information, how to express themselves clearly and have a dialogue, not to say things that can hurt others. We teach them that everyone has a different way of expressing themselves but that they are all similar and all experience the same feelings of fear, anger and frustration.

"The important thing in the camps is that the children are happy. They realise that happiness exists and that they can expect to be happy and they rediscover desires and goals. They rediscover hope ..."

"WHEN I'M GROWN UP, I'LL KILL THEM!"

This afternoon in Ramallah, a few people have braved the curfew and gone out into the streets. The tanks do not patrol the residential areas but stay grouped in the centre of the town, particularly around the Mouqata'a, where Arafat has been held prisoner for several weeks.

Liana, my novelist friend, and I make our way towards al-Bireh, Ramallah's twin city. Suddenly, we hear the familiar rumble of an engine behind us and we freeze: in a cloud of dust, two jeeps overtake us, ignoring the pedestrians and the women talking on the balconies of their houses. We breathe again. Everything is unpredictable here and subject to the orders of the day – but also to individual soldiers. Some of them must resent the role they are forced to play and refrain from arresting a woman doing her shopping or from shooting at passers-by who are just out getting some fresh air. Today there is a semi-curfew – the kind that stifles the economy but which at least allows people to get out and have a break.

It is six in the evening. The sun, setting over the horizon, bathes the town in golden light and to my surprise, I find myself forgetting the siege. Life seems sweet.

The two teenagers whom we have arranged to meet are sitting waiting for us on a low stone wall. Dressed in clean clothes, their hair smoothed down, they have the slightly intimidated air of well-behaved children. Amin is 13 and Hashem 15. They are neighbours and passionate football fans.

"Until last year we went to play every day on the large ground up there, just opposite the Pisgot settlement. Whenever we went, the soldiers would come and shoot, to scare us. One day they shot at a boy who was playing and wounded him in the thigh. He fell and began bleeding a lot; luckily, the ambulance came quickly and took him to hospital. He is alright now but he limps and he can't play any more."

"Why did they shoot at you? Were you throwing stones?"

"No, we were only playing football."

Liana explains that although the ground belongs to the Palestinians, the Pisgot settlers use every means to create an empty space around the settlement.

"It happens everywhere. The settlers prevent children from playing, people from passing by and farmers from working in their fields whenever they think people are too close to the settlement. People are killed every day for that reason."

"We can't go to the big ground any more," laments Hashem. "We have to make do with a small one near the school, where we can't really play properly."

"But we've found a way of annoying them", Amin chimes in mischievously. "We send kites in the colours of the Palestinian flag into the settlement – that makes them furious. Look!"

There in the sky, some five hundred metres away, two large black, green, red and white birds float insolently just over the ramparts surrounding Pisgot.

I look at Amin. Small and frail, he has the worn face of a malnourished child.

"Before I went to throw stones, but I don't do it any more. It doesn't achieve anything, apart from getting children killed. I want to become a fighter, to avenge my father."

His manner is matter of fact, as though pointing out the indisputably obvious.

"Those bastards killed my father when he was out jogging! He was very athletic", he recalls with a proud little smile. "During the day he worked as a house painter and when he finished in the afternoon he would go and train in a sports hall. That day, the hall was closed and so he went running. A patrol saw him and shot him. It was the 5th July 2001. There wasn't even a curfew ..."

"But why did they shoot?" I asked, astonished.

"There had been shooting in the area; soldiers arrived and, in retaliation, shot at the first people who came."

He breaks off, his voice strangled. His friend Hashem throws him a worried glance and then turns towards me.

"Do you think they need excuses? They kill us even when we aren't doing anything. A neighbour of mine, a boy of ten, was in bed when he was shot dead by a bullet through the window. And", – his black eyes flash – "they even killed my dog ... for no reason! If you knew how good he was, and how happy; he wasn't yet two years old. He was with me all the time. One day there was shooting behind our house, near the settlement, and a tank came. My dog barked, the tank slowly turned its arm towards him and fired a shell. My dog was smashed to pieces."

His lips tighten. "When I'm grown up, I'll kill them!"

"By that time there will have been negotiations and, let's hope, peace."

"I don't believe that. We have all seen that negotiations don't do any good. The Israelis never keep their word. The only way they'll leave is by force!"

On the way back, Liana shares her worry.

"The situation has totally changed since the occupation began two years ago. It's no longer just young men who talk about employing violence, but children. And it's not just the poor and the desperate any more – middle class children are increasingly rebelling against what they see happening."

The words of the Israeli lawyer Lea Tsemel[1] come back to me: "The Palestinians did not know what hate was. We taught them. We are good teachers …".

FORTUNÉE'S CHILDREN

I had been trying to meet Israeli children for several days. My friend Naomi had arranged meetings for me with three families, one of which cancelled at the last minute. The other two stood me up at the café where I had waited for them for hours. I was beginning to despair. I can certainly understand parents not wanting to risk their children being upset by having to recall painful events, but it was imperative that I recorded the feelings of young Israelis, to understand how their daily lives are also affected by this conflict.

Someone told me about Fortunée, a mother of three children; I explained my project and, without the slightest hesitation, she agreed to let them take part.

Originally from the Lebanon, Fortunée has the dark beauty of oriental Jews and the elegance of the Lebanese. Married to a journalist, she is herself a researcher specialising in the Near East; she has come into contact with many diverse ideas and opinions, which has given her an undeniably open mind.

"Come to my house tonight. The children will be in – in the present climate, they hardly ever go out – and you will have lots of time to talk."

---

1. See chapter beginning page 223.

Fortunée's house is near the Mahane Yehuda market, in an old quarter of central Jerusalem, where there have been several bomb attacks over the past two years. Leaving the main road, I go down some steps and find myself in a quiet street lined with pretty ochre-coloured houses.

No sooner have I rung the bell at the wrought iron gate than a little girl in a short skirt appears to greet me. She shows me into a shady garden where her older siblings are waiting for me with well-iced Coca-Colas.

Noga, the youngest, is 11. Slim, with long brown hair and green eyes, she has the ethereal grace of a Greek goddess, but the assertive personality of a twenty-first-century child. She cannot contain her impatience and insists on being interviewed first.

"My parents don't let me go anywhere", she complains, "and especially not Canyon, my favourite place in Jerusalem. Before, I went there at least once a week!"

Canyon is a gigantic shopping centre on the outskirts of Jerusalem. Comprising hundreds of shops that import goods from all over the world, it is a veritable temple of consumerism, where Israelis can find all that they could dream of buying. It is also the ideal place for a large-scale terrorist attack. For two years, Canyon has been under the surveillance of an army of police, but one never knows ...

Her brother, Noam, a magnificent teenager of 16 with long, dark hair, wants to add something:

"Life has become impossible. We can't go to the cinema, to the shops in the centre of town, or to the little restaurants and cafés in Jaffa Street and Ben Yehuda Street, where the life of Jerusalem is centred. My parents don't even allow me to take the bus any more – I have to walk everywhere or take a taxi. But there are still exhibitions and concerts, because the Mayor of Jerusalem wants to show that we won't allow ourselves to be intimidated. Quite a lot of people go to them but where is the enjoyment? You are tense, anxious, the police are everywhere, you are searched several times in a row. In the end I prefer not to go!"

"When I'm walking in the street", Noga interjects, "I am often scared, especially when I've seen an attack on television. I am very sad when I see children killed and I am happy that it isn't me!"

"Are you scared when you see an Arab in the street?"

She hesitates.

"A bit, yes ... but I say to myself that it is perhaps an Arab who likes Israelis. Not all the Arabs are wicked; they don't all want to carry out attacks."

"Do you know people who have been killed?"

"Yes, a friend of my parents was killed in the north."

"A girl from my school was killed in a bus attack last year", says Noam. "She was in another class but I knew her a bit. It was a terrible shock."

"What do you think can be done to bring an end to all that?"

"I don't know. I only know that killing Arabs does no good. Sharon stops one or two attacks and then it starts again."

"In two years' time you have to do your military service. Do you think about it?"

"Of course. I want to do it but I will refuse to serve in the territories. The settlers are breaking international law by living in the settlements. Why should soldiers defend them? At school we talk about it among ourselves, but only a small minority think like I do."

Sarit, silent until now, speaks up. Athletic looking, with short hair, she is twenty and is doing her military service.

"I don't think Sharon will manage to stop the attacks, because now the Palestinians are much more motivated than before. In 1996 and 1997, most of them thought that the Oslo negotiations would lead to the creation of a Palestinian state. Nobody believes that any more and the entire population is frustrated. They know we have a weak spot, despite the power of our army: we do not want deaths inside the country. That is why they attack wherever they can, and where it hurts, with these suicide bombings."

"Tell me, what is the life of a 20-year-old Israeli like in such a context?"

"In Tel Aviv, where I do my military service, it's fairly relaxed. You're further away from the problem there, even if a bomb sometimes reminds you of it. But here in Jerusalem the atmosphere is very tense. I love to dance but I don't go to discotheques any more. I know each place where there has been an attack and I think about it whenever I pass them. But we can't live in fear and we are sick of having to be careful all the time. In the end, you just go out. Last week I said to myself, hang it, and I went to a restaurant in Ben Yehuda."

"Do you sometimes meet Palestinians?"

"Rarely. When it happens, we always talk about other things. Otherwise it would be too strained. I hope that one day we will be able to meet each other ... Not me, perhaps, but my children ..."

A friend of Noga's arrives: Morane, a plump little girl with short hair who sits down on the low stone wall and listens to us in silence. Resting on her shoulder is a blue parakeet. With her tilted head, she gently strokes the bird's plumage. Suddenly she speaks:

"My best friend died four months ago in a bus. We were living in Gilo.[1] On the 18th June last year, we were going to get the number 32 bus, which took us to school in Jerusalem every day. But that day, there were so many people that my mother decided to send me with a neighbour, who was driving there. As there wasn't enough room for my friend, we said to each other: 'See you at school!' I never saw her again. She died in the explosion, with 19 other people. Fifty people were wounded.

"I should have died with her", she adds, in a whisper and leans her head forward to feel the softness and warmth of the bird against her cheek.

Morane still takes the number 32 bus every day to get to school. Her mother is divorced and can't afford to pay for taxis for her.

"I'm very scared", she admits. "I always try to sit at the back and, when I see someone who looks suspicious, I hide behind the seat, hoping the seat will explode and not me."

She still seems so traumatised by the event that I ask if she has seen a psychologist.

"Yes, twice. They spoke to me and my mother. We couldn't stop crying. But now", she recovers herself, "I keep my worry inside me and I live normally. I take the bus, I go to Canyon and even into the town centre, to Ben Yehuda."

She is touching, this little girl with a blue parakeet. One senses her confusion, her loneliness as the child of divorced parents and her need for warmth, as she tenderly rubs her cheek against the bird. When I say to her, "Well done, Morane, you are very brave", her face lights up and, as if I have given her a precious gift, she replies "Thank you".

It is almost six o'clock when I leave the house. The Sabbath will begin soon. The shops have lowered their iron grilles and the streets are deserted. As I walk down Agrippa Street to find a taxi, I see a small group of orthodox Jews – a dozen men with side curls and black hats, gathered in front of the entrance to a jazz club. They seem to be waiting for something and are chanting words I don't understand whilst the oldest one, who sports a superb white beard, spurs them on. The door of the bar opens and I glimpse a young man, who closes it brusquely. The group begins to chant more and more loudly and threateningly.

After several minutes, the door opens wide and four young men in jeans, not wearing kippas, appear in the doorway, each with an

---

1. Gilo is a settlement in the municipality of Jerusalem. On the 18th June 2002, a student, aged 23, originating from a camp near Jenin, blew himself up in a bus. Hamas claimed responsibility for the attack.

instrument under his arm – obviously musicians coming out after a rehearsal. The group of men in black surrounds them, screaming. The musicians calmly try to get through but the group will not allow this and pushes them back, menacingly. Urged on by the bearded leader, a puny young man plants himself in front of one of the musicians, insults him and threatens to hit him. Unhappily for him, the man, twice his size, begins to get annoyed; at the first faint sign of aggression, the other withdraws, terrified, to take refuge with his companions, who huddle round him protectively.

The clamour reaches a crescendo and insults rain down on these impious musicians who dare to play on the Sabbath. To my great surprise, they remain unperturbed, even though they could easily get rid of the dozen or so rowdy characters blocking their way. On the contrary, they seem careful to speak to them gently and, above all, not to touch them. They know that they are being provoked, pushed into fighting so that they can be accused of violence against defenceless men of God ...

On the opposite pavement, several passers-by watch the scene disapprovingly. In the end, exasperated, a man wearing a kippa intervenes. After a long confabulation, the men of God finally agree to let the four musicians go on their way.

It is only a small incident, but it demonstrates the huge tensions that split Israeli society. I think of a friend's recent comment: "If it weren't for the Palestinian threat tying us together, our society could implode".

DAPHNE'S CHILDREN

I have an appointment this afternoon at the German Colony, an old district in west Jerusalem, with a young woman I had known 12 years earlier when she was a student and had demonstrated for Israeli Arabs to have the same right to student grants as Jews.

Daphne is waiting for me on the doorstep of an attractive house. She hasn't changed – still the same tall blonde, athletic girl, though now herself the mother of two little girls: Emily, aged six, has long blonde curls and a mischievous little face and Danielle, nine, has brown curls and a reflective air.

We sit on the veranda with a glass of fresh orange juice. After having exchanged our news, we talk about the situation.

"One morning", Daphne remembers, "we narrowly missed being hit by a bomb. It was 7.30 and I was taking the children to school in the car. We were driving down a little side street when I heard a very loud explosion, several metres behind us. Pieces of scorched wood were flying everywhere, and what looked like bits of bodies. I accelerated and got out of the street as fast as I could. There weren't any fatalities; the terrorist blew himself up too soon but a few seconds earlier we would have been right in the middle of it."

"I think I remember him", says Emily. "He was walking and he had a bag."

"Were you frightened?" I ask the children.

The two little girls shake their heads energetically.

"We aren't frightened."

"The father of a friend in my class was killed", Emily tells me. "They were living in the territories. A bullet went into his chest and he was killed. The little boy never talks about it but I know he hates the Palestinians."

"What's all the more distressing", says Daphne, "is that the father was pro-Palestinian and was active in working for reconciliation."

"Do you talk about all that at school?" I ask the older child.

"No. At school they give us exercises to do about all the people who died in America in the Twin Towers. We have to write down their names and what they did."

"And when people die in Israel, do you have to write down their names to remember them?"

"No, never!"

"But America is a long way away! Isn't it more important for you to write about what is happening here?"

Danielle thinks.

"More people were killed there", she says finally.

Her mother suggests that it is perhaps to put the children's problems into perspective, to play down what is happening here and suggest that it is relatively minor compared to what happened in New York.

"In my school, the children are scared of Arabs", says Emily.

"And are you scared of them?"

"When I see one in the street, I shout very loudly, 'There's an Arab, look out, an Arab!'" She bursts out laughing, as though she has made a highly amusing comment.

"So you are scared?"

"No", she says, laughing even louder.

"She is imitating a friend of hers", explains her mother. She turns to Emily.

"I've already told you it isn't nice to do that. Would you like it if people shouted 'a Jew, a Jew!' when they saw you in the street?"

Daphne turns back to me.

"You know, she used to have a terribly racist teacher who kept telling them that the Arabs were dirty, lazy and wicked and that they killed our soldiers and our children. She influenced Emily, who would repeat it all when she got home. I tried to act as a counterbalance but it isn't always easy; they are split between what we tell them at home and what most of their friends at school say."

"How can you tell an Arab in the street?" I asked the children. "It could be an oriental Jew."

They both claim that it's easy: Arabs dress differently, walk differently. They can't explain how, but they can tell.

"Are there any Arabs in your class?"

"The schools are different. Jewish and Arab children aren't mixed", Daphne reminds me. "Although they do meet them in their sports classes."

"I've got an Arab friend that I go swimming with", says Danielle. "I like her a lot even though she's got a really funny accent when she speaks English."

"I've got two Arab boys in my swimming class", Emily comes in. "They are not nice. They fight with everyone."

"Perhaps the others insult them", retorts Danielle. "In any case, the Palestinians are fighting so that we give them their country back. It's normal. The children want to have a home."

Their mother winks at me and says, significantly:

"Danielle has understood what we've told her. Emily is small and she still has to learn."

This produces cries of indignation from the latter.

"You can see the influence of teachers", Daphne laments. "Some of them inject poison into these young, malleable minds. If the children don't have families who can redress the balance, of course they are going to hate the Palestinians when they are adult. Everyday racism is in fact encouraged, not discouraged, by what the highest government ministers say. Moshe Yaalon, the new chief of staff, describes the Palestinian threat as a 'cancer' and declares 'there are all sorts of solutions to cancerous growths. At the moment I am applying chemotherapy'. As for General Meir Dagan, the new head of Mossad and a personal friend of Sharon's, he advocates 'liquidation units'. We are certainly not going to find a solution with these kind of leaders."

"I DON'T TRUST ANY ARABS"

The Albrechts are a well-off family of Ashkenazi origin who live in the residential district of Old Katamon, south of the old city in Jerusalem. When I arrive, late in the afternoon, the whole family has gathered to welcome me to their vast, luminous apartment, which looks out on to a rose-filled garden. The father, Moshe, is in his forties, with a pleasant expression and curly brown hair covered with a kippa. He was born in Israel, to Dutch parents. A paediatrician, he often has Arab patients; he speaks a little Arabic. His wife Rachel, blonde and cheerful, is a researcher in biology. Born in France, she made her aliyah straight after finishing university.

The couple have four children: Rivka, 14; Efrat, 12; Michal, 10; and little Yishai, 2. They are a visibly close-knit family who describe themselves as 'orthodox'. The girls are enrolled in semi-private Jewish schools which give 16 hours of religious teaching a week and they participate in Zionist youth activities.

Moshe describes himself politically as 'centre right' and his wife shares his political views. He tells me that he served his last period of military service as a doctor, during the offensive on the Jenin camp the previous April.

"Soldiers died in my arms", he says, going on to explain that the accusations of a 'massacre', bandied about by the Palestinians and relayed by an anti-Semitic foreign press, are pure lies.

"That camp was a production unit for terrorists. If innocent people were killed during the fighting, I am sorry about it, but we had to do what we did. Indeed, the fact that we had 23 deaths was because we took precautions – we could have bombarded the camp from the air and the matter would have been dealt with without a single loss on our side."

In 1999, Moshe voted for Netanyahu and in 2001 for Sharon. Like them, he thinks that Israel should keep almost all the territories and advances the familiar argument that "we are five million Jews in an ocean of hostile Arabs – we cannot take the risk of giving up the territories as a whole – that would be suicidal".

Impatient to be interviewed, the two girls drum a low table with their fingers. Rivka, the oldest, is a teenager with long brown curls and hazel eyes; she already has the figure of a woman but her expressions are still those of a child. Efrat has a face covered with freckles and a rebellious gaze. She does karate but is also passionate about opera. "She knows dozens of tunes by heart", her father tells me proudly.

I ask them what has changed in their daily lives since the intifada began two years ago.

"When I go to public places, I am always frightened of bomb attacks", Rivka explains. "When we are invited to eat somewhere, for example in a pizzeria, people now put 'security guards on the door' on the invitation. Otherwise my parents wouldn't let me go.

"I especially remember the start of the intifada because it was in October 2000, when I had my bat mitzvah.[1] Over a hundred people

1. Bat mitzvah for girls (aged 12 or 13) and bar mitzvah for boys (aged 13) are the ceremonies in which children are admitted into the adult community.

came to the house, but several families who live in the West Bank"
(otherwise known as the settlements, but Rivka, her sister and her parents do not use this term) "didn't dare come. I had planned a visit for
my friends, to the city of David, the ancient site below the old city. I was
going to be the guide and I had practised for several weeks, but because
of the intifada we had to cancel the tour."

Efrat, bursting with impatience, comes in.

"I'm not frightened. I still go to places I like. Well, not all. Now we
get home deliveries from *Pizza Sababa*, next to the *Moment* café, where
last March a suicide bomber killed 11 people and wounded 54."

"When *Moment* exploded", Rivka takes up, "I was a hundred metres
away, in the building where my youth group meets. We heard the bomb
go off. The people who had been trained in first aid went to help. I went
straight back home. Our premises have been closed ever since."

"Do you know people who have died in the bomb attacks?"

"Yes, but not closely", Efrat replies. "I knew Eran Picard a bit, the 18
year-old of French origin who was killed in March 2002 in the attack at
Atzmona settlement, in the Gaza Strip. He was going to a religious pre-
military academy. His family lived right next door to us: we saw them
every Sabbath. He had a sister my age. When I heard about his death, it
was a shock."

"Two leaders of my youth group were killed in the attack on the
Sbarro pizza parlour in August 2001", says Rivka. "It was a horrible
attack: 15 dead and 90 wounded. I wasn't very close to them but when
we heard the news – we were in a youth movement camp near Tel Aviv
– we were all terrified."

But their most 'outstanding' memory was the bus attack of the 18th
June 2002 near Gilo, in the southern suburbs of Jerusalem.

"It was a horrible day", Rivka recalls, her eyes closed as though reliving the scene. "I was at school and we were just coming out of prayers
when we heard the news. Most of the girls live near Gilo. They were
shouting and some of them were crying because their parents didn't
answer the phone. Everyone was going crazy. Later we found out that
an uncle of one of my friends died in the blast and that several others
had close relatives who were wounded. But, despite everything, I carry
on living like before."

"Me too", adds Efrat. "I try not to think about it. I carry on with all
the things I do – jogging, singing, piano."

"Do you have Palestinian friends, or at least Arab Israeli friends?"

"No, but that doesn't mean I wouldn't", says Efrat, "if they liked
me. I don't think they are so different from us. They have the

same life as us and they do the same things. Of course, their beliefs are a bit strange! But still ... One of us just needs to take the first step – but everyone waits for the other to do it. I don't know what the solution is ..."

Rivka is more cautious.

"Perhaps I could have an Arab Israeli friend ... but after what happened to that boy at Ashkelon, I'm frightened and I think I have the right to be."

"What happened?"

"You don't know the story of Ofir Nahum? He was a boy of 16 who chatted up a Palestinian girl on the internet. When he went to meet her, he was assassinated! In fact, I don't trust any Arabs before I know them. As soon as I see one in the street I am suspicious. I don't think they are all suicide bombers, but there's nothing I can do about it, that's how it is."

"Can you understand that Palestinians of your age are also very frightened of soldiers?"

"Oh no!", Rivka exclaims, indignant. "Our soldiers don't kill children. They only kill if they know that someone is about to carry out a terrorist attack. And if accidents happen, what can we do? If there is a terrorist, you have to shoot, even if there are passers-by near him. Our lives are at stake – it's them or us! What's more, Israeli soldiers never deliberately kill civilians. From that point of view, the Palestinians live in greater security than we do!"

Somewhat flabbergasted by this last statement, I ask her:

"So, what do you make of all the civilians killed at Jenin or at Gaza, when a one-tonne bomb was thrown into a residential district in the middle of the night?"

Very sure of herself, Rivka repeats her father's explanation word for word:

"We had to go into Jenin. We could have bombed the whole camp and then we wouldn't have lost 23 soldiers. As for Gaza, we also had to do that. We had to kill Salah Shehadeh.[2] We had no choice."

"The people who were around Shehadeh weren't innocent", adds Efrat. "When Mr Chirac walks in the street, he is surrounded by collaborators. It's the same thing for Shehadeh. He was surrounded by his collaborators!"

I remind her that the attack took place around midnight, in a residential building, and that nine children, including two babies, were

2. A Hamas leader killed by a bomb on the 22nd July 2002.

among the dead. At which, their father, who has been looking at his daughters with a fond expression, interjects:

"And if they hadn't done it, what would have happened?"

"They would have carried out other suicide bombings", says Rivka, on cue.

Efrat pursues the point.

"They really want to kill us. You've only got to see the explosions of joy in the streets after every suicide bombing – they have a party, distribute sweets ..."

Her father interjects again.

"And what happens here when Palestinians die?"

"We don't distribute sweets and we don't think about revenge!" declares Rivka.

"When we kill a child, we are not happy!" adds Efrat.

Changing the subject, I ask them what negotiations they think will lead to peace. Efrat is categorical.

"I cannot consider for one moment giving them a single one of our towns or a single piece of our land. I don't want to go back to the pre-1967 borders. My country goes from the Mediterranean to the Jordan valley. Many soldiers have died for it. There are enough Arab states – they can go there to live!"

"And Naplouse", I ask her. "Naplouse is one of the oldest Palestinian cities. Does that also belong to the Israelis?"

"Yes, of course it's ours!" declares Rivka, carried away by fervour. "Well ... that is ... it's debatable."

"You must understand that this country is ours", Efrat raps out. "We have the power and it's we who decide! If they don't want to live under our authority, they can leave. I don't understand: we share everything with them, we give them water. They should be grateful. Why do they want to put our state in danger?"

"Perhaps because they think the territories are *their* country", I can't stop myself replying, staggered by her arrogance. "The United Nations have officially asked Israel thirty-eight times to give back the occupied territories."

"Oh, the United Nations!"

Efrat gives a sarcastic little laugh. More conciliatory, Rivka makes an effort.

"They don't all have to be under our authority. The final agreement could give some of them a form of autonomy. But not more than that. After what I have seen since the Oslo agreements and especially since the last intifada, I don't trust them at all any more. We have given them things and they have just killed us. When you give a child a sweet and he hits you, you don't do it again, or you will just be hit again. I don't think we could ever live next to each other – even if they declared they want peace today I would not believe them. You have to think twice before trusting these Arabs!"

I leave the Albrecht family, reflecting on the grave responsibility of journalists, let alone of politicians, who have their own reasons for covering up the truth. I think to myself that if this family, and the majority of Israeli citizens, knew what was really going on in the occupied territories, they would undoubtedly be very upset.

"THEY SHOT ME FOR FUN"

I am still thinking about my conversation with Rivka and Efrat when, the next day I go to Ramallah to visit the Abu Raya rehabilitation centre for the physically disabled, which serves the region around Ramallah, Jenin and Tulkarem.

In the corridors, I pass young people with emaciated faces, walking painfully on crutches or huddled in wheelchairs, alone or surrounded by their families. I avoid looking at them so as not to inflict my pity on them. But isn't it worse to ignore them? Should I smile encouragingly? That could be interpreted as patronising or aggravating ...

Nasser, whom I am meeting, dissipates all my hesitations. His face, striped with a little dark moustache, radiates goodness. He is one of the psychotherapists who have the difficult task of trying to give back hope to disabled youngsters and to persuade them that life is still worth living, even if you are pinned to a wheelchair.

"Here, ninety per cent of the injuries are from the intifada", he tells me. "We always talk about Palestinian deaths, of which there have been over two thousand in two years, but there are also more than forty thousand wounded, of whom five to six thousand will be handicapped for life. And that includes many children. Come, I'll introduce you to Hussam."

In a white room, stretched out on a bed, a small blond boy with a pale face and large blue eyes watches us as we come in.

"Hussam, I've brought a friend to see you, a journalist from France", Nasser tells him, rearranging his pillows so that he can sit up.

At the word 'France', the child graces me with a smile. The French are popular at the moment: some French people assisted Arafat by acting as a human shield and others, by their pressure, stopped the destruction of the Church of the Nativity in Bethlehem.

Hussam comes from Beit An, a village between Naplouse and Ramallah. He is 13 years old. In a quiet little voice, he tells me his story.

"On Friday 5 April, the day the Israeli army invaded Naplouse, I left home to go and see what was happening. I had just got out of the village when I saw three soldiers on a hill. I was alone. They took aim and started firing at me, one bullet after another. First, I was hit in the left hand, then in the right arm. I tried to run, but a bullet got me in the back and another in the right leg. The bullet that went into my left arm travelled through my chest and stuck against my spine. The doctor said that these were 'dum-dum' bullets, special bullets that cause explosions inside the body."[1]

He recounts it all calmly, in a resigned tone and with a sad smile.

"It was as though they shot me for fun, like you shoot at targets in a fairground. An Israeli patrol passed and they stopped to take me. Afterwards I don't know what happened ..."

"They sent him to a hospital in Israel, near Tel Aviv", Nasser tells me. "They removed the bullet near the spine and looked after him. He stayed there for forty-five days."

"Were they kind to you?" I asked Hussam.

"They were normal, like they would be with any patient. My family was able to come and see me, my mother, my older sister and my younger brother. And my father stayed with me the whole time."

"Are you in pain now?"

"Not much. A few days ago I even started studying a bit. I'm trying to revise for my entrance exam to the eighth year. Tomorrow I have a science exam."

1. Weapons that cause cruel and unnecessary suffering are forbidden under the Hague Convention. These include dum-dum bullets, which explode inside the body because the casings are covered with incisions.

I turn to Nasser.

"How is he managing to do that? He can't hold a book!"

"We have developed apparatus that holds the book for him. From time to time we put him in an armchair, so that he can relearn how to sit like that, but it tires him a lot."

"When will he be able to go home?"

"We don't know precisely, but soon", Nasser replies, then adds in a low voice, "careful, he understands English a bit and he doesn't know how serious his condition is."

I turn back to Hussam.

"What do you think about Israeli soldiers?"

"There are good ones and bad ones", the child replies softly. "For example, the officer who picked me up was a good one. The others wanted to kill me, just like that, to amuse themselves. There are different kinds, like among people generally."

I am impressed by such incredible maturity in a child of 13. He has neither anger nor bitterness, but observes and judges his situation as though he were talking about someone else and not as though it is he that is lying in a bed, paralysed by the bullets of some soldiers who 'wanted to have fun' ...

I kiss him on the forehead and leave hurriedly, to hide my tears. This beautiful little boy does not know it yet, but he will be crippled for life.

LIVING UNDER CURFEW

The Sambar family live in the lower part of Ramallah, in an old house consisting of one room of 25 square metres, divided by a tall cupboard – one part for the parents and the other for the eight children, who range from Wassim, 15, to little Malak, three. To get to the tiny kitchen, set up in a shared lean-to, you have to go out of the house; the family uses their neighbour's toilet, a hut some 30 metres away.

On the 28th March, the Israeli army occupied Ramallah and established a military post just opposite the Sambars' house. To be able to manoeuvre its tanks more easily, it blew up two neighbouring houses. The month of occupation was a nightmare for the Sambars.

"They forbad us to leave our room", the mother, a woman of 35 with an emaciated face, tells me. "For twenty-seven days, ten of us had to live in one room, without the right to go to the kitchen or the toilet. I couldn't even go to prepare things to eat. If I opened the door a little, they would point their guns at me and threaten to shoot. The children were hungry and the little ones cried, not understanding why I didn't give them anything to eat. I begged the soldiers to let me go to the kitchen but their only answer was to point their guns at me."

The eldest child, Wassim, a teenager with a fearful air, leans forward on his chair.

"Because the toilets are outside the house", he said, "they refused to let us go to them. My sisters used an empty rubbish bin that we put in a corner of the room. The smell soon became terrible – and we were forced to stay here. I refused to use the bin and I wanted to go to the toilets. My parents said that it was too dangerous but I insisted so much that in the end they agreed. I slipped out at night and ran the 35 metres, very quietly. But when I came out, the soldiers were there. They surrounded me, made me put my hands in the air and threw questions at me, threatening me with their guns: 'What are you doing?' 'What's your name?' 'How old are you?', all the time hitting me with their rifle butts.

"When my father saw them hitting me, he ran out shouting, 'Stop! Stop! He's a child, he just went out to go to the toilets!'. Finally, they let me go. But I've had a lot of pain in my back since then and I can't walk properly.

"The next day, at dawn, the soldiers burst into the house. There were about fifteen of them, shouting like madmen. They went through all our things, upsetting everything, kicking everyone. They shut us all in the kitchen and started to ransack our room. Finally they started searching my father: they made him go down on his knees and hit him in front of us. We were crying but there was nothing we could do. Then they put a plastic bag over his head and took him away, with some other men."

"What were they accusing him of?"

"I don't know. Maybe it was because of the small Palestinian flag they found in the house? We waited for him for days, thinking that they might have killed him. We were sick with worry …"

"And during that month of curfew, how did you manage to eat?"

"I had some provisions", said the mother, "but after they ransacked our room, the soldiers went into the kitchen, broke the windows, threw the food on to the floor and trampled everything. I had to do something, the children were dying of hunger. Through the skylight I could see the soldiers opposite. At night, when most of them were asleep, and there was only one sentry, I waited for him to turn his back and then opened the door very quietly and crept to the kitchen. In the dark, I collected the flour that was spread on the floor, mixed with dust, oil, shards of glass and all sorts of rubbish and I put it in a piece of newspaper. I put some water in a tin can and crept back home with it all, terrified – if they had seen me, they would have killed me.

"In the house, I sieved the flour to get rid of the rubbish, especially the glass, and mixed it with cold water, because they had cut not only the electricity but the gas as well, and we ate that paste. We had terrible stomach aches and by the end of the siege we had lost so much weight that we looked like corpses. But at least we survived."

Tayseer, a boy of 12 with bushy hair and bright eyes, says that he will never forget it.

"People said, 'Soon there will be peace, you will be friends with the Israelis'. I believed it. Now I know it's impossible. They behave like animals: they deliberately piss and shit outside our front door. They are also thieves. One day we were woken up by the sound of breaking glass. We looked out of the window and saw soldiers breaking car windows and stealing the CD players. They broke the window of our car but, thank God, they didn't steal our player, maybe because it's old. And they talk about terrorism! Aren't they the terrorists? I will never forget how they threw my father to the ground and hit him and how they laughed when my mother begged them, and my older brother, who might never be able to walk properly again … and all the people they have killed …

"Before I thought they were like us. Now I know they're not human. I hate them. When I am grown up, I will get revenge."

THE LITTLE FIGHTER

The house, in al Bireh, near the Pisgot settlement, is an old one, made of stone, which you enter through a tiny garden, planted with a fig tree and a medlar. The ground floor, once a stable, has been made into a kitchen; it is meticulously tidy, with gleaming copper and tin pots.

On the first floor is a large living room, full of fluffy animals and plastic flowers, the walls adorned with scriptures from the Koran traced in gold on a black or green background. A refrigerator is on conspicuous display with, sitting atop it, an enormous pink elephant. Mattresses are piled on top of the wardrobes, for at night the room serves as a bedroom.

The house is modest but neat. The father, an itinerant vegetable trader, has been unemployed for two years and the mother takes care of the family by working as a cleaner. Oum Issam is only thirty or so, but her face, framed by a white hijab, is already lined. She has not had a life for two years, she tells me, because of her son.

"He doesn't listen. He wants to throw stones, to fight the Israelis. His father and his uncle have beaten him and his elder brother tries to talk to him but it doesn't do any good. I'm always frightened that I will come home and the neighbours will tell me he is dead. But I can't tie him up or lock him in. If I did, he would escape as soon as he could and never come home again ... Sometimes I follow him and stand between him and the soldiers. That stops him. The boys don't throw stones when there are women there. They shout for us to get out of the way. They are furious, but they don't want to put us in danger."

A small boy with bushy hair, his skin tanned by the sun, has just come in: Ayman. Dressed in a long T-shirt and stained trousers, he is just 11 years old, but already has the air of a muscly little tough guy, with strong hands that can surely throw stones a long way. When I ask if he has come back from school, he gives me a dirty look.

"He doesn't go to school any more", his mother says plaintively. "He just wants to fight. He wasn't like that before. He has become a lot more aggressive since he was wounded."

His grandmother, a large woman with a generous bosom, smiles.

"Ayman has grand political theories. He says to us: 'Presidents of the world come and go as they like yet the Israelis stop our president from going anywhere. We should go and liberate the Mouqata'a!' And he tries to get us to go and demonstrate: 'It's your duty. Abu Ammar [the familiar name for Yasser Arafat] is in prison and you are staying at home in the warm. You should be ashamed of yourselves!'"

I later find out that Ayman often goes back to her house in the evening, to wash and to get rid of the signs of his misdeeds, before returning to his parents.

"Actually", she adds, taking off her white veil and wiping her face, "I myself went to demonstrate last night. There were thousands of us in the streets of Ramallah, banging saucepans so that Arafat would hear us from the Mouqata'a where he is imprisoned.[1] The Israeli soldiers were furious, but because it was a peaceful demonstration, with no stones being thrown and with us keeping our distance from them, they couldn't really shoot at us."

"We were there too", say the aunts proudly.

The mother gives them a disapproving glance and says to me, "I tell Ayman: 'Wait until you are grown up. What good has it done him, your friend who died? He is in the earth now, he doesn't exist any more!' He responds: 'No, he's in heaven'. What can I say to that?"

Ayman sits in the midst of this tribe of chattering women – mother, grandmother, two aunts and sister – with his arms crossed and the indifferent air of a man leaving the women to gossip. Despite all his bravado, however, he cannot change the childishness of his face.

I stand in front of him, so that he has to look at me.

"Ayman, tell me how you were wounded."

To my astonishment, he does not play the hero. In his hoarse voice, which is beginning to break, he contents himself with relating the facts, as though he were talking about the most normal thing in the world.

"It was in January. The soldiers had surrounded Arafat's office and people were saying that the soldiers were going to harm him. Bulldozers were putting up earth banks all around. I was with a group of children and I was encouraging them. 'Come on, don't let them do this to Abu Ammar', I said, but they were frightened. It was the

---

1. The whole of Ramallah came out on to the streets for the 'saucepan protest' of 25th September 2002. Spontaneous demonstrations went on for three days in support of Arafat, as Palestinians feared for his life. The Mouqata'a was bombed continuously and the elderly leader's office riddled with bullets.

first time we had gone to the Mouqata'a – normally we go to the checkpoint near Qalandiya. They went and I was the only one left to throw stones.

"Then children from the Qalandiya camp came. They're no weaklings! The Israelis threw a canister of tear gas at us but it didn't go off; I picked it up, took the pin out and threw it back at them. They had to move back. We took advantage and moved towards the bulldozers, but two jeeps arrived. The Qalandiya lot threw a Molotov cocktail at one of them, which caught fire. The soldiers started shooting and I was hit. I fell and I couldn't breathe. My friend Jihad and a paramedic took me to hospital and the doctor operated on me."

He lifts his T-shirt and shows me a large scar on his left side, near his heart.

"He was incredibly lucky", his mother says. "The bullet went into his ribs and lodged itself two millimetres from his heart. He was in intensive care for forty-eight hours and then in bed at home for three months."

"Were you in pain?" I asked Ayman.

He assumes a casual air.

"It stung."

"You weren't frightened of dying?"

"No. If I die, I will be with all my friends who have died. Seven of my friends have been killed. One of them was in the car with his father, who was a militant. Another one was looking out of the window. I visit their graves, I put flowers on them and I water them."

"But what will your mother do if you die?"

He hesitates, gives her a look full of tenderness and then, lowering his head, replies:

"She will cry."

Oum Issam lets out a deep sigh.

"He says to me all the time: 'If you find out I'm dead, don't cry – you should sing'. When he says that, I start crying."

"What do your elder brothers and your father say?"

"My brothers say to me, 'stay here with us' and when my father knows that I'm going out he hits me to try and stop me. He is right; he wants me to grow up and he can't accept that I might die. I'm not frightened of dying but I don't want to be handicapped."

Here, finally, is the chink in his armour. Ashamed of the advantage I am about to take of it, I tell myself it's in a good cause and plunge ahead.

"But if you carry on, you might be disabled for life!"

He stares at his feet for a long time. When he finally speaks, it is in a pathetic little whisper.

"But I have to carry on throwing stones! They are occupying my country and killing our people. It's natural that I throw stones! I can't accept them being here in our country. They don't belong here!"

"Even when he was at nursery school", his mother interrupts, "he threw his bottle of juice at a jeep."

Why did it occur to me to ask him if he goes to the mosque? Doubtless because of the simplistic Western idea that attributes all nationalist struggles involving Muslims to a *Jihad*.[2]

"I used to go to the mosque but I have other occupations now", he declares; the responsible man who leaves prayers to women and old folk.

I stop myself from smiling.

"And before you were wounded, did you have problems with the soldiers?"

"Yes, several times I got rubber bullets in my arms and legs, and also tear gas, but that's all nothing", he said in the manly tones of an old warrior.

"And have you been arrested?"

"Yes, twice. The first time, the others ran off. The soldiers caught me and beat me, asking why I threw stones. I said to them, 'You are on our land, so I have to throw stones at you!' They tied me up and took me to Pisgot settlement. The settlers there laughed at me because I was little. I was eight. They lit a lighter under my nose to try to scare me, but I wasn't frightened. More recently, last June, they caught me near the al-Amari camp, after they had bombed houses in the camp. I had an iron bar. I tried to tell them that it was for jobs in the house but they'd got photos of me throwing stones.

"They took me in a jeep and all day they made me pick up stones on the road they were building for the settlers. Then they took me to their headquarters, near the camp. They humiliated me. They stopped me going to the toilet, gave other people water but not me and stopped me sleeping even though I was very tired. They wanted me to give them the names of my friends. They hit me and put my head down the toilet while they asked 'Who was throwing stones with you?'. I said 'Nobody'. After a while I started crying; then they said, 'We'll let you go but next time we'll keep you'.

2. Jihad literally means 'holy striving' but has come popularly to mean 'holy war'.

"When I was leaving, a soldier held out his hand and I refused to take it. They said, 'If you don't shake his hand, we will keep you here'. An old man from the camp came and tried to intervene, saying 'Leave him alone, he's a child'. Then the soldier pushed me on to the old man so that I would make him fall, but I moved to the side and fell on to a soldier. I took him down with me."

At this memory, Ayman's face lights up and, forgetting his grown-up air, he begins to laugh like the child of 11 that he is.

"The Israelis were furious. Luckily the internationals[3] arrived to speak to the officer and when they surrounded him, I escaped."

"Do you know how to make a Molotov cocktail?"

He shrugs his shoulders.

"All the children around here know how. It's easy: petrol, a bit of sand, a piece of material that you set alight, and then you throw it."

"Do you really think children can make the Israeli army withdraw?"

"Well, at any rate we frighten them. The other day a soldier called us over. We said to him: 'Put down your gun and come here if you're a man!' He put his gun down and we threw stones at him. He ran off. And then their Merkava tanks aren't invincible. We only have to jump on top and they can't shoot at us any more – then we undo the lights and the loudspeakers and take them."

Ayman's mother, profiting from our presence, begins to give him a long lecture. He doesn't respond but just sits politely, with a bored expression. He is obviously not listening and his mother may as well talk herself hoarse for all the good it will do. Adult lectures are not going to stop him. He patiently waits for the storm to abate so that he can join his friends ... to go and throw stones.

On the way back, the teacher who had accompanied me explains that they have noticed that the children who throw stones have the fewest psychological problems.

"They sleep well at night. They feel they are doing what they have to do. Their actions fit in with their way of seeing things. They feel useful and not guilty, as so many others do, about not doing anything. At any rate, if you try and stop those who want to throw stones, they go in secret. You won't even be able to try to protect them any more. They also do it with their friends, which means that if they don't go, they will be excluded from their group. My son does it ... you can only say to them, 'Those who died, died for nothing.'"

3. The various NGOs.

She sighs, then goes on.

"I am not sure if we should have spoken like that to the kid. He had tears in his eyes. Now he doesn't know what he should do any more. It's not easy for a child to see his friends being killed without reacting. It is a real trauma that he can only overcome by acting to avenge them. One can really see that it is a need for Ayman. If he doesn't avenge his friends, he feels like a coward. And that is, no doubt, worse for him than death."

7

◆

Gaza

Surrounded by electric fences and military posts, completely isolated from the outside world, the Gaza Strip is often described as a gigantic open-air prison. Almost a quarter of its 363 square kilometres has been confiscated for use by 7000 settlers, while 1.2 million Palestinians are crammed into the remaining 288 square kilometres.

Confined in this space from which they cannot get out, without work or sources of income for two and a half years, almost eighty per cent of Gazans live below the poverty line and depend for their survival on UNWRA or on aid provided by Europe, the Arab states and various charitable organisations.

The United Nations agencies have issued a warning signal and are urgently demanding an increase in aid to avert a humanitarian disaster. Israel, however, opposes this, declaring that the aid might be used by terrorists and their families.

JABALIYA CAMP

Jabaliya Camp, in the north of the Gaza Strip, is one of the biggest Palestinian refugee camps. It provides shelter to several hundred thousand people, most of whom have come from neighbouring villages situated in the zone that now belongs to Israel.

To avoid getting lost in the maze of identical little dusty streets, you need to be accompanied by one of its inhabitants. My guide for the day is José, a Spanish photographer who is writing a book on life in Jabaliya and who has lived here for a year. The Palestinians think of him as one of their own.

We stop in front of a humble house, made of breeze blocks, where his friend Nabil lives. José has just photographed his daughters – classic examples of Palestinian beauty, he declares. We go into an internal courtyard, made of concrete and completely bare of greenery. In the corner is a water point where a pregnant woman, surrounded by three or four children, is washing dishes; on the opposite side, a mat and several mattresses serve as sofas.

Nabil, a small man, with a face full of energy, comes to greet us. In 1948, when he was three years old, he arrived in the camp with his parents, from a village north of the Gaza strip. His two daughters, smiling and shy, are with him. They are ravishingly beautiful, as José had claimed; tall and delicately built, as refined and alluring as princesses.

Yassera, who is 16, has immense grey eyes, and a very pale complexion framed by brown curls. She seems as lively as quicksilver. At the moment, she is preparing for her matriculation exam – the brightest student in her class, she dreams of going to university. "If", she murmurs, "Daddy lets me." Her elder sister Djamilla has the air of a Madonna, with plaited hair gathered into a low chignon and a gentle smile. Married, she has a little boy of a year old, and has just taken up studying again to prepare for a secretarial exam.

Nabil is proud of his daughters. Unlike many Middle Eastern fathers, he thinks that they should receive as much education as boys.

"I have sweated blood to get all my children to their matriculation certificate, but I can't do more, especially as I don't have any work now."

Nabil was a driver for a Palestinian politician, but the barricades that cut the Gaza Strip in three and which stop people, even officials, from leaving the enclave to go to the West Bank, have put him out of his job. If the situation is better next year, he will do all he can to pay for his daughter to go to university.

"Have you ever been back to your family's village?" I ask him.

"Yes, after 1967, when the borders were opened. I even went to work in my own village, picking oranges. I remember that I was working with a Hungarian Jew, who asked me one day, 'Where do you come from?'

"I replied, 'From right here'.

"'But there aren't any houses here – where do you live?'

"'In Gaza.'

"'So why don't you say you're from Gaza? Why do you continue to say you're from here?'

"'Do you think I would forget that my father, my grandfather and all my ancestors were born and lived here, and that they have cultivated this land since time immemorial?' I said to him. 'I also tell my children that this is where we are from!'

"He was furious. I felt like saying to him, 'You're from Hungary', but I didn't dare, for fear of losing my job or even being arrested."

"It must be hard to be an agricultural worker on land that belonged to your parents'."

"I was very small; I don't remember much. It's much harder for those who lived there all their lives. When we went back in 1967, my grandmother knelt on the soil in her garden and covered her head with earth, weeping. She died not long after.

"When I worked there, I had a Yemenite Jewish boss with whom I got on very well. But there was also an American Jew in the village who had bought land and built a little house, where he came for a month every year. My boss and I didn't understand what he was doing there. That Yemenite and I were the same – only our religion was different and that doesn't matter. The problem between the Jews and us isn't one of religion or of understanding. The problem is that we claim the same land.

"After that, I worked for ten years in a factory at Ashkelon. There were some Moroccan Jewish workers there with whom I used to discuss things fairly openly. Once, when he was manoeuvring a tractor, one of them didn't watch what he was doing and ran into a very old tree. I said to him, 'Leave that tree alone. It was planted by my ancestors – why are you knocking them down for fun?'.

"He replied, 'Stop bothering me with your ancestors!'

"At least you can talk to Middle Eastern Jews. We speak the same kind of language!"

Nabil sighed.

"Now we can't go and work in Israel any more. We are completely shut in. We cannot even move inside Gaza!"

His daughters have never been out of Gaza. Their dream is not to go to Paris or New York, like other girls. They dream of going to their own country, Palestine – and above all to Jerusalem!

"But it's not possible for the moment. They have refused all exit permits for three years!"

Nabil comments that relations with the Israelis were, none the less, less difficult before.

"We could go and work in their country – in manual jobs, where we were often mistreated and always underpaid, doing the toughest work, but at least we earned a living. Now we live in destitution. As soon as we began demanding our rights, a real country and not a 'reservation' under the control of their army, the Israelis began acting violently. We can't bear being in this overpopulated camp any more; we are suffocating and we want to go home. Before ... [his voice breaks]. Before, every family had their garden and grew vegetables. We had a life with dignity."

"But if all the Palestinians returned home, that would be the end of Israel ..."

"I know", Nabil said bitterly. "I am longing to go back to my land and my roots, but I know it's impossible ..."

He lets out a long sigh and looks at me, his eyes shining.

"What I really want, now, is for the occupied territories to be given back in return for peace. To have normal relations with the Israelis. I don't ask more than that. I just want to live like a human being!"

All the Palestinians to whom I spoke expressed the same profound desire to return home, while the majority accept that it isn't possible.

"One of the main obstacles to peace", I ventured, "is that the Israelis are frightened for their security."

"And our security, doesn't that count?" exclaimed Nabil angrily. "Every day children are killed on their way to school, every day women are assassinated while doing their shopping! Do you think that, if we had the opportunity of living decently, our young people would turn themselves into human bombs?"

Yassera interjects, trembling:

"When I see the soldiers destroying houses with families inside, it makes me want to go and blow myself up in the middle of Israelis, to avenge those innocent people. Before I didn't think like that, but for a year I have heard about all these horrific things, especially at Jenin, and it makes me feel guilty. The important thing is not to kill Israelis – it's to frighten them so that they can't live normally and can't go out without fearing a bomb attack. That is what will make them find a solution. They are not going to give us back our land out of the goodness of their hearts."

"You know", said Djamilla, cradling her baby, "even a cat, if you hurt its young, will scratch and bite and do all it can to defend them. It's a natural instinct. Why should we accept our children being killed without defending ourselves in the same way? And since we don't have weapons, our only defence is these bomb attacks. I am not willing to do that because I have a baby but I don't have a life any more. I live near an Israeli checkpoint, with tanks, and machine guns firing all the time; my child is terrified, he doesn't sleep. We live in constant fear that one day the soldiers will come in, destroy our house, shoot, like they often do, for no reason, because they are in a bad mood or because one of them has been wounded and they want to take revenge on no matter who. Believe me, I have no intention of blowing myself up but if something happened to my child, I wouldn't hesitate to go up in flames, with as many Israelis as possible, to avenge him."

"But you, Yassera, you're 16 and you've got your life ahead of you – could you do such a thing?"

Without hesitation she replies vehemently:

"If things get even worse, with all our people suffering, being killed, there would be no alternative. You, in the West, you talk about suicide. It isn't suicide. It's resistance."

"But Israeli babies are not your enemies! Do you think there is nothing wrong with killing them?"

Their mother, who has come over, speaks. Barely 35, she is a very pretty woman, who is, she tells me, expecting a baby boy – 'the weapon of population', she smiles.

"I cannot feel happy about a death, even of an enemy. I think of that child's mother and I understand her pain. We also experience pain. We feel it – it isn't an abstraction. Those who rejoice are those who have never been down that road, but every Palestinian family has known at least one death."

"A year ago, I thought the same as my mother", said Yassera. "But now, with all the horror that we have lived through, most of us have changed our minds. The Israelis have sown hatred in our hearts."

KHAN YUNIS

Khan Yunis is a large, animated village, its streets swarming with bright-eyed children and lined with open-air cafés where, under shady palm trees, men in galabiehs smoke hookah pipes and play backgammon. Girls wearing the hijab and women dressed in long robes and black veils wander among the shops, while, amid a cacophony of horns, small donkeys trot along, ridden by little boys proudly taking their vegetable-laden baskets to market.

We are far from the West Bank. In Gaza City – the principal town and administrative centre of Gaza – one feels as though one is in a different world, but here it almost feels like Egypt, from which we are separated by only another checkpoint and Rafah, the urban area in the far south of Palestine, where several deaths occur every day. Tragedies that the international press has long since stopped bothering to report.

I have a meeting with Marwan, a young man who studied in Lyon and who speaks perfect French. He returned a year ago and is without work, like the great majority of Gazans. For ten hours he will be my indefatigable guide and interpreter, reacting angrily to my offer of payment at the end of our day together. Throughout my stay in Palestine I encountered the same kindness and generosity from people who often hardly had enough to eat.

First, Marwan wants to give me a tour of the market. The Gaza Strip is a fertile place and in the market one finds magnificent vegetables at truly bargain prices: two shekels for a ten kilo crate of tomatoes, three for a crate of cucumbers and five for peppers.

"Most people in Rafah and Khan Yunis used to make a living from the land", Marwan explains, "but now they are destitute. Israeli bulldozers often destroy their fields, on the pretext that they are near a settlement; sometimes the Israelis let them cultivate the land, spend money on irrigation, seed and manure – and as soon as the harvest is ready, the bulldozers flatten everything. It happens so much that many farmers have given up. And those who continue to farm can hardly export any more. For almost three years the West Bank has been completely closed to us and with all these checkpoints, it is difficult to get produce even to Gaza City. So prices have plummeted.

"But even so, there are few customers. People don't have any more money. They can't find work, have spent all their savings and sold all that they can sell. Many families survive solely through international aid, with a twenty or thirty-kilo bag of wheat every two months, a bit of sugar and some tea ... For the first time since their eviction in 1948, Palestinians are reduced to a state of quasi-beggary. If it weren't for the children, I think that most would prefer to starve to death, from pride."

We have now left the market and are making our way towards a large white building, the sports and cultural activities centre for Khan Yunis, where we have an appointment with a Fatah youth leader.

Zeid is, at most, thirty, with a scarred face and a haunting, grave expression. Born in Khan Yunis refugee camp, he comes from a previously wealthy background. His father's side of the family owned a textile business and his mother's were large landowners.

"In the summer of 1948, my family, like hundreds of thousands of Palestinians, lost everything in the space of a few hours. My father told me that he was in school when they learnt that the Israelis were massacring people in neighbouring villages. His family and all their neighbours fled towards Gaza, which at that time was held by the Egyptians. Like a lot of young people, for a long time I criticised my father for not staying behind to fight, and then I read the work of the Israeli 'new historians' and realised that the Palestinians, with their poor weapons, had no chance. To have stayed would have been suicidal and they had to survive, to safeguard the future.

"At the beginning, we lived in tents left by the English Army and then in 1949 UNWRA gave us better ones. Later on we built small houses. My father, who had never worked with his hands, became a construction worker. He worked himself to the bone to be able to bring us up and to enable us to study. When I got my political science degree, he was proud and very sad all at once: 'If we still had our country, you could have gone on studying, but now I can't pay for you any more'. He still talks to us about life in the old days ...

"When the organised struggle began, around 1965, my father left for Egypt, where he fought in the 1967 war. The Egyptians subsequently imprisoned him for four years because he was part of the Palestinian Liberation Army and they didn't want trouble with Israel.

"In fact", Zeid concludes, sarcastically, "three nations are responsible for the suffering of the Palestinian people: England, which gave our land to the Jews, the Israelis, who occupied and massacred us, and the cowardice of the Arab countries ..."

"And how did you become involved in politics?"

"I was ten years old at the time of the Sabra and Shatila massacres. The victims were poor, defenceless people in camps, like us. I asked my teachers a lot of questions about it, and also my father, who was then working as a manual labourer in Israel. It is hard to work for those who have forced you out of your home ... He had to feed his children, he didn't have any choice – but it made me feel bad for him.

"When the first intifada began, in 1987, I began throwing stones. When you are very young you have no fear and I used to stand three metres in front of the soldiers! I was imprisoned twice, the first time when I was 16. It was under Begin, who had given the order to break demonstrators' arms and legs. The soldiers followed that order so well that they didn't even interrogate us any more – they merely hit us. They broke the hands of thousands of prisoners, saying 'Now you won't throw any more stones!' As for me, they hit me on the head with a baton. I had to have 13 stitches."

He parts his black hair and I see a scar running along the top of his skull.

"They beat me to a pulp and then threw me into a tent. It was in the middle of winter and we were very cold, but the feeling that we were heroes gave us some comfort. There was an extraordinary solidarity between us. When I was released, I cried because I had to leave my friends behind.

"The second time was harder. They arrested me for belonging to Fatah. Even if you didn't have any weapons – and at the time we just had stones – you had only to be a member of a party, any party, to get a prison term of at least two years. They caught me writing slogans on walls. It was in 1990 and I was 18.

"They tortured me for 22 days. At first they put me in a tent with other prisoners who, I quickly found out, were collaborators. They tried to frighten me by saying that they were going to break my arms and legs and subject me to horrific torture ... Then the Shin Beth started calling me for interrogation, always at three o'clock in the morning, the time when you have the least resistance. They would say, 'You are guilty but if you help us, we can come to an agreement'. As I refused, they threw me against a glass window; I was cut everywhere. Then they hit me in the face with a club, breaking my nose and teeth.

"They interrogated me every day, kicking me with their boots, especially in sensitive parts of the body. As I did not give in, they shut me in a tiny hut, completely dark without any light or air, and left me there for five days. I was suffocating. They gave me nothing to eat, apart from rotten eggs that they sometimes threw in. When they brought me out, they took me into a room where a man was lying, covered in blood, and said, 'That's what will happen to you if you don't co-operate'.

"Sometimes a soldier put a gun to my head, saying, 'He's dangerous; we have to finish him off'. But I knew it was just to frighten me; they never kill in that way. Other times they made me kneel down, my hands behind my back, bent forwards and pressed my face down to the floor with a boot on my neck. It was a painful and degrading position but it would allow me to sleep for a few seconds.

"As they were still getting nowhere with me, they began to inflict their speciality: the 'suspension bridge' torture or the 'arc', which they are particularly fond of because it leaves no external marks. They put you out in the cold, naked, with your head covered with a stinking hood that suffocates you, and then they tie you to a small chair, a few inches high, your legs pulled back, your arms pulled up, very tightly bound with handcuffs that cut off your circulation. The body forms an arc, strained to the maximum. The tension of all the muscles and the lack of oxygen act like poison and lead to terrible pain. Every five hours or so, they release you for a few minutes, so that you don't die.

"And then they begin again. If it is practised over a long period, that torture will disable you for life. A friend who underwent it in the prison at Chatta, near Haifa, told me that a mural painted on a wall in the entrance declared to Palestinians: 'You enter proud as lions but you will leave like rabbits'."

Zeid relates all this calmly, as though it had happened to someone else. But I know that just telling me about it is painful for him. Palestinians who have experienced torture very rarely agree to talk about it, through modesty, unwillingness to present themselves as heroes when so many others have endured the same, or worse, suffering and also because they need to forget. But the man sitting opposite me knows that giving his testimony is part of the struggle and he takes the risk. I cannot stop myself asking where he found the courage to resist.

"I thought of my family, above all of my brother, who had been killed two weeks before I went into prison and my anger towards his murderers gave me strength."

"What had he done?"

"Nothing! Settlers killed him while he was asleep. He was 28. He was working in Israel and as it was impossible to spend hours travelling there and back every day, he slept in an empty warehouse with other workers. That was forbidden, but at the time, in 1990, a lot of people took the risk – otherwise they couldn't have worked and fed their families. One evening, after work, his friends went to buy food. They told me that when they got back they found him swimming in blood. Zionist settlers had shot him. At the time, all the Israeli papers had to say about it was 'We must stop all these murders, or we won't have a Palestinian workforce, and they are indispensable to us'."

"And you, how long afterwards were you released?"

"I was sentenced to two years in prison and I came out in 1992. I stayed at home to recuperate for some time and then began my studies at Bir Zeit University. However, I had to leave because I couldn't afford to pay any more. Later I joined the leadership of Fatah Youth for the Khan Yunis area. Today we look after six thousand young people."

"Have you ever tried to avenge your brother?"

Zeid gives me a look of annoyance.

"Good Lord, no! I am not going to kill Israeli people to avenge my brother! The problem isn't getting revenge but liberating Palestine. In any case, I think that life is precious and I am totally against the suicide bombings. There are many desperate people among the Palestinians who go to the political leaders of various organisations and offer themselves as volunteers. A recent survey showed that of 300 people questioned in Gaza, 285 said that they wanted to be martyrs. But in Fatah we do all we can to dissuade them. We are opposed to this kind of action."

"But what is the solution to the situation?"

"The Israelis have no choice but to negotiate. They can't kill or transfer all the Palestinians. The experience of 1948 is enough for us. We will not go, even if they use force."

Someone knocks at the office door. A man in his forties appears: he has the strong, rugged hands of a manual labourer. He explains calmly that a bulldozer has destroyed his house and everything inside; he is on the street with his family and has no means to live. Can they help?

More than what he is describing – a situation that has, unfortunately, become commonplace – it is the calm with which he speaks that is striking, as though he were talking about just another everyday problem. At no time does he complain.

Where does this attitude, so common among Palestinians, come from? From being so used to misfortune? From the constant tragedy all around, which makes you realise that you are just one case among many, that there are worse – such as losing a child – and that crying is

only a waste of your remaining energy, when those in charge need precise details to be able to help you?

All that is doubtless true, but such an absence of reaction to suffering is also sometimes the sign of a tragic absence of feeling, as if one
has been hit so often that one has ceased to feel pain. It is an escape from
a world that has become unbearable, a latent depression that affects
more and more Palestinians.

Khan Yunis Camp

Zeid calls on Wassim, a lanky young man who works with the
organisation *Enfants réfugiés du monde*, to act as my guide to Khan
Yunis camp, which shelters 60,000 refugees in a few square kilometres.

Wassim is 28 and was born in the camp, where he now lives with his
nine brothers, two sisters and parents. His father is a welder who, until
the second intifada, worked in Israel. I ask him what his brothers do
and whether they are politically active.

"Only one is militant. He has been arrested five times and the
Israelis are looking for him at the moment; I haven't seen him for three
months. He is a true fighter – he is prepared to die in the service of his
country. I serve in other ways, by studying psychology and looking after
children."

As we talk, we wander along dirt roads lined with houses made of cob
or rough concrete. Many are unfinished, with iron bars pointing to the
sky. Some of these abandoned shells have two or even three storeys, an
indication of the years of hope that followed the Oslo agreements. It was
during that period that Gaza's port and airport were built, with money
from the European Union; the Israeli government has never allowed
them to operate and, after being bombed in 2001, they are now unusable.

But it is the walls of Khan Yunis camp that, like all the walls in all the
camps in Gaza, grab the attention. These walls relate the history of
Palestine, its struggles and its 'martyrs'. Since the second intifada,
between September 2000 and March 2003, there have been around
2,700 deaths, 2,100 of them Palestinians. Primitive paintings depict the
war with its fighters, tanks, planes and rockets but also peace, symbol-
ised by idyllic landscapes with gardens full of oranges, olives and palms
and lambs grazing near clear water. Here and there are portraits of
Feday'een,[1] wearing *keffiyahs* (a scarf worn over the head by Arab men)

---

1. A feday (singular form of Feday'een) is in Palestinian terminology a fighter who sacrifices
his life for the liberation of the homeland.

and armed with Kalashnikovs, as well as a dove of peace, the black stone of the *Ka'aba* on the house of a *hajji* (someone who has made the pilgrimage to Mecca) and slogans proclaiming: 'You can destroy our houses but you will never destroy our souls', and 'With the Koran and the gun we will win independence!'

And then there are the posters of 'martyrs' everywhere. The names and portraits of these men, women and children, endlessly reproduced, have been printed against a background of the golden dome of the al-Aqsa mosque in Jerusalem – uniting them, in death, with the holy city of which they had dreamed.

After walking around the narrow streets of the camp for half an hour, followed by swarms of children curious to know whether I am American or Israeli – but who at no time show any aggression – we come to the extreme west of the camp, where Wissam lived.

His house is no more than a pile of stones, next to other ruins. All the houses within a radius of about a hundred metres have been destroyed. Only some empty shells, riddled with bullets, are still standing.

The Israeli military zone stretches into the distance in front of us, surrounded by walls that are a dozen metres high, topped with watch towers.

"Why did the soldiers destroy your house? Was it because of your brother's activities?"

"No, that was nothing to do with it. They also destroyed the houses of about twenty neighbouring families. The reason they decided to 'make a clean sweep' was because militants were trying to stop them taking land that belongs to the camp and were shooting at them from behind the houses.

"It was on the 12th April 2001. They came in the night, without warning. I remember being woken by the noise of the bulldozers. At first I didn't pay any attention to it and it was only when they started to come really close that we realised what was happening. We just had time to get out, without taking anything with us.

"They shot at people who tried to escape, with high calibre machine-guns. It was a real massacre, with four dead and 24 wounded – old people, women, children ... One of my brothers who tried to intervene was shot in the head. He survived but is seriously handicapped. It happened over a year ago but I still wake up screaming ... I wouldn't wish it on anyone, seeing what I saw that night!"

"Why did the soldiers confiscate your land? Was it to protect the settlements at Gush Katif?"

"Supposedly", Wissam retorts, shrugging his shoulders. "In reality, behind those walls there is nothing but dozens of hectares of empty land. The Gush Katif settlements, where people live, are much further away. The so-called imperatives of security are simply an excuse that the Israelis give to appropriate more and more land and to deny us access to the sea."

Returning to the centre of the camp, we stop in front of a simple cob house. A small, thin man, his head covered with a *kofia,* the cotton skull cap worn by Muslims, welcomes us. Salim Mohammed al-Bas radiates an air of infinite sadness. He ushers us in to an inner courtyard, empty apart from two mats thrown directly on to the ground, on which we sit. His wife, Niafa, joins us. She seems tougher than her husband. It is she who tells us the story of their son Bassel, who was killed on 19th March 2001, when he was just 12 years old.

"We were living in a small house next to the sea, not far from the military camp. Just behind the house we had a chicken coop and a run and Bassel used to feed the chickens and play with them when he got back from school."

She breathes deeply before going on.

"That day, a chicken escaped. He tried to catch it and a tank fired a shell at him ... he was blown to pieces."

Niafa stops, staring into space. She was there and she saw everything. In a strangled voice, she mutters:

"They could see from the control tower that it was a boy playing with chickens! He didn't throw stones or anything like that. He was a very quiet boy."

She hands me a poster showing a small boy with bright eyes, set against the golden dome of the al-Aqsa mosque.

"Of course he never went to the al-Aqsa", Wissam explains, "but portraying him like that is a way of sanctifying these young victims, of implying that they died for their faith – which isn't true. Yet it comforts the parents to have the death of their child connected with a noble cause such as the liberation of holy sites."

The al Bas family were originally farmers, from a village near Gaza. In 1948 they became refugees. When Salim, the father, was grown up, he worked as a farm worker in Israel and the settlements.

The man seems broken. He tells me that he has two other sons, aged 15 and 18, neither of whom is an activist and that Bassel was the most gifted of the family.

"He was excellent at maths and he wanted to study. I was saving so that he could. He was counting the years until he could take his matriculation exam and said that it was he who would take care of us later ..."

He begins to cry, silently, his head to one side, wiping his eyes with the back of his hand, apologising to me for letting himself be overcome in this way.

Witnessing such self-effacing pain, I feel like an intruder in the life and the hearts of these people. I arrive, I plunge them back into memories of their tragedy, and then I leave ... Ashamed, I ask my interpreter to tell them how important their testimony is and that I am going to tell people about it so that they understand what is happening here, to try to bring about change.

Can they still believe that? So many journalists and politicians have come and gone and their situation has done nothing but worsen for fifty-four years ... At any rate, they have the generosity to pretend. The mother hugs me tightly and insists that I take the photo of their son. The father continues staring at the floor, his eyes wet with tears. Making a superhuman effort, he accompanies me to the door of his house and manages a weak smile of farewell.

Twenty hours to travel ten kilometres

It is only three o'clock in the afternoon, but if I want to get back to Gaza City before nightfall, I should leave now, Marwan warns me.

We pile into a shared taxi that has come from Rafah, near the Egyptian border. The person I am sitting next to, a man in his fifties, tells me that he owns a nail factory – the only one in all Palestine. He used to employ eight people but since the start of the troubles he has only three, and soon he will have to close down. He imports his raw materials from China to Israel by freight, at a cost of $800. But for some time the Israeli government has made him pay $800 extra for the short trip from Israel to Rafah.

"It has ruined me. I am going to have to shut my factory down and let go of my workers. Which means there will be three more families with nothing to eat ..."

Although he is bitter about it, he is anxious to stress the difference between the Israeli government and Israeli people.

"I have an old Israeli friend. We used to work together and, before the incidents, I even lent him money. Jews and Palestinians love life and we can live together without problems ... If it weren't for these politicians!"

The driver jumps into the conversation.

"We've had enough of this intifada! It's brought poverty to people and there's no work anywhere. A bit earlier on I took three men from Rafah to Khan Yunis; they used to be construction workers who earned a good living but now they didn't even have three shekels to pay for the taxi ride. They were very embarrassed and asked if I would accept just one shekel. Of course I did, but I felt really bad about seeing their shame."

At last, we arrive at the Khan Yunis checkpoint, which has been closed for almost four hours. A compressed line of cars and vans stretches back for two kilometres; we walk along it in the heavy heat. Most people have deserted their cars and sought out a shady place in which to sit or lie on an old blanket. The atmosphere is curiously relaxed. People are drinking tea, talking, eating ice cream and some even smoking a hookah – reviving the practices of a bygone era when one had all the time in the world. Mothers, sitting slightly apart, nurse their infants. Along the dusty route, stalls have appeared, selling all sorts of drinks and food. There are even toys for the children.

The driver of a van carrying fruit and vegetables tells me that the previous week he had waited forty-eight hours, sleeping there for two nights; when he finally reached his destination on the other side, almost all his cargo had rotted.

At last, we are among the first cars. Ahead of us, the high walls of the Gush Katif barricade loom up again – a towering monolith punctured by holes three-quarters obscured by sandbags, through which machine guns are pointing. I get out my camera but am instantly reproved by my companions:

"Don't do that! They can see everything from the other side through binoculars. You'll get yourself shot!"

In front of us, raised up a little, stretches a wide road, built for Israeli settlers. It is deserted.

"What are we waiting for?" I ask my neighbour.

The look he gives me makes me want to disappear into the ground. Have I still not understood that life here revolves around waiting on the whims of the occupier?

Finally, a car goes by on the settlers' road and, ten minutes later, another. On the two sides of the checkpoint, thousands of pairs of eyes follow them; humiliated, and frustrated. In the space of an hour, three other cars and a bus that is almost empty will use the settlers' road while, behind the barricades, the line of vehicles stretches out of sight ...

It is almost six o'clock and, as the sun sets over the horizon, good humour begins to give way to weariness. An insistent bleating is coming from a lorry carrying sheep, to which caged chickens cackle in response. The animals are thirsty and there is no means of watering them.

"I have seen entire loads of chickens die from dehydration", a lorry driver tells me. "So we don't often risk transporting them now. It's the same thing for fruit and vegetables, which rot very quickly. The only solution is to sell what you can on the spot."

Practising what he preaches, he perches himself on the back of his lorry and signals to the women, who come running: crates of tomatoes, cucumbers and water-melons are offloaded for a few shekels, to the great joy of these housewives.

"I don't make anything and sell at cost price", the man tells me, "but at least their children can eat something other than bread!"

A thin man next to me, who has been lighting cigarette after cigarette, agrees.

"I did my engineering studies abroad. After the Oslo agreements I came back because I wanted to help build my country. But I don't know how much longer my family and I can keep going ..."

"We will keep going", a woman interrupts, "and our children will take over the struggle. I've got two daughters. I called one Horya, which means 'freedom' and the other Kifah, 'armed struggle'. They have known nothing but occupation but they have only one idea in their minds: to fight to be able to live in freedom!"

All of a sudden, there is bustling in the crowd. "The barricade! The barricade is coming up!" We run back to our cars. But shots suddenly ring out and the order is shouted into a megaphone 'Rouh! Rouh! – Back! Back!' Terrified, people move back and take shelter behind the vehicles.

"They usually fire blanks", the engineer reassures me, "but you never know. People have been wounded, even killed. The soldiers then say that the crowd threatened them! They are almost untouchable – the army never tries them, unless foreign witnesses report a blatant case. Then the authorities make out that they are holding an inquiry, because they want to maintain the fiction that they are a just government."

"But why did they shoot just now? People were just going back to their cars. It doesn't make any sense!"

"No, it doesn't make sense", he agrees gravely. "It never makes any sense ... It is that inconsistency and injustice which, minute by minute and day by day, eats away at us perhaps more than the real tragedies. When someone dies, his family can make a hero out of him, a martyr for independence, whereas a life that is simply ground down and degraded is a life that isn't worth living, that's good for nothing."

The alarm over, people recover themselves and a group of young men at the front begin to dance and sing, accompanied by hand clapping, right beneath the soldiers' gaze. Their response is not long in coming. From the watch-tower, a voice thunders out. The Palestinians freeze and then, to a man, they begin to boo this voice from the sky.

"What did he say?" I ask my neighbours.

"He insulted Arafat. He said that he is corrupt, a swine, that he is exploiting us, that it is because of him that we are in this situation and that we should get rid of him."

"People don't seem to agree!"

"No, and yet Abu Ammar is not viewed as a saint, particularly in Gaza. He has allowed too much corruption. But no one will permit foreigners to tell us who our leader should be. Israeli and American pressure has only made us unite around Arafat who remains, despite everything, the symbol of our struggle for independence. No one else, at the moment, can unite the Palestinians – which is why Sharon wants to get rid of him."

Night has fallen and it is beginning to get cold. Laughter and defiance has been replaced by tiredness and irritation. Thankfully, mobile phones exist and people phone for reassurance: no, nothing serious, just ten hours at the checkpoint, almost routine. The lines are so heavily used that the exchange is blocked.

"Unless it's an Israeli trick", grumbles the engineer, who is called Khaled and who speaks perfect French. He offers me shelter in his car. His earlier brightness has disappeared and he seems exhausted.

"We have to wait longer and longer. I am frightened that the Israelis will close the checkpoints altogether soon and won't allow us to move around at all. To avoid an international protest, they are adopting this strategy bit by bit. First of all, it has become almost impossible to obtain a permit for the West Bank, when they had promised us a road connecting the two parts of the Palestinian territory; then there was the total closure of Gaza – for two and a half years, no one has been able to leave – and lastly these internal checkpoints. Tomorrow, it may be total imprisonment ..."

In the black of the night, the only lights are the glow of our cigarettes and the paraffin lamps of several stalls.

Finally, at half past nine, the megaphone springs into action again and announces, "We will not open tonight. Go back!"

All those hours of waiting, for nothing! And then there is a quandary – where will I stay the night? I haven't managed to get hold of Marwan and I have been told that there isn't a hotel at Khan Yunis. Perhaps a few guesthouses, but they will be packed ...

Seeing my predicament, Khaled offers to take me with him to his brother's home, two kilometres away. I accept gratefully. Gratefully? In truth, I have got so used to the generous hospitality of the people of the Middle East, particularly Palestinians, that I had not doubted for a moment that he would look after me. Yet I had not expected such a warm welcome from his sister-in-law, who insists that I take her bed.

The next morning, at six o'clock, I take to the checkpoint road again. Passing the line of cars, I see men and women with worn faces and swollen eyes.

We wait for another four hours. This time, an ambulance offers me a seat; no one is allowed to cross the checkpoint on foot. Inside, a young pregnant woman is sweating heavily. Her contractions have started and a nurse holds her hand, trying to calm her. I know that the soldiers are usually inflexible but can't we try to sway them?

The paramedic shakes his head, disgusted.

"I've tried a hundred times but it only annoys them and perhaps makes the wait even longer. There is an Israeli saying: 'A good Palestinian is a dead Palestinian.' They are hardly going to let ambulances through."

Behind us, we suddenly hear a voice saying, in a strong American accent:

"It's scandalous! I'm going to speak to them!"

Turning round, I am astonished to see a tall blond fellow wearing a cowboy hat, surrounded by Palestinian teenagers who are clearly delighted with this unexpected sight.

John has been to Rafah, where he was on a reconnaissance mission for a charitable organisation. He tells me that he saw two children killed in one day. He is brimming with anger – the American press report nothing of all this, he could not have imagined such things ... he is going to write a report. It is his first time in Palestine. New to it all, he is still filled with idealism.

And off he goes to the checkpoint, his arms in the air, waving his American passport. The megaphone screams 'Rouh! Rouh!' Unperturbed, he continues to advance ... Everyone holds their breath. Finally, two soldiers emerge from the little fort, machine guns at the ready. John continues walking towards them. Will they shoot? He is so obviously American: can they shoot at a citizen of their unconditional ally, even if this madman stands on the 'wrong side'?

They are not going to do anything so stupid. At a respectful distance, the machine guns still pointing, a dialogue begins.

Several minutes later, the blond giant comes back to us, shaking his head. He is immediately surrounded by enthusiastic youngsters: an American who supports their cause! Their eyes shining with emotion, they almost carry him off in victory. Even if he did not succeed, he has tried to help them and such a gesture, in the helplessness Palestinians feel, heartens them.

The soldiers refuse to let the ambulance through but promise that the checkpoint will be open in half an hour. It is in fact two hours before they open it, at 11 o'clock.

At which point a rush ensues. The drivers, at the end of their tether after this interminable wait, cannot bear to lose another second – they sound their horns wildly, accelerate, cut in front of each other and then stop at the last moment with a terrible screeching of brakes. It is a miracle that there are no accidents.

In the middle of this giant traffic jam, sitting quietly near their sentry hut, three young soldiers snigger. They have the cold expression of conquerors, in which contempt for this sub-human population is evident – people who can be penned in at will and then, when let loose, stampede and crush each other.

Of all that I had seen over the previous twenty hours, it was that expression of effortless contempt of the strong towards the weak that revolted me the most.

TAREQ, EX-FEDAY

After returning from Khan Yunis, I have a meeting, in a quiet café in Gaza City, with an ex-feday, who is still on the wanted list of the Israeli and American Secret Services – and even of various Arab countries.

Fifty years old, thin, with fine features, the man, whom I shall call Tareq – one of his many pseudonyms, – has the air of an intellectual more than a fighter. He gauges me with his grey eyes, while I explain what my book is about. Gradually, his blank expression relaxes.

"You're sure my life is of interest to you?" he asks, surprised. "You know, I have never talked about it to anyone, except my wife."

I begin to explain why it is of interest, but he stops me.

"You have been recommended to me and I trust you. Just change the names, because", he says with the mocking smile of a teenager, "quite a lot of people are still out for my hide.

"My family come from Jaffa, the modern city – the Paris of Palestine. It was a very rich town. Its port, the largest in the eastern Mediterranean, was the point of transit between Europe and the Middle East and also exported citrus fruit that was known throughout the world. At the time of the First World War, Jaffa had around 120,000 inhabitants and a lively cultural life with cinemas, theatres and newspapers. All that was before the Jews arrived from Europe and built Tel Aviv just next to it, which began to be a competitor.

"At the time, there were farms and animal husbandry even in the towns. My father owned several cows, which he kept to sell. He ended up a wealthy trader. My mother was 16 when she married my father, who was 52. She was his third wife – he had divorced the first two – and she gave him 12 children, in addition to the six he already had.

"Before 1948, around Tel Aviv, there were many clashes with the Jews who had come from Europe. They were buying up more and more land, usually from big absentee landlords, throwing the farmers off and building kibbutzim. They didn't behave like refugees, whom we would have welcomed with open arms, but like settlers who wanted to take our land from us.

"From the 1930s, there were serious conflicts between Palestinians and extremist Jewish groups. Bit by bit, everyone started buying weapons. But we didn't have any organisation or strategy. To defend yourself, you bought your own gun and formed small groups. My father bought a Bren machine gun and gave it to my brother, who was with a group of militants. We didn't own cannons or anti-tank guns – only rifles and a few machine guns.

"In 1948, Jaffa was heavily bombed. There were fires everywhere. People fled, taking with them the minimum necessary to survive for what they thought would be one or two weeks, while they waited for things to calm down. My father told me that they shut everything up and hid their valuables. At the time we lived in a big, two-storey house with a little garden. On the ground floor were some shops – a baker, a barber, a grocery. Everything was boarded up.

"After a while, we realised that we couldn't go back. My family decided to go to Gaza. But what to do with the cows? My father hired some trucks to transport them: as he couldn't take them all, the weakest had to be slaughtered and sold for meat. He only took five or six.

"In Gaza, these cows, which were our only source of income, posed a problem because they meant we couldn't go to a refugee camp. So my father rented a small house in an orange plantation for two years, until we were able to go home. Later on, when he realised that our exile would continue, he bought an orange grove where he built a house and a stable and started his life all over again.

"I was born in 1950, the eleventh child. I remember envying those who lived in the refugee camp. It was like a big family; people had lost everything but there was a real sense of solidarity and fraternity among them. They understood each other; they had shared experiences and a common past. It was a real community that had kept its customs and its identity, whereas we felt like foreigners among the population of Gaza. We were 'the refugees' in that fairly wealthy and extremely conservative society. Because we lived with them we had to act like them, even if we didn't have the means to do so.

"The Gazans were quite rough and ready compared with the people of Jaffa and they despised us for not being 'men', tough like them. And then there was the problem of language. The dialect of Gazans is cruder; I remember as a child being forced to speak in different ways, in the street and at home. I didn't know where I was any more. When I went to the camp to visit my cousins and my elder brothers and sisters who lived there with their children, they thought of me as a Gazan. That really hurt me – I felt rejected. And when I went back to my district, people said, 'Here's the Jaffaite!'."

Tareq's face clouded over and he sat silently, lost in his thoughts. After a long pause, I asked him.

"What was your relationship with your parents like?"

His face lights up again with a child-like smile.

"I was their favourite son and I adored my mother. She was calm and gentle. But I criticised my father bitterly for having left Jaffa. Even now I can't accept that they fled. I asked them, 'Why didn't you die there? That would have been better than the life we lead!' Now I can see that I was torturing them with my questions. My father never stopped dreaming that he would return to Jaffa; he talked about it until his death. He even refused to go to the mosque, although he was a practising Muslim. He blamed the Lord for what had happened. He said, 'I will only go to the mosque in Jaffa'. He never forged relationships with people in Gaza and he gradually withdrew into himself."

"Did they have photos of Jaffa?"

"No. Before 1948, cameras were a luxury item owned only by the upper classes. But I had all the images in my head because my father, mother, sisters and neighbours spoke about nothing but Jaffa! It was as if we didn't live in Gaza. They would recall people, places, events and I stored it all up. So when I went there, three years ago, I already knew everything – the Clock Square, the mosque, the Alhambra cinema ... Unfortunately, the Israelis have made it into a tourist destination, a museum-town. Everything seems artificial; the place has lost its soul."

"Was your father politically active?"

"He was very interested in politics but had no involvement in it. He read all the papers: his hero was Nasser, the great nationalist who promised to liberate Palestine. I was mad about science, particularly space travel, and also literature. With my pocket money I bought all of Arsène Lupin,[1] as well as Balzac, Zola and Victor Hugo – in Arabic of course! I began to be interested in politics at school around the age of 13. Our teachers were mostly Arab nationalists; one of them used to invite us to his house and talk to us about Palestine. After 1967 he was put in prison.

"The war of 1967 was the turning point of my life. We were convinced that Nasser was going to liberate Palestine. We had begun to pack our bags – 'This is it, we are going back home!' we said to the neighbours. My parents started making plans – what we would do with the cows and so on.

---

1. A character in a series of novels by Maurice Leblanc, Lupin was known as the 'gentleman thief' and was the literary antithesis of Sherlock Holmes.

"When we heard about the defeat, my father had a heart attack. I was 17. Gaza was being bombed by Mirage planes and cannons. We didn't have a car. I put my father on the farm cart and took him to hospital through the bombardment. It was night-time and I was alone in the streets; everyone was holed up in their houses. By some miracle, I was lucky enough not to meet an Israeli soldier, we got to the hospital and my father was saved.

"Everyone was suffering from shock after the defeat. Soldiers from the Palestine Liberation Army – the army created by the PLO in 1965 – had taken refuge in the orange grove where we lived, but they had nothing but rifles in the face of the Israeli arsenal. I would take them food and we would talk about the resistance. Very quickly some of these soldiers, boys aged 19 and 20, formed a group to begin resisting. I wanted to join them but they said that I was too young. Instead, I helped them and acted as their guide.

"It was they who organised the struggle against Sharon when he came to Gaza in 1969 to crush the resistance. He was a general at that time and had the same strategy of indiscriminate violence that he uses today. He sent tanks and bulldozers into the camps to demolish houses, arrested thousands of men, from children to old people, ordered the targeted assassination of militants, killing their families into the bargain ... In my little group of friends, two were killed and five were imprisoned.

"I had just passed my matriculation exam. After the resistance had been crushed, I left Gaza to study business in Cairo – that was my father's choice, but I would have studied anything to get to Cairo, the beacon of the Arab world!

"Several months later, in autumn 1970, the events of 'Black September' took place: Hussein's army crushed the Palestinian resistance, based in Jordan. I could no longer stay where I was. I went to the PLO office to sign up to fight with the resistance. They refused: I was a student and I should continue with my studies; we needed people to build our future country. I insisted so much that in the end they gave in. One hundred and eighty Palestinians enrolled, of whom eighty were students. We were taken to Libya and given a 'commando' training for six months. It was very hard. But before the end of our training, the Palestinian resistance in Jordan collapsed. So we were taken to Syria, on the border with Jordan, which is where my military career began. We launched rapid commando operations from Syria against the Israeli forces."

Tareq does not want to give details of that three year period of his life, for security reasons. But when I ask him if he had taken part in aeroplane hijackings, he shakes his head energetically.

"Never! I am against this kind of action and always have been. I have always opposed aeroplane hijackings and suicide bombings – and all attacks against civilians. As a soldier, that is not how I conceive of war."

He leans towards me and looks straight into my eyes.

"Sometimes, when you have to, you kill. That has to happen in a military context and there may, unfortunately, be civilian victims. In a war, soldiers shoot and if they die, that is normal. But civilians are civilians. I am against fighters blowing themselves up among civilians; among soldiers, OK."

Tareq's argument is exactly the same as that of Itaï, the Israeli conscientious objector whom I had met in Jerusalem. Both are honest soldiers. If they met, they would undoubtedly get on.

"Even if Israelis kill civilians – and they kill many – I am totally against the killing of unarmed people", Tareq adds.

Settling into his armchair, he goes on:

"After many were massacred by the Jordanians in 1970, the PLO fighters took refuge in Syria and Lebanon. But in May 1973, relations between the PLO and the Lebanese army deteriorated. We also had problems with the Syrians, who expelled us, until they called us back because they needed us in October 1973 to fight in the Yom Kippur War. You know, a foreign army creates problems, even in a friendly country. On top of that, our struggle against Israel resulted in reprisals that often affected the Lebanese people, which is why many of them wanted us to leave, despite the fact that the majority supported us.

"I fought in the Yom Kippur War in a special unit in the Golan Heights. I was wounded in the hand and arm, which was actually fortunate as it immobilised me for a time and enabled me to stand back from the situation. After our defeat, a number of us began to reflect and to get more interested in politics. We had had enough of being simple warriors, employed here and there, expelled or annihilated by our Arab allies when we posed them a problem and called back when they needed people to fight against Israel! We had had the experience of defeat in 1967 and then in 1973, while our elders had experienced the defeats of 1948 and then of 1956 when the French, British and Israelis had occupied Suez – the Israelis occupying Gaza as they passed through, massacring a large number of people. The experience of the Palestinian resistance was also not very conclusive: we had been driven out of Jordan and had had many problems in Lebanon.

"I left the commando life and settled down to a more stable existence. I found a job in Beirut, as the manager of a training centre for students and militiamen."

"What were these militiamen supposed to do?"

"They had to protect the Palestinian camps, which the Israelis were bombing regularly. They also had to provide protection against the special units dispatched to assassinate Palestinian leaders in Beirut. The Fatah leadership sent us volunteers, whom they had briefed in minute detail, for us to give them a basic military training."

His face suddenly lights up.

"That is where I met Naïma, my future wife! One day, they sent us three upper class Lebanese girls, who hardly spoke any Arabic", he recalls with a laugh. "Naïma was one of them. She was 20 years old and wanted to join Fatah. I was just 24 myself, but I had had a full past. I had been a fighter for six years and had led a monastic life. When I was wounded I had stayed in hospital for two months. And now here I was finding myself, after years of leading an almost primitive existence – in Beirut, to top it all, which was at the time a very lively place, the most glittering city in the whole of the Middle East.

"I remember that when I first saw those three pretty girls, who had been sent by a political leader, I looked at them and said to myself, 'What's this?' We had Palestinian girls, fighters, who came from the camps and also several middle class Palestinian girls, mainly from Kuwait, but at least they spoke Arabic! These three just spoke French and cobbled together a bit of Arabic between them. I didn't take them seriously. I was even a bit contemptuous: 'Why are you interested in all this?' I asked them. 'You don't have any problems – why do you want to fight?' Their response didn't convince me. I entrusted them to one of my instructors so that they could learn how to handle a rifle. I would observe them occasionally. These refined people who came to play at war annoyed me – what were Lebanese Christians doing there? For me they were a bit like hippies, people looking for new, exotic experiences!

"One day, I made them shoot, to see what they were capable of. I remember that Naïma closed the wrong eye to take aim and I said to her: 'Close both eyes and shoot!' She was furious ... It was only later, when I saw her in action in difficult circumstances, that I said to myself, 'She isn't so bad, after all, this little Lebanese!'

"All this time I was talking about plans for the future with my comrades at the training centre. We thought the Arab regimes were rotten institutions and the PLO ineffective, but our greatest enemy was the Americans, Israel's unconditional ally. In the face of repeated failures, we had become radicalised – too much, probably."

He gives a gently mocking smile at the memory of his former passion and naivety.

"In Beirut at that time there were parties and cliques from all over the world: Irish, Kurds, Armenians, Indians, Red Indians, Red Army, Red Brigades, blacks, yellows, everything! We set up a clandestine organisation and began to organise attacks against American interests in Lebanon, Syria, Jordan and of course against the Israelis. But never against civilians! That lasted a year and a half, from the beginning of 1974 to July 1975.

"In July 1975 we were arrested by the Lebanese and Syrian police, who were working in close co-operation. We were accused of conspiring against the national security of Lebanon, Syria and Jordan, which normally attracted a sentence of death by hanging, or at least life imprisonment. The Syrian security forces took all the Palestinians back to Syria, where they were hanged. I had the good fortune to be imprisoned in Lebanon, without being tried, because the Civil War had erupted.

"It was a modern prison, clean, in the mountains and in the middle of a Phalangist stronghold. I began to organise the other political prisoners in an escape attempt. We got hold of revolvers through wardens who belonged to political parties sympathetic to us. We failed twice. The third time, it was New Year's Eve. They discovered our plan, beat us up and put us in solitary confinement. Then they decided to separate us. I was sent to an old Ottoman prison, not far from Sabra and Shatila, right in the heart of a PLO district. Those were three very hard months; it was damp, dirty and full of rats. I also tried to escape from there. Fourth failure. For three days, I was beaten and tortured with an electric baton and then for a week shut into a dark cupboard, called 'the oven', which they alternated between extreme heat, so that you thought you were going to suffocate to death, and an icy cold."

Tareq would not give any more details. A man does not speak about his suffering. He has the modesty and the dignity not to complain.

"Several weeks later, the Lebanese *coup d'état* of 1976 took place. Crowds came and broke down the prison doors; everyone got out. I was cautious and didn't go out by the door but jumped the wall, got across the barbed wire, and hid. I had done the right thing, because the Syrian Intelligence Service was waiting to catch political prisoners. I had to disappear for a while because I was being hunted not only by the Israelis and the Americans but also by the Arab deterrent forces who had entered Beirut. Naïma had also come out of prison. We hid for forty days. Then the deterrent forces gradually withdrew and the PLO and Lebanese left-wing nationalist groups began to control Beirut.

"During this time my relationship with Naïma began. Before we had shared the same apartment for months, as comrades. Gradually I realised that I was in love with her. The little Lebanese girl whom I had at first laughed at had seduced me with her courage, charm and vivacity."

He laughed. "She has been seducing me for twenty-eight years now!"

Tareq continues his narrative.

"In 1976, Beirut was the centre for all the political movements but also for the intelligence services of the entire world. Our group of militants had dissolved; most of them had been killed. I needed to take stock of things.

"So, we decided to leave for Europe. We boarded a Cypriot ship with false papers – and thought a hundred times that we were about to be discovered. In the end we stayed in Europe for two years, teaching Arabic and working as translators. But that life in exile was unbearable for us and we missed Lebanon. We came back in 1978, travelling via India, then Jordan. It was a crazy venture, but it was the only way. We had reflected a lot and realised that we had to find another way than armed struggle.

"I didn't take up a gun again until 1982, when the Israelis invaded Lebanon and Beirut was surrounded. But that was a case of self-defence. I set up a group of fighters and for two months we fought back intensely.

"During that siege, Naïma gave birth to our first child. I remember taking a few hours off to get to the hospital. It was a boy! I can't describe my feelings. I kissed them, telling myself that it might be for the last time, and went back to fight.

Several weeks later, the PLO and all the Palestinian fighters had to leave Beirut to go into exile in various Arab countries. The families were going to join us afterwards. But Naïma insisted on leaving with me and our new born baby, who wasn't even two months old. We ended up in Tunisia, with Arafat's HQ. There I became a journalist for the Palestinian press. My past as a combatant seemed distant and I was passionate about my new profession. I thought the most important thing now for our people was education, particularly political education."

"What was your life in Tunisia like?"

"I liked the country, but we were foreigners ... We stayed there for twelve years. In 1994, after the Oslo accords, we came back to Palestine, with many other Palestinians. That was a very hard decision for me to take. Imagine going to live under the Israeli occupation! Until then my relationship with the Israelis had been one of 'I'll kill them or they'll kill me'. But all my friends wanted to come back. They were proud and happy to be going home. They thought the Israeli occupation would not last much longer and that the country would finally be ours. I wasn't so sure. In the end I agreed to go back, for the sake of my wife and children – in the meantime I had had a daughter and another son.

"I was the first to go with friends, through the border at Rafah. We went back officially, after the Oslo accords. None the less, we had to wait for four days and nights at the border, in the worst conditions. The Israeli soldiers screamed at us as though we were dogs. I could never have imagined such humiliation. It was horrible to have to submit without reacting; I died inside several times during those four days. I stuck it out for Naïma and the children, who were going to join me later.

"Finally, the Israelis let us through, at one o'clock in the morning. I was totally lost; I had left Gaza at the age of 19 and this was twenty-five years later. My family were like strangers. My nephews, whom I had last seen when they were small children, now had babies of their own. I had no idea who the children I was kissing were. It all seemed totally artificial. They wanted to carry me in triumph to my mother's house; on the way, everything seemed to me small, inadequate. The street, the trees, the people, the space – they had all shrunk. I remembered the orange groves and the orchards, donkeys pulling a cart, memories of calm and beauty. But it had all become hideous, concreted, with cars everywhere and everything covered in dust ... I was overwhelmed by it.

"My mother was waiting for me at the door. She didn't speak; she looked at me and took me in her arms. We sat down next to each other and she just kept looking at me and touching me, as though I was from outer space. And I didn't recognise anyone except my elders, now aged and surrounded by dozens of children. I can't say I was disappointed; I felt nothing but a great emptiness, as if I had fallen down a well. Everything was different. Even the air seemed stifling.

"To them, too, I had become a stranger. To try to fill the void, the adults talked to me as though I had never gone away, telling the same old jokes, trying to pick up where we had left off. I felt very, very distant.

"A month later, Naïma arrived. It was terrible. While she was replying to the questioning, the children waited in a yard where other young Palestinians were joking about. Soldiers in civilian dress came and insulted and kicked them. My children, who were aged between eight and 12, were completely traumatised by it. Before we had left, I had said to them: 'Soon we will be in Palestine; you'll see, it's magnificent, the sea, nature ... and soon we will have our own state and a normal life. You'll see, we'll be so happy!'."

"And they were greeted with violence ...

"But we forgot about it very quickly. We were back home! The large towns had been liberated. As for the rest, things were going slowly but we kept our hope. I found work in a cultural organisation. Does that surprise you? But culture isn't just Stendhal or Picasso; it's a huge, open space in which one can do anything, particularly educate people politically."

"So, have you left armed struggle altogether?"

"Yes, unless of course I one day have to defend my family. Returning to Palestine was, for me, a political decision. I am now convinced that the sole means of achieving peace is by negotiation. The current failure should not make us give up. Our generation may not see an independent Palestine but our children will."

Palestine ... his eyes cloud over.

"Several months ago, I would get up every day at dawn and go for a walk. After my return, I walked in the countryside all the time, breathing the fresh air deep into my lungs, drinking in the light of my country. I didn't get tired of it; I had dreamed of it so much. It was my way of making up for all those years of exile and the expropriation of my land. Every tree, every bush and every wheat field filled me with happiness and pride. It was our country, more beautiful than any other country in the world. Often I would stretch myself out in the grass and breathe in the smell of the earth and even – you will think this is idiotic – sometimes put my lips against it so as to be one with it ... and wept with happiness."

"But now..."

He got up, his expression grave.

"For two years, I haven't been able to leave this town and, half the time, not even our apartment. I am suffocating. One day we will brave the guns, like some people have done in Naplouse and elsewhere because they cannot bear this imprisonment any more. One day we will go out and get ourselves killed simply because we want to breathe!"

A RATHER DIFFERENT LITTLE BOY

In Gaza, to the north of the Jabaliya refugee camp, the village of Beit Lahiya stretches along the coast. It is surrounded by sand dunes filled with rubbish, for neither waste nor human beings are allowed to leave this tiny enclave, encircled by barbed wire, into which more than a million Palestinians are herded. But these dunes, contaminated as they are with detritus, are a godsend to a boy of 13. You can go down them, securely fastened to the skateboard that your dad has put together; if you tumble, it doesn't matter because the sand will soften your fall. The problem is you can't get back on the board or climb back up the dune for another slide; you have to wait until your mum comes to put you back on or picks you up to carry you home again, when you are a little boy whose legs have been amputated.

Slight, fair-skinned, her black hair modestly covered with a veil of white cotton, Najwa al Sultan's natural elegance is striking. She is 28 years old and the mother of four children. Mohammed is the oldest, a beautiful boy with dimples, brown curls and a childish smile that is contradicted by large, thoughtful eyes.[1] Najwa was 15 when he was born. "In our families, we marry young, especially in these troubled times. Parents are frightened for their daughters."

She and her husband, Fadel, invite me into their home, a rough concrete building that is, like a good many Gazan houses, unfinished because money has run out. After serving a welcoming cup of coffee, flavoured with cardamom, Najwa sits opposite me, her hands crossed across her knees, like a schoolgirl waiting to be questioned.

I have qualms about speaking in front of Mohammed but he doesn't seem to be listening, preoccupied with the remote-controlled toy man that I have brought him. Does this steel figure, that he can move about as he chooses, give him a sense of greater freedom? Or does it emphasise his lack of freedom? I had hesitated for a long time in Gaza City's sole toyshop, but for the moment my fears have evaporated: he seems overjoyed with his new toy and smiles his beautiful, grave smile

---

1. Mohammed is the subject of a very beautiful film by the Israeli director Ram Loewy.

as he monitors its comings and goings. I imagine that he has not laughed like a child for a long time.

In a barely audible voice, Najwa tells me their story.

"One day, when Mohammed was four, he woke up with a foot that had gone blue. He was in pain and crying. I took him to all the doctors and hospitals in Gaza but no one understood what the problem was. I was advised to go and see a specialist in Jerusalem. I asked for a permit from the Israeli authorities, with the doctor's letter, but they refused. That was in 1994, after the Oslo agreements. It was a period of calm and everyone believed that peace was going to come soon. But the Israeli checkpoints were still in place and you couldn't leave Gaza without special permission. Mohammed was in more and more pain and so I decided to go to the checkpoint and plead with the soldiers to let me through. The child was writhing and screaming in pain, I was crying and begging them to have pity. In vain. They pointed their guns at me and made me go back; if I tried to approach, they took aim at us.

"Finally, on the fourth day, my doctor managed to get permission for Mohammed to go to Jerusalem with my mother. He had stopped crying. He didn't hurt any more; he couldn't feel anything in his legs. But when he got to Jerusalem, it was too late. The blood had stopped circulating and the specialist couldn't get it going again … He had to amputate my son's legs!"

She bursts into sobs. "He said to me … if we had arrived a day earlier, he could have saved him."

She cries, while her husband takes her hand. On the jute mat where he has been placed, Mohammed lifts his head. He looks desolately at his mother, as though he longs to comfort her.

"But why didn't they let you go through at the time?"

Najwa dries her tears and looks me straight in the eye.

"Because, during the first intifada, when I was 17, I went to prison."

"What had you done?"

"Attacked soldiers."

I look at her, staggered. This fragile little woman?

"At the start of the intifada, in 1987, I was 13. My parents weren't politically active but my mother's brother was in the resistance. We didn't see him often because he was continually in hiding. One day, when he had gone to see his wife and children, he was killed, in front of his house, by a missile fired from a helicopter. Two other uncles then joined the resistance. Because of them, soldiers often came to our house. I remember knocking on the door in the early hours, and the intrusion of those men wearing boots, armed with machine guns, into the room where we slept, and our terror and shame ... I think they married me so young to protect me."

She turns to her husband, who is sitting next to her. He is barely older than she, a man with a sunny smile from which emanates a gentle strength.

"My family are not at all political", he says. "I have never carried a gun. I fight by resisting day after day, through my words and my endurance and by continuing to live and to keep my hope alive, against all odds. Controlling oneself and one's weaknesses is what we call in Islam the big jihad, as opposed to the little jihad, which is war."

She gave birth to Mohammed very soon after her marriage, Najwa tells me.

"He was an adorable baby who laughed all the time. Although we were poor, I was very happy. But how could I ignore what was going on around me? My two uncles had been imprisoned and we knew that they had been tortured.

"The day everything turned upside down was when Israeli soldiers beat up an old man who was going past my house on a donkey. He begged them to stop; his face was bleeding profusely. When they finally left him, I ran out and brought him inside to look after him. He said to me, 'No, leave me, they'll kill you!' From that moment, I decided that I had to do something. Suddenly, I wasn't a frightened young girl any more; I was overtaken by anger. I had to act, or I couldn't have lived with myself. My cowardice would have been too unbearable to me.

"Next to our house at Abu Khadra was a military complex. I managed to procure a Molotov cocktail that some youngsters had made; I hid it under my shawl, walked towards the complex and when I was quite close to the entrance, I threw it."

We listen, hanging on to her every word – her husband, who obviously knows the story by heart but especially Mohammed, who is staring fixedly at his mother. The shy young woman has turned suddenly into an intrepid resistance fighter.

"I tried to escape but they soon caught me and took me to prison, where I was beaten up. They hit me in the stomach and on the head. Then they shut me up for days in a dark cupboard, bringing me out only to interrogate me. But fairly soon they realised that I didn't belong to any group and that I had acted on my own initiative because I was so revolted by what I had seen. So they stopped interrogating me and transferred me to Ashkelon prison. I lay down in that cold, foul-smelling cell, without receiving the slightest care or attention; I thought I was going to die. The soldiers mocked me, saying 'Poor imbecile – you're suffering while your president is lazing around on his honeymoon!' Arafat had just married Soha.

"Luckily, one day, the Red Cross announced an inspection. They quickly gave me a bit of care and put me into a comfortable room, threatening to put me back in the dark dungeon if I complained. 'But if you say nothing, you will be well treated and you'll stay in this lovely room.' I was frightened and I lied to the Red Cross. Which I regretted afterwards because they put me back into that horrible cell."

She addresses me angrily.

"Why don't the Red Cross make surprise visits? It's not exactly hard to work out that they change everything for the visits and threaten the prisoners to prevent them from talking!"

In the weeks before her trial, Najwa was in a barred cell.

"It was like a cage. Everyone could see me. I was the only woman and the people who went by looked at me as if I was a strange animal. It was completely humiliating."

At the trial, the judge sentenced her to only ten years. By arguing that she had a two-year-old child who needed his mother, Najwa's lawyer had managed to get a reduction in her sentence.

"My Molotov cocktail hadn't hurt anyone, or I would have got a lot longer. It was in prison that I was educated politically. There were groups there of the various organisations; the leader of each group dealt with the prison authorities. If there was a problem or if they were not happy, the soldiers would take the leader into a dungeon and torture her with an electric baton, while they tied the rest of us prisoners to a wall and hit us."

"Which group were you in? Fatah? Hamas?"

"No, I belonged to Islamic Jihad because I liked the leader, Safiah. Her face radiated warmth and sincerity, she had a deep faith and was very intelligent. She taught me a lot. One time we went on hunger strike for 11 days, to get visiting rights for our children but above all in protest at the mistreatment to which a mentally retarded girl had been subjected by the warders. Every night they took her off, tortured her, had fun with her and every morning she would come back injured and covered with bruises. The whole prison went on hunger strike with us, in solidarity. At the end of it, they gave us raw carrots to eat. And we all vomited blood."

I glance at Mohammed. What a strange expression is on his face as he stares at his mother. It is no longer the admiration of earlier, but the serious gaze of a child for whom suffering holds no secrets.

Najwa came out of prison in 1994, after one and a half years, as part of a group of prisoners who were released after the Oslo agreements. She was 19.

"At that point I gave up being militant. I believed in peace. I said to my children, 'We have to make friends with the Israelis. From now on we are going to live in peace with them'. I convinced them that they were going to have a good life and interesting careers."

She nods towards Mohammed's younger brothers, three lively boys who are playing marbles.

"One of them wants to be an engineer, one a doctor and the other a soldier. I told them that would help build their country, Palestine, and that from now on there would be nothing to fear, that we were going to live peacefully next door to each other."

She lowers her head.

"I reproach myself for having giving them false hopes. I was too innocent. The Israelis will never let us have our homeland, unless they are obliged to do so by force!"

"Do you really believe that killing civilians is a solution?"

Her expression clouds over and for a moment she looks helpless and overwhelmed.

"When I see an Israeli mother on television, crying for her child, I want to cry with her ..." she murmurs.

It is eight o'clock and night has fallen. I get ready to leave, but my hosts protest. "You must stay and have dinner!"

I try and give all sorts of excuses, worried about causing them additional expense, but Najwa will not hear of it.

"Go and take the air on the terrace. It will be ready soon."

I guess that she has already prepared everything. To refuse her hospitality would be an insult, even if it means that tomorrow they have nothing to eat. In the orient, the poorer people are, the more they want to share what they have. It is the only luxury they can afford.

We go up on to the terrace. Fadel apologises for the state of the stairs and the house in general. Instead of doors and windows, there are just openings, some of them covered with a piece of material – scant protection against bad weather.

"I started building years ago but I have never had enough money to finish. Now less than ever; there is no more work ..."

Outside, everything is quiet and we savour the first cool of the evening. Not far off we can see vast islands of light.

"That's the settlements of Eli Sinai and Nissanit", Fadel tells me. "The settlers are armed to the teeth. One of these days, they will attack and occupy us."

A little further on, violently lit up, is the Erez Passage, the frontier post between the Gaza Strip and Israel, through which no one, apart from diplomats and journalists, has passed for two years. The contrast between the sparse glimmer from the Palestinian villages and the profligate expanse of light on the Israeli side is striking, reminiscent of some huge theatre. Hardly has this thought entered my head when we are suddenly plunged into total darkness.

"There are cuts all the time", Fadel says resignedly. "The Israelis have allocated Gaza a very small voltage. Whilst their settlements are fantastically well lit all night and they have air conditioning everywhere, we don't even have what we need to work a fan. During the summer we suffocate and in the winter, with no possibility of heating, we freeze."

From below, an apologetic Najwa asks us to excuse her: the meal is going to be late because now she has to prepare everything by candlelight. We have the time. The night is beautiful and I gaze at the stars, caught up – despite the tension, the problems and the intermittent grumbling of F-16s above our head – in the poetry of the moment. Above me, a planet gives off a brilliant glow.

"Venus?" I ask.

"No", Fadel corrects me, "it's an Israeli spy satellite. They can see us and make out the smallest details. They have us under constant surveillance."

The rumbling noise of aeroplanes gets closer – F-16s start to circle above us. People on their terraces point them out to each other.

"You never know if they are going to drop a bomb", Fadel remarks. "Look down there!"

Lights are moving near the Erez checkpoint. It is a column of tanks entering Gaza.

"They are going into a village. It's the same thing every day. Even if there is no reason, they do it to terrorise people. But they succeed only in stirring up hatred. The other day, two young people from Jabaliya camp, next to here, wanted to enter a settlement. They were caught and killed. Their mother went to ask for their bodies. Instead of giving them over, the soldiers unleashed dogs on to the corpses, which devoured them in front of the screaming woman …"

He shakes his head.

"To kill them is one thing, but that … how could one ever forget it?"

Dinner is finally ready. Najwa has prepared us a veritable feast: kefta, hummus, stuffed aubergines, sayadieh (fish with rice and onions) and delicious sweetmeats – ka'ak, krafelt and baqlawa – all accompanied by fresh sugar cane juice.

"I wanted you to taste real Palestinian cooking so that you know we have very ancient traditions and are not wretched nomads like the Israelis claim so as to deny us the right to a country."

"But there are Israelis who try to help Palestinians – Ram, for example, who came to make a film about your problems."

She concedes that, yes, there are good Israelis but in general they do not want peace. If they really wanted it, they would not have voted for Sharon in the elections. Sharon's manifesto stated that he rejected the Oslo agreements and an independent Palestine. Before, they voted for Rabin, who had opposing policies. Their politics change all the time!

I turn to Mohammed, who is sitting next to me.

"What do you think of the Israelis, Mohammed?"

"They are traitors", he replies in his clear voice, which has not yet broken. "They promised us a country but they lied. They kill children with planes and rifles. We are frightened all the time, we can't sleep because of the noise of the planes ... and ... I lost my legs because of them", he concludes, lowering his head as though acknowledging the indecency of referring to his disability, his suffering.

I persist.

"But the film-maker, he's your friend?"

"No! Even if Israelis do good things for me, I still hate them and don't want to talk to them. If they want peace, why do they go on occupying our land?"

"But if one day there is peace, do you think you could have Israeli friends?"

"No!" he insists once more, without a trace of hesitation. "First, I don't believe there will be peace and second, I don't want to live with the Israelis. Never! I want to live in Palestine with Palestinians!"

What will Mohammed be when he is an adult? His father told me that he would like him to be educated, trained in a profession such as computer technology. If, of course, there is the money to do it ... But apart from his occupation, what kind of man will this beautiful little boy, whose two legs have been amputated, become?

The evening lengthens. After dinner, lit by candles, Mohammed's little brothers want to sing us the national song of the Palestinians, *Biladi* (my country).

When we take leave of each other – will we ever meet again? – Najwa takes my hand and looks at me for a long time.

"You know", she murmurs, "here, even when there is peace, our people have fire in their hearts."

Two months later, in the early morning of the 6th August 2002, thirty or so Israeli tanks invaded the village of Beit Lahiya amidst heavy machine gun fire. We know only that a Palestinian policeman was killed and two other people arrested. In the early months of 2003, other murderous invasions took place.

What became of little Mohammed and his parents?

8

◆

Being an Arab–Israeli

Arab–Israelis are Palestinians who remained in their homes when the State of Israel was declared in May 1948. There are today around one million Arab–Israelis, constituting twenty per cent of the population.

Although they are Israeli citizens with, in principle, the same rights as their compatriots, in reality they suffer daily discrimination under a semblance of legality. Access to university grants, mortgage loans and various forms of credit are all dependent on the completion of military service. Even access to employment depends on it, with most job advertisements specifying that applicants should have completed their service.

However, the Israeli government exempts its Arab citizens (with the exception of the small Druze community – a non-orthodox Muslim minority living in Syria, Lebanon and Israel) from military service and they therefore have no rights to these benefits, in distinction from orthodox Jews who refuse to undertake military service but nonetheless enjoy the same advantages as other Jews.

A recent study carried out by two sociologists, Ramsis Gharra and Rafaella Cohen, shows that salaries are thirty-five per cent higher among Jews than non-Jews and that thirty-seven per cent of the Arab population live below the poverty line, as opposed to thirteen per cent of the Jewish population.

Other statistics reveal that, as a result of land confiscation, the twenty per cent of Arab–Israelis possess a total of only two per cent of the land.

THE ASSASSINATION OF A PEACE CAMPAIGNER

Asel was killed in his green T-shirt printed with the words *Grains of Peace*, an international peace movement. A soldier shot him in the back at point-blank range. He was 17 years old.

An Israeli Arab, who spoke fluent Hebrew, Arabic and English, he had campaigned since he was 14 for reconciliation and understanding between Jews and Arabs. He had dozens of friends in the two communities, as well as in Switzerland and the United States, where he had taken part in youth camps for peace and where he had been sent several times as a delegate, notably to a meeting with Kofi Annan.

His elders had placed much hope in him. His tolerance and dependability, as well as his sense of humour and ability to get on with everyone, marked him out as a future leader in the difficult Israeli-Palestinian dialogue. So many people talked about him to me that I wanted to know more. I decided to go to Araba, a village near Nazareth, to meet his family.

Late one summer's afternoon, I took a car that drove me across the winding roads of a green Galilee. The gently rolling hills, the silvery tones of olive trees and the graceful cypresses all exhaled a quiet serenity. Seated on a stone, an old man wearing a black and white *keffiyah* contemplated the sun setting on his field, with its perfectly straight furrows. All along the route, I noticed with surprise how meticulously these fields were cultivated.

"We Palestinians do not have much land but we put all our heart into it", my driver had remarked. "The land is our blood and our child. But for how much longer? Year after year they take it all, for the 'needs of the state'."

It is nearly dark when we arrive in front of a pretty house, surrounded by a garden. A small man in his fifties and a young girl are waiting for me on the veranda: Hassan Asleh and Aysha, Asel's father and elder sister. His mother, a woman whose face is heavily lined, comes to greet us but soon leaves, saying that she has work she must finish.

"It is two years since our son was killed, but she still cannot bear to talk about it", her husband explains.

Asel died on the 2nd October 2000, during a peaceful demonstration of Israeli Arabs.[1] The demonstration followed Sharon's visit to the Esplanade of the Mosques and the shooting that had killed seven Palestinian protestors and wounded two hundred others.

Hassan Asleh, helped out by his daughter when he cannot find the words in English, recalls what happened.

"The demonstration took place at the northern entrance to the village. Neighbours came to tell me that there were a lot of people but that things were calm. That was when I realised that Asel wasn't in the house. I had a premonition and I took a taxi to go and see what was happening. There were a lot of young people shouting slogans against Sharon. Policemen in uniform threw tear gas and shot rubber bullets but people went on demonstrating. I finally spotted Asel, who was easily recognisable by his height and his green T-shirt. He was sheltering under an olive tree, watching the demonstration. Suddenly I saw a jeep coming; three men in khaki got out and began to run, pointing their rifles at the demonstrators. They began shooting, while the other policemen shot at the sides of the road. The demonstrators were totally unarmed! We were stunned: the police never shoot at demonstrators in Israel!

"Then I realised that Asel had his back turned to the armed men coming in his direction. I shouted to him 'Come here!' He heard me and stood up but the police had got to him. I saw him trying to run towards the trees but the police caught him and surrounded him; one of them hit him with a rifle butt. He fell and I couldn't see him any more, but I heard him crying, "Dad! Dad!' Then I heard a shot behind the trees and I saw the three policemen coming out of the grove. I remember thinking it was odd that they were leaving without taking Asel. And then I realised that they had killed him ... I fainted. When I came to, I was told that my son had been taken to the neighbouring hospital at Sakhnin. He died there almost immediately."

The man stops talking and stares at the table, his jaw clenched. His daughter takes his hand. We sit in silence. On the wall, a young boy with a laughing, round face and sparkling eyes gazes down at us.

"For him, everything could be resolved through dialogue", Aysha tells me. "He had set up the *Grains of Peace* network on the internet and

1. There were 13 dead and 700 wounded. It was the first time that the army had shot at unarmed Israeli Arabs, since the 'day of land' in June 1976 when soldiers killed six people during demonstrations against land confiscation.

spent hours at his computer discussing the issues with people of all views. Because he accepted their arguments and calmly explained the Palestinians' situation, he established a real dialogue. Gradually, understanding was being built. After his death we received hundreds of messages, particularly from young Jews all over the world, mourning his loss."

"Was an inquiry held into his death?"

His father shrugs his shoulders.

"We lodged a complaint, like the families of the 12 other people who were killed, and of the wounded. After a month of demonstrations, and interventions by human rights organisations, we succeeded in getting an official inquiry commission set up, whose members were chosen by the president of the Supreme Court and were independent of the government. The commission received dozens of testimonies from people who were at the scene and who reported the police's refusal to talk to the Arab leaders, who could have calmed things down, and the completely disproportionate use of force. But, as always when it is a matter concerning we Israeli Arabs, the hierarchy covered up for those men and did not name anyone as being responsible."

"In your opinion, were those 13 deaths due to individual blunders or to an order from above?"

"I still ask myself that question: why did the police shoot at unarmed people who were not threatening them in any way? It all seems to point to a deliberate provocation. I even think it could have been a test of a future policy: the Israeli authorities envisage, more and more openly, driving out the Israeli Arab population into the West Bank and Gaza. Even Labour Party leaders such as Barak now think of us as a major strategic problem. He has proposed the exchange of the Um el Fahem region and its surrounding villages, mainly populated by Israeli Arabs, for settlements in the West Bank. Everyone has their own idea. They talk about us like bundles that can be shifted from one place to another!

"You know, October 2000 was a great turning point. Until then we believed that bit by bit we would be accepted as full citizens. Despite all the discrimination we suffered, we hung on to that belief. The massacre woke us up out of that dream and we realised that as soon as there is a problem, we are treated like enemies. The fact that the soldiers shot at us like they shoot at the inhabitants of the West Bank and Gaza, and that the majority of the Jewish population approved of it, was a terrible shock for all those who believed in reconciliation and integration. It was proof that they didn't think of us as compatriots but as Palestinians from outside, as enemies."

"We have to be very careful in the street", Aysha comes in. "If we speak Arabic, we risk being attacked or at least insulted."

"It has almost always been like that", her father recalls. "We lived our childhood in fear even of saying our name. I remember going to Haifa when I was ten, to find work; someone asked me what I was called. I said 'Moshe' because I was frightened they would beat me up. They believed me because I spoke Hebrew well. I had learnt it at school."

"You were working at ten years old?"

"Yes, as an agricultural worker in a kibbutz, while I continued to study. But I only got as far as secondary school", Hassan adds, in a tone of regret.

"My father is an extraordinary man!" proclaims Aysha, with a touching vehemence. "He has worked since he was a child and today he has succeeded in establishing his own building firm. But more than anything he helps people around him, including Jews that he knows."

"The Israelis killed your son; what are your feelings about them?"

"I hate the police and the Israeli authorities, but I will never hate the Israeli nation. I have good Israeli friends. But I admit that at the moment I am very frustrated by the silence of the liberals. Where are they now, when massacres are being carried out in the West Bank and Gaza? I am worried about the future. Racism is now part of the young Jews' education and no one is doing anything to stop these evils ..."

"You speak of a possible transfer. But the Palestinians of Israel and Palestine all tell me that they aren't ready to forget the experience of 1948 and that they will continue to resist."

"With what?", Hassan looks at me with an air of desperation. "Resist with what? Without weapons, how can we defend ourselves? Soldiers can come into this village, round up all the families into the square, load us on to lorries and deport us. And what would the democratic world do? Nothing! Just as they do nothing to stop Israel massacring all these civilians in the occupied territories ...

I search in vain for words to encourage him. I have already heard his fears many times, expressed by Palestinians, and even by the Israelis to whom I have spoken. We drink our tea in silence. Looking around me, I note the details of this comfortable room, decorated with love. Like Hassan, I wonder: 'For how much longer?'

It is ten o'clock at night. The family accompany me to my taxi. They tried hard to persuade me to stay to dinner, but I declined their invitation. I have to be on the road very early the next day.

"So, we will meet again next year!" says Hassan Asleh, looking straight into my eyes. An intense energy radiates from him once again.

"Next year, that's a promise!" I reply, returning his smile.
In Sh'Allah ...

I returned to Nazareth, the biggest Arab town in Israel, divided between the old city, huddled into the valley and covered with sanctuaries commemorating the annunciation and the childhood of Jesus, and the new Jewish town of 'Nazareth Ilith' on the heights.

I had to make a tour of the old city before I could find accommodation for the night. Since the troubles of October 2000, when the Israeli army killed thirteen Arab demonstrators, there aren't any more tourists, the shops are empty and most of the hotels are closed.

The taxi finally deposits me in front of a brand new hotel. When I ask for a quiet room with a view of the holy sites, the manager replies with a sad smile:

"You can have anything you want. There are 350 rooms and you are the only guest."

He explains that they had opened in January 2000.

"We were full until October. But since the incidents, no one comes, even though everything has been quiet here. The problem is that Israeli journalists continue to write about them. Gradually, the Arabs who can afford to are moving abroad. That is what the Israelis want – for us to leave, voluntarily or by force."

9

◆

Jenin

A MARTYRED TOWN

Early next morning I leave Nazareth for Jenin,[1] despite the warnings of the hotel manager, sorry to see his only customer leave. Jenin is only three hours' drive away and no curfew had been announced.

However, when we arrive at the checkpoint, several kilometres outside the town, we are stopped by some very agitated soldiers.

"No one can go through!"

"Why? The town is not sealed off! I have to get through; I am a journalist."

I know it is not the best argument. Journalists are detested – they see and report what the Israelis want hidden from the world and above all, perhaps, wiped from their own memory. Things of which most of these young soldiers doubtless disapprove deep down. Journalists, particularly from the foreign press, are discouraged at all costs and perceived as anti-Semites who criticise Israel, not understanding that all Palestinians are terrorists in the making ...

I get out my authorisation, issued in due form by the Israeli Ministry of Information. The soldiers hesitate. The order is to block the road, but nothing has been specified for members of the press. I insist that they let us through and finally, tired of arguing, they authorise us to proceed, on condition that the driver gives them his identity card until he returns. Now it is the driver who hesitates. After discussion, he agrees to take me through the checkpoint, but will not hear of taking me as far as Jenin.

At the first village, we find the owner of the local minibus, busy gardening. With the current blockade, customers are, rare and he readily abandons his spade.

"Let's go – there's always a way of getting through!"

---

1. In April 2002, the assault of the refugee camp at Jenin made the headlines in all the press. For 12 days, the camp tried to resist the Israeli forces that had invaded it. The behaviour of the Israeli army was severely criticised by the international community and certain leaders spoke of it as a war crime.

We have not gone three kilometres before we are stopped by a group of men and women.

"You can't go on. The Israelis have blocked all the roads."

We learn that, that very morning, an attack against a military bus near Jenin has killed 16 people. Those responsible came from the neighbouring village, El Yamun. The whole region is now under tight control.

"The only solution", one of them tells us, "is to go cross-country. It's possible with a minibus."

In a few minutes, we are in the middle of the countryside. Everything is quiet: a strange, heavy quiet, as if even the landscape were holding its breath. There is not a soul on the horizon – not even a dog. Inside the bus, the passengers joke but they are clearly nervous: at any moment, we could be shot at.

The narrow road we are on is nothing but holes and bumps and the driver zigzags, while unleashing a torrent of swearing. Suddenly he comes to an abrupt halt: a wide ditch splits the road. We will have to continue on foot.

After an hour, covered with sweat and dust, we arrive within sight of Jenin, the martyred town that held out against the Israeli army for 12 days and which is now a symbol of resistance, not only for the Palestinian people, but for the entire Arab world. As we enter the town, we are greeted, with sinister irony, by a monument displaying a dove of peace, in sad evocation of the lost illusions of another era.

I want first of all to go to the hospital. Seeing me hesitate, the man who has helped me to carry my bag during the walk offers to accompany me. He introduces himself: he is president of the farmers' association for the Jenin region.

"Here, as in Gaza, thousands of farming families have seen the desecration of their land", he tells me. "At the slightest suspicion of anything, the soldiers arrive with their tanks and bulldozers, destroy the land, the houses, the wells, kill the cattle – not only of the person they suspect but of all his relations and often of the whole village – and then make multiple arrests. Since the beginning of the intifada, Israel has carried out these collective punishments, which are prohibited under international law.

"What is more, they control our borders and ban us from exporting, under the pretext of security. The region has been ruined. The Palestinian Authority has to talk to the Israelis, find a solution. It's essential!"

He is trying to hang on to the idea that the Authority can engineer a solution; the situation is so serious that he cannot allow himself to lose all hope. But it is obvious that he doesn't really believe it.

When we arrive at the hospital, I am told that the hospital director is busy putting in place the emergency plan in case there is another Israeli attack. If I come back in an hour, I might be able to meet him.

Close by stands a large white building, the al Quds University. I go into the canteen, which is heaving with talking, laughing students – a group of young people as lively, noisy and carefree, it seems, as in any other university in the world. There is just one difference: boys and girls sit in separate groups. I approach a table at which three girls wearing hijabs are sitting. They welcome me with a smile.

"Talk about the situation? Yes, no problem!"

Leaving the raucous canteen, we seat ourselves on the little wall in the courtyard, in the shade of an olive tree. Suha, Zahira and Iman are 18 and 19 years old. The first two live in Kabatiya, a nearby village and are studying accounting, the latter lives in Jenin refugee camp and is training to be a teacher.

The conversation is hardly under way when half a dozen boys, curious as to what the girls are going to say, join our little group. In this town, many young people now talk about sacrificing themselves in suicide bombings. Are these just expressions of protest and pain, or is it more than that?

Suha has the crystalline voice of a teenager, in contrast to the vehemence of her words.

"With all we have gone through recently, I am ready to go into Israel to carry out a martyr operation!"

The three had brought me up sharply when I had spoken of 'suicide operations'; they do not think of it as committing suicide but as giving one's life for the cause of Palestine.

"My cousin was killed in the recent incidents", Suha goes on. "She had gone out to get food because her children were crying with hunger in the house. She said to herself that if she took the little street behind the house ..."

Suha stops, overtaken by tears, and her friend Zahira strokes her shoulder. In a small and trembling voice, she continues.

"They shot her. We don't know if she died straight away or if she suffered for a long time. We couldn't get her body back for several days ..."

Iman, a blonde girl with the face of an angel, says that she too is ready to die and she is not afraid of death.

"Today I'm alive but the Israelis might come and kill me tomorrow – I would rather be a kamikaze fighter, so that at least my death has some purpose and serves my people. You don't need to be religious to believe in a future life. Religion can be love of one's land, love of one's country. Of course there is a fear of death, but to choose my death is to not be a victim any more – a slave at the mercy of the Israeli master. It's an escape from their whims and arrogance, from their power to do what they like with our lives."

I wade in.

"Every time there is a kamikaze attack" – with relief I use this word, which avoids the choice between 'suicide' and 'martyr' and the risk of offending raw sensibilities – "the Israelis retaliate by killing many more Palestinians. The figures show that for every Israeli victim there are four Palestinian. Do you really believe that the kamikaze attacks are a good way of getting them to withdraw?"

Behind us, a young man chimes in passionately:

"Our country is occupied – are we supposed to do nothing?"

His vehemence is in direct proportion to his despair. One would have to be made of stone not to feel his suffering. I nod my head to show that I sympathise, but I persevere.

"Isn't it more realistic to try and negotiate?"

"What negotiations?" Zahira, a tall girl with a serious expression, replies sharply. "The Israelis don't want to negotiate because they would be forced to give us back our territory. They pay lip service to entering negotiation but each time international pressure makes them sit around a table, they make sure everything breaks down. Proof? There are dozens of examples. Last winter, for example, Sharon asked for a week of peace so that negotiations could start again. On the 16th December 2001, Arafat ordered a truce, having managed to persuade the extremists to respect it. For 24 days, there was peace. But on the 14th January, the Israelis assassinated Raed al Karmi, the leader of the al-Aqsa brigades of Tulkarm, who had managed to keep peace in the region. Because of that, obviously, everything started up again!

"Several months later, on the 22nd July, when the secret negotiations initiated by the British were about to reach a conclusion – Sheikh Ahmed Yassin,[2] the spiritual leader of Hamas, having agreed to stop the attacks – a bomb was thrown into a building in Gaza in the middle of the night, killing a Hamas leader, Salah Shehadeh, and numerous

2. On 22 March 2004, Yassin was assassinated by Israeli forces in a so-called 'targeted killing'.

civilians, including nine children. How can we believe in the sincerity of the Israeli government?"

A boy cuts in angrily.

"If there's an Israeli death, the papers all talk about it but it's hardly mentioned if it's one of ours. My cousin, who was 20 years old, was recently killed in Jenin. He didn't have a gun and he wasn't even throwing stones."

When they describe their relatives who have been killed by the Israelis, these young people no longer dare say they were activists or even that they were throwing stones. They want to portray all Palestinians who die as lambs led to the slaughter, because the propaganda is such that they do not know how to deal with it. If they say, 'X threw stones', they fear the world will judge that sufficient reason for their death.

I thought of the words of an Israeli friend, Michel Warsawski, who has been a campaigner for Israeli–Palestinian peace since 1968, and is president of the Alternative Information Centre in Jerusalem:

"The perversity of the Israeli approach is that they have wiped out the whole history of what happened before the invasion and occupation, with its succession of cruelties and humiliations. They use a volley of stones as a pretext, saying, 'We have been attacked, we need to defend ourselves', while saying nothing about the fact that this attack is nothing but a response, and a very weak one at that, to a much greater aggression. What they are doing is so huge that if one analysed what has happened, from the beginning, one would not believe it; the imbalance of power and of actions is so great that one cannot understand why the world does not see the screaming injustice of it. The Palestinians are hopeless at getting information across while the Israelis are past-masters in the art of propaganda and media manipulation.

"You just have to look at how the failure of Camp David was reported: all the blame was put on to Arafat for refusing when Barak 'offered him everything'! It wasn't until a year later, that Bill Clinton's special adviser on the Middle East, Robert Malley, and three members of the Israeli delegation – Oded Eran, Amnon Lipkik-Shahak and Ami Ayalon – challenged that official version of events. But the harm had been done and everyone remembered Barak's version."

Sitting a little way away, a man of thirty or so, his emaciated face framed by a thin, narrow beard, joins the conversation. He is an English teacher, a real feday, say the students, who urge him to speak. When I assure him of anonymity, he laughs: "I'm past caring!"

Ahmed Fayed was born in the camp at Jenin, to a family that had fled their village, Affula, in 1948.

"I lost two brothers in April during the last invasion. One was a Palestinian policeman who, under the provisions of the Oslo agreements, worked with Israeli police to keep the peace. When the army went into the camp, with its Merkava tanks and bulldozers, after having bombed the police headquarters, what could he do other than take up a gun to try and defend his family? They killed him in front of me ... My other brother had cystic fibrosis. On the eighth day of the invasion, at 5.30 in the morning, the Israelis threw in fire bombs, which set fire to our house. We got out quickly and saw a bulldozer coming down on our house. My mother shouted, "Stop, a disabled person is inside. Let us get him out!' The bulldozer carried on.

"Then a neighbour who spoke Hebrew intervened and begged the officer to let us go and get my brother. He agreed. My mother and sister had just entered the house when the bulldozer started moving again, crushing the walls. We screamed. They just had time to get out, without being able to get my brother, who was buried under the rubble ...

"He remained alive for two days", he continues, his voice distorted by grief. "We could hear him shouting and calling for help. With pickaxes and our bare hands we did all we could to try and free him. In the end, his shouts stopped ... We never found his body, even though we dug and dug ..."

He is silent for a while and then continues, in a very low voice:

"During that invasion I also lost two cousins and my three best friends. We are expecting my cousin's body back today. He was 60 years old, very gentle, had never been involved in any political activity. When the soldiers entered the camp he was in his house with his children. They took him and tortured him, simply because he was my cousin. Then they took him to prison, where they must have continued torturing him. Three days ago, an Israeli hospital phoned to tell us he was dead.

"I also have a young brother who was arrested and put in prison at Ofar camp, near Ramallah. They have been interrogating him for two months. Someone saw him 15 days ago; we haven't had any news since."

He straightens himself up and looks deep into my eyes:

"But we will continue to fight until we are free. We don't have any choice. This war is a clash of two wills and as long as we do not say we are beaten, they cannot win. Even if they have the most sophisticated weapons and we just have our slings and rifles, in the end we will win because we have right on our side. It is a fight between two principles: the principle of humanity, the struggle for freedom and for basic human rights on the one hand and Zionism, which believes that the Jews are the chosen people and therefore superior, on the other. Even their Palestinian fellow-citizens, whom they call 'Israeli Arabs', are second-class people. Religious discrimination, is that their democracy?"

"But couldn't negotiations prevent all these deaths?"

"In the Oslo negotiations, we accepted two states, one Israeli and one Palestinian, that would live side by side, in peace. Since these recent events, it is clear that we were naïve and that the Israelis do not want a Palestinian state at any price."

"But don't you think the kamikaze attacks are counter-productive because they unite Israelis against you, even the most moderate?"

Ahmed stiffens, as though bitten by a snake:

"Let's talk about the moderates! Where was the Israeli peace movement? Where were they during this invasion? I believed in that movement; I even had dealings with them. They betrayed us. Through their silence they have supported Sharon.

"You have to understand one thing: you do not become a kamikaze through desperation, because you are in too much suffering. It isn't an isolated act; it's an act of war, a political act to demand justice and dignity. The gesture of a kamikaze is less bloody than the policies of America, which launches bombs and causes thousands of deaths and mutilations or hundreds of thousands of permanently sick people, as with the radiation of Hiroshima. We are ready to stop the kamikaze actions if we have other means of fighting. As a Hamas leader said recently, 'Give us F-16s and we will stop the human bombs'."

Two boys have joined our small group.

"The army is coming to invade the town; you should go back", they tell us.

Ahmed gets up with Olympian calm, as if the approach of danger or the risk of dying, this very day, is of no import.

"Well, I'll leave you. I have to get back to the camp. Everyone has stayed there, despite the destruction. They have resolved to fight – they want to avenge their dead."

After he has left, I turn to Iman.

"You can't return to the camp now! It's too dangerous. Why don't you stay with friends?"

She seems embarrassed by my suggestion.

"No, I want to go home. I prefer to be with my family, whatever happens. I feel dependent on them."

The boys around us smile.

"It's impossible for her to stay out – tradition demands that a girl stays at home, especially at night."

These young roosters seem to find nothing wrong with the idea that a girl's life should be put at risk for the sake of propriety.

"But she will be at a girlfriend's house!" I object.

From their expression I understand that a girlfriend has brothers and that just staying the night under the same roof would be enough for her to lose her reputation. Even in this time of war, danger and horror, a woman has to continue to sacrifice her life for this narrow notion of virtue ...

As I have not yet seen the camp, I decide to accompany Iman, despite the protestations of my interpreter, who wants to leave Jenin as quickly as possible and get back to his village, several kilometres from the danger.

The centre of the camp is now no more than a pile of ruins. These are not the remains of houses that have been gutted or pitted with holes by shell fire or sections of falling walls, such as I saw in Beirut in 1982 during the Israeli invasion or in Grozny, the Chechen capital that was bombarded for months by the Russians. What we see here is something else: it is as though a mad giant has broken up methodically, piece by piece, everything that had constituted his enemy's habitat and life, so as to do away with every trace of it and to wipe out all possibility of recognition or memory. This is now nothing but rubble in which only rats can live. More than a desire for destruction, this is a desire to deny a people's existence.

Two months after the fighting, a yellow dust and odours that one would not want to identify still render the air unbreathable. An Israeli newspaper had published the account of the brute who had cheerfully worked on the centre of the camp for an uninterrupted 72 hours, boasting that he had driven his bulldozer into houses that he knew were inhabited and flattened the houses and pulverised the ruins so well that he had given the Palestinians the gift of a beautiful football field ...

Apache helicopters circle above our heads.

In the camp, panic has reached fever pitch. Housewives, their robes billowing, run to the main shopping street and return laden with trays of eggs, followed by children holding squawking chickens by the feet. A dense crowd, jostling to buy the round bread piled up in pyramids, assails the bakery stall. Everyone is hurrying to buy provisions. They know from experience that helicopters can shoot at them at any moment, but they take the risk. The last curfew effectively lasted 40 days and the population had suffered grave hunger; of those who dared brave the curfew, many were killed – like the baker who went out one morning to make bread because he could not bear to hear children crying with hunger any more. The soldiers had shot him and he had lain bleeding in the street; no one had been able to go to his aid. He bled to death.

At the entrance to the camp, several young people armed with Kalashnikovs prepare to defend their families: tragic heroes. What can their pitiful weapons do against helicopter and tank fire? I approach them, without any great hope of being able to speak to them; in the general frenzy, it is not really the right moment. But, to my surprise, they agree. They want to bear witness, to say what is in their hearts, conscious that it may be for the last time.

"Let's take shelter behind the wall. It's too dangerous here; the helicopters shoot as soon as they see the glimmer of rifles."

There are three of them: two social science students and a farmer, all around twenty-five. They put on a show of bravado for the foreign journalist.

"We're waiting for them. We've got secret plans to defend Jenin. The road is mined to stop them getting in – the street, not houses, as some of the press makes out. How could we kill our own people?" they ask angrily.

"How many combatants do you have?"

"A lot, distributed throughout the camp."

In fact, very few of them have access to anything other than stones. Many were killed or wounded and hundreds taken prisoner during the 40 days of the siege. Those who remain are desperadoes, ready to give their lives.

"Do you really think you can stop the Israelis entering?"

The young man who seems to be their leader has a face tanned by the sun and the look of a hungry wolf. He belongs to the *Tamzin*, the combatant youth wing of Fatah. Arrested during the first intifada, he spent six years in Israeli prisons.

He responds to my question with a world-weary smile – what's the good of play-acting?

"I know I'm going to die. Today, tomorrow, in a month, it doesn't matter. What does matter is the way in which I die: like a man, fighting, or like a coward, trying to protect myself inside a house."

None of them has illusions. They know they can do nothing against the power of the Israelis and they no longer believe in the intervention of the international community. But rather than getting arrested and tortured, they want to die with a gun in their hand, having inflicted losses, however small, on the enemy.

In the sky over Jenin town, F-16s make ever-decreasing circles. Those with cars have crammed their family inside, with food and equipment essential for survival for a few days or weeks thrown in and mattresses piled on the roof. In the middle of a symphony of car horns and infernal traffic jams, everyone hurries to leave town.

But I am still absolutely determined to go to the hospital to see the head doctor. My interpreter, Salah, begrudgingly agrees to come with me. A Middle Eastern man, he wants above all to conceal his fear – but he must curse the image that has been stuck on Palestinians ... why must they all be heroes?

Dr Abu Khalil receives me in his vast office on the top storey of the hospital. An attractive man in his forties, his face is stamped with goodness and simplicity. He speaks perfect French, having studied paediatric surgery in Algeria; he returned to Jenin in 1993. Throughout the interview we hear the whirring of helicopters flying above the town.

"Until two years ago there weren't major problems in Jenin. It was a large agricultural and commercial centre where Israeli Arabs came to do their shopping because, in normal times when there aren't checkpoints, it's not a long journey from Haifa and Nazareth.

"But here, like elsewhere, people have stopped believing in negotiation. Things have really started to deteriorate over the past year with these repeated Israeli incursions and then this appalling siege. They are talking about 54 dead but, given the intensity of the fighting and the number of missiles and tanks, I think there must have been many more. There must still be a lot of bodies under the debris. I say that because in the morgue there are bodies of several people who were found in various places and who have not been claimed; that indicates that the whole family has been killed. There are also indications and testimonies that the Israelis have taken bodies away with them. But the most terrible thing is not so much the number of dead as the way in which the wounded have been left to suffer in agony. These are crimes against humanity that should be judged by an international tribunal.

"For 12 days, no one was allowed to enter the camp. The Red Crescent and the International Red Cross pleaded with the Israeli Army to let us out to look after the wounded. We weren't even allowed to cross the hospital door. From my window I could see the centre where the prisoners were rounded up; the soldiers forced them to take off all their clothes and then beat them up. The wounded were taken there too, and also hit.

"It is impossible to describe your feelings as a doctor when you see wounded people suffering in front of you and you can do nothing to help. The hospital was empty and yet, a few metres away from us, the wounded were bleeding to death!

"Only after five days were we given permission to go with the Red Cross to the outside of the camp. Hardly had we picked up three people, who were seriously wounded when the soldiers 'confiscated' our ambulances and had the men, who were virtually dying, taken to prison! We were driven back to the hospital under military escort.

"One day they even shot through the window while we were in a meeting with the Red Cross delegate and several doctors."

He gets up and shows me the bullet marks in the wall.

"But they have done more than just threaten. They killed Dr Khalil Suleyman, the director of the Red Crescent. He was a wonderful chap. With the express permission of the Israelis, and accompanied by the Red Cross, he went to pick up the wounded in the camp; he was in an ambulance, with a little girl whom he was taking back, when the Israelis fired an incendiary bomb at them. He was burnt alive. He had screamed and called for help, but the soldiers shot at anyone who tried to get near. Afterwards they said, as usual, that it was a mistake ..."

The telephone rings and Dr Abu Khalil replies at length; he seems to be trying to reassure someone.

"My children are panicking", he tells me when he has hung up. "They are aged between 10 and 13. They get frightened when they hear the helicopters. It's very hard for them ..."

"I apologise, I'm taking up your time. I'll leave now; you doubtless have things to prepare."

"No, everything is ready: gas, water, instruments. At the moment there are 30 doctors in the hospital. Last time the Israelis even destroyed our oxygen equipment but this time we have put a security system in place. All that, of course, on the assumption we can get out ..."

We can hear the helicopters approaching. The telephone rings again; the children are demanding their father. It is time I left. Dr Abu Khalil gets up to accompany me out. He has an air of immense sadness.

"We had put so much hope in help from Europeans, but they don't dare go against Israel, which has succeeded in portraying criticism of its policies as anti-Semitism. How can your intellectuals accept this blackmail? How can you remain passive before the crimes per-petrated by Sharon's army? Where is Europe's humanist tradition?"

During the interview, Salah, my interpreter, has managed to find a car to get us out of the town. I had tried to persuade him to stay if we took precautions but he had asked me mockingly whether I wanted to be holed up there for weeks and assured me that if I did, it would be without him. We were among the last to leave Jenin. Half an hour later, a column of tanks invaded the town.

10

◆

Common Cause

A certain number of Israelis dissociate themselves from the policies of their government and a small number fight, with admirable generosity and courage, for the recognition of Palestinian rights. I met several of them.

AN OPTIMISTIC REALIST

Small, square-faced, Moshe Misrahi is no Apollo, but he is charm personified. His large black eyes radiate intelligence and a real goodness and, when he smiles, you feel privileged. An Israeli film-maker of French cultural origin, he remains, despite his clear-sightedness about the world, a representative of that rare species, the true humanist. Or, as he says, an 'optimistic realist'.

"I was born in Alexandria, in 1931, into a Judeo-Spanish family. My mother was born in Jerusalem; my maternal family had settled in the city in the 15th or 16th century. They were Jews who had come straight from Spain, under Isabel the Catholic. My maternal grandfather was born in Corfu, my father in Rhodes, which was under Italian influence at the time; my paternal grandfather was born in Imperial Turkey and my paternal grandmother was of Italian origin. A real hotchpotch! I hardly knew my father, who died, aged 30, when I was nine. I know only that he loved life and was a great gambler."

"Did he gamble with money?"

"Yes. Mainly at the races. It was his mania. My uncles too, who were bookmakers. I remember them taking me to a racecourse, with their pockets full of stake money.

"So my mother was a widow at 28. We were four children; I was the oldest. My grandfather, who was a carpenter, took care of us. We spent the entire war in Alexandria, in the extraordinary atmosphere of that garrison town in which, between 1940 and 1943, soldiers from all over the world lived – the British, detachments of the Free French Army, South Africans, New Zealanders, Australians ..."

"Did you hear about what was happening to the Jews in Europe at that time?"

"Yes, but for us Jews of Alexandria, it was a bit abstract. We knew that the Jews were being arrested and sent to camps. But in Alexandria, the intersection of so many different communities, we knew nothing about anti-Semitism. There might be conflicts and Jewish kids might fight with Arab, Greek or Italian kids, but the different ethnic groups respected each other. Everyone was free to live their life. We fought, but we weren't persecuted.

"I had Greek and Armenian friends. There was also an Italian family who lived off the same hall as us. I remember one of those absurd incidents that could only happen in Alexandria at the end of the 1930s. I was very friendly with the children of the Italian family, who all belonged to a Fascist youth movement, with its black shirts, berets, pompoms and ribbons ... One day, in 1938 or 1939, an Italian submarine turned up in the port. The war hadn't begun yet. All the Italians, very proud, wanted to visit the submarine. I wanted to go too. They dressed me up in a black shirt and took me along! You can imagine the sort of atmosphere! But in 1940, they came to take the family away to a concentration camp because Italy, as an ally of Germany, had suddenly become an enemy power.

"I went to a French high school until the age of 14. I read a lot, and went to the cinema all the time. One day, for family reasons, my grandfather decided to go and settle in Palestine. We had a lot of family there, all over the country – in Jerusalem and also in Tel Aviv. My grandparents had gone to visit them in 1945 and had come back full of enthusiasm; they decided that we would all go and live there together.

"So, we arrived in Palestine in 1946. Having grown up in the cosmopolitan environment of Alexandria, I hadn't envisaged going anywhere but Paris to study when I was 18, after my baccalauréat. I didn't know exactly what I wanted to do but I sensed that gaining access to culture was the key to freedom. I therefore did not in the least want to go to this Palestine, that I didn't know and with which I had no personal connection!"

"Were your family practising Jews? Was that one of the reasons they left for Israel?"

"They were very strong believers, but not in an orthodox way – as is typical of Jews of Spanish origin. My family spoke Ladino, a rather archaic Spanish that had borrowed Italian, Greek and Turkish words over the centuries – those countries into which Jews had been assimilated. The religious side of this form of Judaism was very liberal and open; it was a very joyful kind of religion – to such a point that when I decided, at the age of 13, that God did not exist, it was not a case of rebelling against a restricting religion. The sense of sin was not highly developed. It was a religion of the heart. For me, being a Jew does not consist of respecting the letter of the law of the Torah!"

"What is it, exactly, to be a Jew?"

"Essentially, it is a culture of memory. It is actually quite extraordinary that wherever they went – to Poland, Austria, Norway, Spain, Iraq or North Africa – the Jews maintained, through their religion, a culture that embraces all aspects of life. The Jewish religion – and the Muslim religion resembles it in this respect – is not just a set of dogmas; it is also a code. A civil code, primarily – you marry in this way, divorce in that way; if you buy land, the religion prescribes the form of contract and if you harm your neighbour, it tells you how to compensate him and so on."

"Is this code still followed now?"

"Yes, it is. It always has been. Which creates a paradox because all legislation in Israel is modelled on current law in democratic countries – except for that governing the personal domain. So civil marriage or divorce does not exist, for example. If you don't go before the rabbi, you are not married, which means that it's impossible for an Israeli Jew to marry someone from another religion. The couple have to get married outside Israel and while such a marriage would be valid in every other country, in Israel it would not – with all the problems that that involves for the children. It is said that the spirit of British law has had a strong influence on the Israeli judicial system – but so has the Bible.

"One of the great problems of the state of Israel is that it is defined in the declaration of independence as a state that is both democratic and Jewish. The concept of a 'Jewish state' means that it is a state not only for Israeli citizens but for all Jews in the world. The law of return allows them to settle in this country and to be immediately accepted as citizens, a right that exists nowhere else. But there is a contradiction between the desire to be democratic, which it is, and this notion of a 'Jewish state', which implies that it is essentially designed for Jews, while officially granting minorities the same rights. In practice, these are often not respected but the law exists and an Israeli Arab citizen can have recourse to it to protect himself.

"Israeli Arabs, who are citizens of Israel, are right to raise this problem. Israel will have to decide one day whether it is a Jewish state or a state that is, like all other democratic states, made up of all its citizens."

"If the Holocaust had not happened, do you think there would have been a Jewish state?"

"Absolutely. The foundations for the State of Israel already existed in Palestine in the 1930s when five to six hundred thousand Jews lived in Israel – farmers and workers who spoke Hebrew, a language that had been dead for 2000 years. The national corpus existed in Palestine well before the Holocaust. The Judeo-Palestinian conflict, the Palestinian revolts of 1929 and 1936 against Jewish colonisation, the *Haganah*–the basis for what would become the Israeli Army – all that existed well before the Holocaust, which only accelerated the process, not initiated it."

"And despite these conflicts, it was claimed that Palestine was a land without people?"

"That was a lie! When I came to this country as a teenager, I said to myself, 'My God, how can this be possible? How can they call Palestine *Eretz Israel*, the Land of Israel, when so many Arabs live here?' I saw Barbary fig trees, houses built of clay, peasants on their donkeys ... To justify their ideology, the Jews had to put on very selective glasses: the landscapes they saw were Biblical landscapes, from ancient times, empty of people, that they had come to liberate and develop through their work and their sweat. They didn't see the reality.

"I was soon overtaken by what we today call a leftist ideology. At thirteen and a half I read the *Communist Party Manifesto* and books on the problems of equality between nation-states. I felt that I belonged to all the peoples that I loved. Because I had shared their life in Alexandria and because I had friends from all over the world, I didn't see why I had to think that my family were better than others. However, from the age of 14 or 15, I wanted at all costs to belong to this country that was fighting for itself, that was in the act of becoming. After several months, I spoke Hebrew and my political ideas had begun to take shape.

"First of all, I thought that the solution was a bi-national state but I quickly understood that this view – shared only by certain Jewish and Palestinian Utopians – actually hid an extremist concept. The Jews wanted a bi-national state on condition that there was a Jewish majority and the Palestinians on condition that there was a Palestinian Arab majority.

"I am absolutely convinced that the only solution is partition. The bad genie must never be let out of the bottle and that is the role that politics should play – to establish boundaries. This is my home here and that is your home there. There must be a border. According to the American proverb, a good wall makes good neighbours. It's true enough."

"When you arrived from Alexandria, what kind of relations did you have with the Arabs here?"

"Very idealistic ones! With a friend my age, who came from Syria, I tried to organise Arab road workers politically. As we spoke a bit of Arabic, we could talk to them. We even created a communist cell, because there was an Arab communism at that time."

"As Jews, were you well received?"

"Yes, especially if you spoke Arabic. But around 1947, after the United Nations' decision to partition Palestine, hostilities began and the situation became more and more difficult. The last time I went to Tulkarem, at the end of 1947, to meet some friends and talk with them, I quickly realised that I had to leave because it was becoming dangerous to walk around the town. It was just after the Arabs had rejected the decision to partition Palestine. After that, war broke out.

"In 1947, the Arab leaders made what was, in my opinion, an historic mistake: they did not understand that what was already being called the Judeo-Palestinian entity was an emerging state and that the migrants could not be driven into the sea."

"But the Palestinians had been there for at least fifteen centuries. They could accept a certain number of Jews coming here and buying land, but not dispossessing them of everything."

"It's true that if I were a Palestinian, I would find it unjust if people came to my home, asked if they could rent a room, to which I agreed, asked if they could rent another, to which I also agreed, then rented the whole house and ended up by taking it over and driving me out."

"And what is your perspective on the situation now?"

"We are in front of a brick wall but the reality called the State of Israel is simply not going to be dismantled."

"But the Palestinians have completely renounced that! Arafat has accepted Israel's existence for more than ten years."

"He has accepted it but he hasn't been able to prevent his extremists – Hamas, Islamic Jihad – from continuing to demand, loudly and clearly, 'all Palestine'. There was also a group of people who rejected the Oslo agreements and there was military as well as political opposition. Rabin had to fight on those two fronts, trying to convince his people that we had to continue the Oslo process, despite the acts of terrorism."

"When the Palestinians believed that the agreements leading to independence would be respected, wasn't there a lull in the violence?"

"It lasted hardly a year! The first attacks against the settlers led to Goldstein's massacre at Hebron.[1] From a desire for vengeance – which was perhaps legitimate – the Palestinians then perpetrated the bloody attacks of Tel Aviv and Jerusalem. That was during Rabin's leadership; he tried, with every means at his disposal, not to break the thread of Oslo but then he was assassinated by the extreme right – which had,

---

1. On the 25th February 1994, a Jewish settler Baruch Goldstein killed 29 Arabs during prayers in the mosque inside the Tomb of the Patriarchs.

204 OUR SACRED LAND

because of those attacks, the political strength to mobilise and to stir up hatred against him. It was then easy for Netanyahu to say 'You see what happens – give them rifles and they respond with bombs ...'. If the attacks had continued, Rabin would probably not have been re-elected. Later on, Shimon Peres wasn't elected because of the attacks. So Netanyahu came to power and he did everything he could to break up the Oslo agreements."

"Don't you think that if the Israeli government had kept its promises, the peace process would have continued, despite acts of violence on both sides?"

"I feel a bit schizophrenic talking to you because deep down I agree totally. For me, the fault has, from the start, lain mainly with the Israeli leaders. Oslo was a thunderbolt that shook public opinion and filled us with hope. In reality, such things don't last and you have to act quickly. The big mistake was to have given ourselves five years in which to resolve the problems when we should have withdrawn from all the territories immediately, freeing as many political prisoners as possible and opening discussions straightaway on the status of Jerusalem and the dismantling of the settlements. The Palestinians would then have realised the advantages of Oslo. We should not have been so lenient towards the settlers – they are not so numerous; twenty per cent of them are unshakeable but the rest would agree to leave if they were given the necessary compensation in Israel itself.

"But it would be unjust to put all the responsibility on Israel. Arafat, who is the supreme head of the Palestinian Authority, has not been able to say, like Ben Gurion at the time: 'Our state is on the way. It has a sole authority and a sole military force. I will not allow dissidents to carry out their own individual policies'. The Palestinian side does not have just one spokesperson or a strong power. Arafat doesn't control Hamas or Islamic Jihad and so we can't trust him. Ben Gurion forcibly got rid of those extremists who refused the UN solution and who wanted Greater Israel, and even Jordan, such as the Irgun group led by Begin and the Stern Gang, to which Shamir belonged.

"In my opinion, Arafat has got his fingers in too many pies. It is the misfortune of our two peoples not to have, at a critical time, leaders of scope and vision who can cut through the Gordian knot without looking over their shoulder all the time – and without being chiefly preoccupied with their place in history. Perhaps Rabin, if he had lived ... I don't know. But in any case no one who has come after him has had the necessary calibre."

"How do you see the situation evolving?"

"In the 1960s, very few people fought for Palestinian self-determination or for the refugees' right of return. And demonstrations were rarely allowed – you had to confront the police. The differences today are that the police protect the demonstrators, rather than repressing them and the majority of people think there will one day be a Palestine next to Israel. It is absolutely vital to have two states in which everyone can express themselves and let off steam. I don't know what the result of that will be; I know only that people prefer to be hit on the head with their own clubs rather than foreign ones!"

"So do you think peace is possible?"

"Of course! The solution exists. When Begin made peace with Sadat, when Rabin made peace with Jordan, peace was based on the principle of all the territories in exchange for complete peace. There is no reason why that principle should not be the same for Israelis and Palestinians. It is the only valid solution. We would need to negotiate the exchange of territory, as we did with Jordan – three square kilometres here would go to the State of Israel in exchange for three square kilometres there to the State of Palestine. We can discuss the arrangements. But the principle is clear and simple: that is the price that we must pay for peace.

"We have to give up the dream of Greater Israel, just as the Palestinians have to give up the dream of a Palestine with the right of return. We are not going to force the Palestinians to abandon their right to a proper state and they will not succeed in driving us into the sea. The solution has been outlined in detail: give back all the territory that was occupied in 1967, with a few modifications here and there. We need simply the willingness to apply it and to make the necessary concessions: Palestinians will only get back twenty-two per cent of the original Palestine and the Jews will not have Judea and Samaria.

"We also have to accept the partition of Jerusalem and to give up the Esplanade of the Mosques where the Temple once was. All that is possible but the problem is that the Israelis think that the Palestinians see the borders of 1967 as only a first step and that they will later demand everything, as far as Tel Aviv."

"On their side, the Palestinians say, 'Sharon has never wanted to give back the territories, he has made official declarations about it, and yet the Israelis elected him.'"

"It's true, Sharon is not the one who can or wants to negotiate. But there will be negotiations; it's inevitable. On the other hand, no one here will agree to negotiate while there are suicide bombings. The Palestinian cause was much stronger when youngsters used nothing but stones. The Israelis were completely destabilised by that because Israel is a very moral society – they can't bear to think of themselves as monsters who execute children for throwing stones. That was when the big demonstrations started that led to the Oslo agreements.

"The Palestinians are deluding themselves if they think that violence is going to make the Israelis think again. They believe that Hezbollah drove the Israelis out of southern Lebanon when in fact Israel had no interests there and wanted to leave. The suicide bombings do nothing but unite everyone around Sharon. The Palestinians completely underestimate the depth of trauma and fear that still exist as a result of the Holocaust. When Israeli civilians are attacked, Israelis immediately think 'They want to annihilate us'. They don't reflect on the fact that they have much greater power and that they have the United States behind them.

"If the Palestinians concentrated their attacks against soldiers and settlers, the message would be clear: it would be a campaign against the occupation and not for the abolition of Israel."

"To come back to you, Moshe Misrahi, how have you defended the rights of Palestinians and Israeli Arabs over the past 20 or 30 years?"

"Before I began making films, I was an active militant and was in charge of the Socialist Left party in Jerusalem. I was the parliamentary correspondent for a communist daily paper at the time; I was what was called a paid official. But when I was 26, I left the communists, having realised that Marxism led nowhere – it was the time of Khrushchev and the events in Hungary – and I started wanting to make films, as another way of expressing the things that I held dear."

"But with your name and your notoriety, your openness to the Middle Eastern and the Arab world and your humanism, why have you never made a film about the Palestinian problem?"

Moshe Misrahi shakes his head. It is a question he has often been asked.

"I experience the problem on a daily basis, on a gut level, but I have never been able to express it as a film-maker. I still feel a bit guilty about it but I cannot make militant films. You can incorporate all sorts of subtleties into a book but in a film it's very difficult. You can't show all the ambiguities and ambivalences. And a militant film – which by its nature is going to be a somewhat over-simplified treatment – does not correspond to how I am, to my way of seeing things. As a film-maker, I avoid generalisations. I try to get to those precise, individual human details in which the truth lies.

"As a citizen, I express myself through petitions, like anyone else. I am not a politician and I can't go beyond my role but I express myself wherever I can in interviews and debates. Everyone knows my stance.

"In my films I pass on my views in another way. I let myself be guided by intuition and personal experience; I speak about the roles of the child and of women in society. In fact, when I think about what has really influenced my vision of the world, I realise that it isn't political books or films but those wide human portraits, like the works of Balzac or Stendhal's *Le rouge et le noir* ... I hope that my films help people, in another way, to experience greater openness towards others and renounce violence."

THE WOMEN IN BLACK

"Can you take me to Hagar Square?

The taxi driver looks at me, bemused.

"Never heard of it", he grumbles.

Is this deliberate unhelpfulness? Taxi drivers in west Jerusalem do sometimes refuse to take you to east Jerusalem, which is mainly inhabited by Palestinians.

I enlighten him.

"It's a big square, on this side. You know, where the women in black gather every Friday!"

"Oh, those nutters! Why do you call it 'Hagar Square'? They carry on their pantomime in Paris Square!"

A quarter of an hour later, he drops me at a roundabout in the centre of the city where several dozen women dressed in black have begun to assemble. I go and find Ruth, the Israeli woman whom I have arranged to meet.

"Why did you say 'Hagar Square'? I almost didn't make it."

She laughed.

"We have forgotten the real name. We christened it that, after the name of the founder of the movement. But above all, Hagar is the name of the mother of Abraham's eldest son, Ismael, who is said to be the ancestor of the Muslims, while the second son, Isaac, born of Sarah, his lawful wife, is the ancestor of the Jews."

"Ah yes! Hagar, Abraham's first wife", I concur.

"No", Ruth corrects me sharply. "Not his wife, his servant!"

This clarification disturbs me, as it disturbs all Muslims, who obviously dispute it, refusing to accept that they are descended from a servant, unlike the supposedly legitimate descendants, but most of all I am surprised to hear it from Ruth, a liberal. Why is it that people on the same political side cannot speak of their origins except in terms of arrogance or rumpled sensibilities?

Once again I have to face the fact that, with rare exceptions, Israelis – even those of goodwill – feel a strong sense of superiority over the Arabs. Beyond the questions of borders and economic problems, this is perhaps the deepest obstacle to future coexistence.

Every Friday at one o'clock the Women in Black meet to demonstrate against army involvement in the occupied territories. The movement was started by mothers of soldiers killed in southern Lebanon and has continued for 14 years.

Today is the 20th September 2002, the day after a suicide bombing in Tel Aviv that killed six people and wounded 40 others. Jerusalem is filled with high tension; people expect more incidents. These attacks against civilians make the position of Israeli pacifists even more difficult; many people do not hesitate to call them traitors or even 'anti-Semitic Jews'.

There are fifty or so women here, aged from around 20 to 70. Dressed head to toe in black, they will stand at this very busy roundabout for an hour, holding placards depicting a hand of Fatma painted with a dove of peace and the simple words 'Stop the occupation'. They stand there, implacable, in the face of motorists' gibes and insults: 'Sluts of Arafat!' and 'Go and get f***** by the Arabs' being among the nicest ...

Several men stand at the side – very useful in case of fisticuffs; the women have sometimes been physically attacked.

"But mostly they tear up our placards", a lively grandmother reassures me.

Just three or four metres away, a dozen or so extreme right-wing demonstrators, the 'Women in Green', are agitating. They are wearing green hats or T-shirts and are accompanied by young men wearing kippas and wielding the Israeli flag.

Without even glancing in the direction of the women they call 'whores', the 'Women in Green' hold up long banners on which is written 'Eretz Israel belongs only to Jews' and 'The only solution: get rid of the Arab cancer' – taking up the word used by one of Sharon's ministers a few days earlier – and 'Kahana was right!' – the late Rabbi Kahana was the founder of an extreme right-wing group that demands the 'transfer' of all the Palestinians outside the territories. I have never understood why what is called elsewhere 'deportation' becomes the euphemistic 'transfer' when applied to Palestinians.

Around the square, four policemen equipped with mobile phones survey the scene with a mocking air. They are accompanied by a young recruit who has the beautiful face of an oriental Jew, a girl in sky blue short-sleeved shirt and tight trousers who seems to be enjoying herself hugely. But they are all vigilant: if violence breaks out, they will be held responsible. There is no question of letting Jews fight one another – this isn't an Arab demonstration!

Among the 'Women in Black', a tall one, her strong face framed by short grey curls is giving orders. She is Gila, one of the organisers.

"If the others get violent, we don't retaliate, because that is what they want. We move to the other side of the square. We don't respond to provocation."

At this, several people mutter disapprovingly. A man shouts out, "In that case, I'm not staying. Last time I clouted a youngster who was insulting a grandmother and I'm not going to tolerate that today!"

He gives back his placard and leaves, shrugging his shoulders.

I walk up to the women in green and approach a young girl, who refuses to talk to me. She has seen me with the other group and is wary. Eventually my French accent wins her over – she is a native of Lyon – and she throws out in a defiant tone, "According to the Bible even Jordan is *Eretz Israel*. The Arabs have no right to be here – they should just go to other Arab countries."

An older woman intervenes: "Why are you talking to her? It's not worth it. Foreign journalists are all shits!"

With that, both of them turn their back on me.

I return to the women in black and am called over by a little blonde, Sarah, who has witnessed the scene.

"Don't be surprised – they are always that aggressive", she says in perfect English. "The woman you've just spoken to dared tell me I'm not Jewish because I don't think like her ... I am certainly more Jewish than her – she has just come here from France and hardly speaks any Hebrew. I was born here – in a kibbutz!" she specifies proudly. In Israel, that is like having an aristocratic title; the kibbutzniks were the pioneers, the real, pure Israelis.

"That woman", she goes on, "knows nothing about the true country. She just repeats all the religious slogans of the newly converted. And she dares tell me what my country should do!"

A thin man is threading his way through the group to get to the women in green.

"He lives in my street. He's called Itamar. He's a poor wretch who has had nothing in his life. He was adopted. He's full of hatred. Really poisonous flowers grow in that kind of soil ... The word 'negotiation' isn't in his vocabulary – the only word he knows is 'kill'. His ideal would be to live in a world with no Arabs and his dream is to drop an atomic bomb that would annihilate them all. In his sick mind, anyone who is not a Jew doesn't have the right to exist. If he had lived sixty years ago, he would have been the worst Nazi imaginable. Unfortunately, he isn't unique – there are a lot like him."

As Sarah is talking, an old man in a kippa passes close by and throws out, "Shame on you!"

"He's nice", she remarks. "Most of them say, 'Slut! How much does Arafat pay you to sleep with him?' and much worse."

As if to prove her point, a woman wearing a hat, in the manner of practising Jews, passes by with a child on her back; coming close enough to touch her, she hurls an insult. Sarah looks flabbergasted.

"What did she say?" I ask.

"I can't repeat it – a pornographic obscenity. Where did she get that from? They don't use those sort of words in their world!"

Cars drive past, sounding their horns. A woman lowers her window and, her face full of hatred, shouts at a white-haired woman standing next to us, "So, you old slut, do your Arabs make you come?"

"You hear that?" asked the lady angrily. "And now she will calmly go and say her prayers and blow out the Shabbat candles! They hate us because we remind them that Judaism is a humanist religion and that they are trampling all over it."

I realise that the women in black, whom I had thought were a left-wing group, come from very diverse backgrounds. They are made up of religious believers who, like my neighbour, deplore the way in which the ideals of Judaism are being distorted, humanists, free-thinkers, men in kippas who prefer the peace dove to the slogans of Kahana and even rabbis from 'Rabbis for Human Rights' which criticises current Israeli policy for trampling all Jewish moral values underfoot.

At two o'clock the demonstration ends. Everyone folds up their placards. This time there have been no excesses, perhaps because the extreme right-wing group were very much in the minority.

We arrange to meet Gila, the organiser, later.

At 55 years old, Gila Svirsly is a beautiful woman with very pale green eyes, an aquiline nose and a dazzling smile. She has chosen an isolated table on the café terrace.

"With what I'm going to say, I prefer to be discreet so as not to be insulted or even attacked."

At the time I thought she was exaggerating, but I subsequently saw Israelis being physically threatened for expressing opinions contrary to the general consensus – and Jews in France attacked by extremist coreligionists for daring to criticise Sharon ...

"I belong to the 'Coalition of Women for a Just Peace', which was created in November 2000 and is an umbrella group for nine Israeli and Palestinian organisations. We are demonstrating to demand an end to the occupation and the resumption of negotiations, but above all the lifting of the military blockade of Palestinian territory.

"Our actions are non-violent: we dismantle temporary barricades, fill in ditches that prevent Palestinians leaving their villages and sometimes lie in front of army bulldozers to prevent the destruction of Palestinian houses or fields."

She gives a small, ironic laugh.

"In reality we don't prevent anything – we only hold it up. But above all we attract public attention and that is essential. The Israeli government is enormously attached to its image."

"Last month, you tried to force the barricade which has for weeks cut off Bethlehem from the rest of Palestine. What happened?"

"Oh, that was a great moment", she said, laughing and shaking her curly hair. "Around seven hundred Israelis and Israeli-Palestinians had gathered for a non-violent demonstration. At the barricade going into Bethlehem, large numbers of soldiers were waiting for us with a water cannon. As we advanced, we were pushed back by the torrents of water but we carried on. So then they used a powerful means of attack: masked horsemen, armed with whips, who charged us at high speed, steering their horses into us and hitting us with their whips. It was terrifying! Many of us were wounded, though not seriously, and one woman was taken to hospital.

"After we had fled the scene, we came back and sat on the ground for an hour, in the August sunshine, to prevent other armed vehicles from getting on to the site. Then we advanced to the barricade, all linking arms so as to make a tight wall, chanting 'Yes to peace, no to the occupation'.

"Thousands of people were waiting for us in the town, on the other side of the barricade, in the Square of the Nativity. As there was no question of our getting through, we held our peace meeting on mobile phones. We heard the speech of the Governor of Bethlehem, thanking us for our solidarity and we replied on a mobile phone that we would continue the struggle for peace. All under the noses of the furious soldiers. They could stop our bodies going through, but not our voices or our thoughts!"

Her enthusiasm and optimism are infectious. She could make me believe that the situation is not so bad after all ...

I wanted to know more about her.

"Where were you born? In Israel?"

"Not at all! I was born in the United States and only came to Israel, for religious reasons, when I was 19. I was an orthodox Jew and a

Zionist. My mother had lost all her family in the Holocaust, at Ponary in Belarus, where 100,000 Jews, gipsies and communists were executed. She went to live in Palestine in 1934. My father's family had left for the United States in the 1920s but they were unhappy. It wasn't Jewish enough and so they too came to Palestine, which is where my mother and father met, in 1936. After their marriage they left to live in America.

"You will understand that with such a heavy past on the two sides, my environment and my education were very Jewish. I had the profound belief that Israel was my motherland, a moral society of which Jews could be proud and to which I had to return. I arrived in 1966, a year before the Six-Day War. I didn't question anything. I was happy to be in a model country that was to be a beacon for other nations. I admired the kibbutzim and dreamt of being a pioneer like my mother had been before the creation of Israel."

"What made you change your mind?"

"I began to worry about Israel's actions in the 1970s, when more and more settlers occupied the Palestinian territories. I had married a man who was neither religious nor right wing ..."

She laughs.

"They say that women espouse the ideas of the man they sleep with! That was in my pre-feminist days. But at that time I was not very critical. I was studying philosophy and looking after my children. When they were older, we divorced and I became the head of a foundation that looks after oppressed communities in Israel, including Israeli Arabs.

"I was stunned to find out how our Arab fellow citizens were treated and the conditions in which they lived. Before, I had thought – like everyone else around me – that the Arabs were dirty. I began to realise that the government didn't give them the funds to install water or mains drainage in their villages or districts."

"Had you met Arabs – at university, for example?"

"No. Israeli society is much more divided than South Africa was under apartheid. Even today we don't meet each other.

"But I still didn't make the link between the problems in Israel and the problem of the occupied territories. For me, as for everyone, Israel would occupy the territories just long enough to make peace and then we would withdraw. That was until the first intifada in 1987, when we realised that the occupation was neither benign nor transitory, as we had believed.

"That intifada was a big shock to the liberal community. It began with a little demonstration in Gaza, then a bigger one, then stones started being thrown, then someone was killed; then someone was killed every day. Which was when we realised something was wrong and that the violence had to stop. Through a friend, I joined the 'women in black' movement against the occupation, in January 1988. Little by little, with other women, we began to educate ourselves polit- ically and to realise that violence has its reasons and that it doesn't emerge from a vacuum. We invited Palestinian women and they took the risk of crossing the green line to come and speak to us.

"Rita Giacoman was the first of our Palestinian guests whom I met. I still remember the shock: I couldn't believe my eyes or ears. I was fascinated. She was so different from my image of what a Palestinian woman would be like! Sophisticated, relaxed, intelligent, educated, eloquent – she was very cultured, much more so than me, and than most Israelis or Americans! A woman like that a Palestinian? I couldn't get over it!

"I remember that she said: 'We Palestinians are not opposed to the State of Israel. We want a Palestinian state next to Israel'. That was in 1988. I asked her: 'Is that your personal position?' She replied, 'No, it's the official position'.

"I had never heard that in Israel – not in any newspaper or radio programme and in none of our leaders' speeches. Nowhere! At the time we were prohibited from even mentioning the PLO and we knew absolutely nothing about their views. So that opened my eyes. That is just an example of the many events that made us understand the reality of the problem and become activists.

"We formed a coalition of nine organisations: one keeps an open dialogue with Palestinian women and children, another maintains a presence at barricades so that soldiers do not badly mistreat Palestinians, there are the women in black and so on. There are only a few hundred of us but we have an important influence and we can unite thousands of people."

"But there are no demonstrations against what is currently happen- ing! Most Israelis seem to support Sharon."

"Yes, that's the terrible difference between this period and previous ones. After the Sabra and Shatila massacres, the country demonstrated *en masse* to show its indignation. But now it is silent about Jenin, for example, and even goes as far as justifying what the army is doing. Even the enlightened movement Peace Now has been absent ..."

"Is that because Palestinians are now using weapons?"

"No. It is primarily because of what we call the 'great lie': the myth that Barak offered everything to Arafat who refused because his aim was the elimination of Israel. That was the point when things broke down; the Israelis believed their government and the Americans and they supported Sharon's repressive policies.

"The second reason for the liberals' silence is, of course, the Palestinian attacks inside Israel. People are very frightened. I am also frightened ... That fear unites Israelis from all sides against the Palestinians. It is a bad strategy.

"However, since the first intifada 15 years ago, there has been a big shift in Israel. More and more people understand that peace is impossible if we keep the settlements, that we have to return to the 1967 borders and that there will one day be a State of Palestine. People support repression at the moment because they want to stop terrorism, without understanding that terrorism is the response to the government's refusal to negotiate. Sharon has said on numerous occasions that he refuses to implement the Oslo agreements and that he will not give up the settlements. So who are we fooling when we put all the blame on Arafat?"

"What do you think of the Israeli-American demand that Arafat should go?"

"It's repulsive to try and dictate to the Palestinians who their leader should be. If Bush and Sharon did not act in such a crude way, people would doubtless criticise Arafat a lot more. As it is, they are uniting and will continue to unite around him.

"I also don't understand Sharon's insistence, because if Arafat goes, who will he be able to blame? What excuse will he have for continuing to refuse to negotiate?"

RABBIS FOR HUMAN RIGHTS

At the 'Women in Black' demonstration, I had been told about another very active group, 'Rabbis for Human Rights'. Motivated by the desire to safeguard Jewish values of justice, they are at the forefront of the peaceful fight to support the Palestinians.

On the telephone, Rabbi Jeremy Milgrom's voice sounds energetic and clear.

"I would be happy to meet you, but at the moment I am harvesting olives. We are trying to protect Palestinian farmers from being attacked by settlers. If you want to meet me tomorrow morning, I'll take you there. We can talk in the car."

The following morning, at six o'clock on the dot, I meet Rabbi Milgrom in the lobby of my hotel. Or, rather, at first I look around for him because the only person there is a man of forty or so, dressed in jeans and wearing his long curly hair in a ponytail, who looks more like Christ or a hippy than a Rabbi ... However, it is him. Conscious of my surprise, he laughs.

"You were expecting me to have a hat and sidecurls, but only the ultra-orthodox wear those. You know, there are a thousand trends in Judaism, just as in Israeli society."

"Why did you choose to become a rabbi? Were you born here?"

"No, I was born in the United States, in Virginia. My father was a rabbi and wanted his children to learn about their own culture. Every morning, over breakfast, he would speak to us in Hebrew and teach us the Bible. When I was 15, I won a prize in a religious competition: a trip to Israel. I intended to stay for a year, to study in a *yeshiva*,[1] but ended up staying three years. I did my military service here, in 1971, during a period of peace. Then I went back to the United States. My parents were living in Berkeley then and I really wanted to discover California's liberated society. But I soon missed Israel and I came back. After studying maths and history, I eventually decided to become a rabbi.

"I wanted to bridge the gap that exists in this country between orthodox and modern Jews, but I quickly realised that the widening

1. Yeshiva religious school.

gap between Israeli Jews and Israeli Arabs was much more worrying. In a country that is supposed to be democratic and tolerant, and in which citizens are supposed to have equal rights, I realised that a real apartheid existed.

"I have been a rabbi for 25 years and my work consists of trying to establish a dialogue between the two communities. Seven years ago, I joined 'Rabbis for Human Rights'. From Israeli Arabs we naturally progressed to a concern for Palestinians. We think that if we are faithful to our religion, we should oppose the human rights violations that occur constantly in our country. How can we claim to be a Jewish society if we torture, inflict collective punishments and destroy houses, throwing whole families on to the street?

"People listened to us during the Oslo period but now it has become more difficult. The Israelis are convinced that whatever happens we have no future together and that the Palestinians hate us."

"Are there many of you in the organisation?"

"There are a hundred or so rabbis, mainly American immigrants, including several women. Our organisation was created 14 years ago during the first intifada, to protest against the order given to soldiers to break demonstrators' bones. The religious kept silent about it, and the religious establishment supports the government. So our group fulfils a vital need, giving moral direction that affirms the ideals of justice and human equality. There are not many of us, but we are influential.

"We supported the Rabin plan but it is now obvious that Israel used the Oslo process to consolidate its control of the occupied territories. We are doing in the territories exactly what the South Africans did – creating Bantustans, controlling them and keeping total control of water. The Israelis do not want to share anything. The great majority of them do not live in the Middle East but in an artificially created European island. We have a negative attitude towards this region, its culture and religion. We have built our own luxury ghetto. That is a mistake. In fifty years, the Palestinians will outnumber us and we will be a minority governing a majority. That cannot work and will inevitably lead to disaster.

"At the moment, the world does not react because the Jews are influential and people are frightened of being accused of anti-Semitism. But it is we Jews who are today responsible for anti-Semitism. We are causing people to doubt the moral value of Judaism."

"You are a religious minister; what do you think of those settlers who refuse to evacuate the settlements in the West Bank from religious conviction, claiming it to be their sacred land?"

"They do not so much believe in the sacredness of the land of Judea and Samaria as they do in a certain idea of Zionism. It is a way of Jews saying to the world, 'We have suffered so much; now we can do what we want. That argument has nothing to do with the Bible or religious faith. They have the deeply ingrained notion that they have the right to commit the faults that others have committed before them. It is as if they are catching up on horror ... I find that unbearable. Instead of being more sensitive to others' suffering because of our own and instead of keeping faith with our Jewish ideology, which two thousand years ago was more advanced than others – notably Roman law – our morality lags behind that which exists everywhere else.

"While the entire world has now rejected colonisation, we colonise, on the pretext that we are in danger, but in reality because we think that Israel should be a country first and foremost, and if possible, exclusively for Jews. We are doing all we can to get rid of the Arab population by making their lives impossible and perhaps by expelling them one day, if they rebel."

We approach the village of Kafr Yussef, near the settlement of Tapuah, where we are to join up with human rights organisations.

"The farmers have been trying to get to their fields for two weeks", Rabbi Milgrom explained, "but the settlers have been terrorising them by shooting at them, as they do almost everywhere in the West Bank. That has been going on every October for three years, just as the crop is ready to be harvested. Olives are a vital source of revenue for hundreds of thousands of Palestinians and olive fields make up almost half of all cultivated land, because they demand very little water, which is severely rationed by the Israelis here: eighty per cent of water in the West Bank goes to the settlements!

"The Palestinian economy has been devastated by two years of blockades and curfews and preventing olive harvesting has very serious consequences. Amos Gilad, the general in charge of the territories, recently admitted that sixty per cent of Palestinians are living below the poverty line. In many villages, particularly those next to settlements, farmers cannot bring in their harvest without risking their lives. People have been wounded and even killed. Two weeks ago, on the 6th October, a man aged 24, Hani Yussuf, from the village of Akraba, was shot dead while he was in his field quietly bringing in his harvest!"

Perhaps Rabbi Milgrom is exaggerating; perhaps this Hani Yussuf had got too close to a settlement and had been taken for a terrorist ... What difference could it make to the settlers if the farmers picked their olives?

Several hours and several gunshots later, I understand.

It is around 7 am. when we arrive at the village of Kafr Yussef – or rather, near the village because the road is blocked by a huge barricade of earth and blocks of stone, erected by the Israeli Army.

It is still cool and, in the soft October light, we set off at a good pace towards the village. My attention is suddenly seized by graffiti on a wall proclaiming 'Death to Arabs!' in red letters.

"It's the settlers", says Jeremy, shrugging his shoulders.

"Why don't the Palestinians remove it?"

"They do, but it always reappears, so they just give up. They have got other fights on their hands."

The village of Kafr Yussef has around two thousand inhabitants and, like all Palestinian villages, it is over-populated. Every scrap of land has been converted into a makeshift dwelling.

As soon as we arrive in the village, we are met by swarms of children who lead us, amid much shouting and laughter, to the main square, where hundreds of people have already gathered. Most of them are farmers, men and women armed with poles and large sheets in which to collect the olives but I also make out a handful of militants from various Israeli peace movements and several French, British and American sympathisers.

They have been trying to gather the harvest for two days but the settlers from the neighbouring plantation of Tapuah have stopped them by throwing stones and shooting at them. The army had intervened but, rather than protecting the farmers, instead forced them to withdraw.

Today, the villagers have once more decided to try their luck. The situation is serious: if they do not harvest their olives, not only will they have lost their principal source of revenue for the year but they also risk losing their fields, which could be confiscated as 'uncultivated' and given to the settlers.

Just a week earlier, the village of Hirbet Yanum, not far from here, was forced to give up the fight. It is said to be the first time since 1948 that an entire village has been emptied of its inhabitants by this 'soft' transfer. The Palestinians fear that the settlers, fortified by their success, will intensify their attacks against all the small villages of the West Bank.

Hirbet Yanum is an isolated village comprising 26 families: around two hundred people. Unofficial settlements – unauthorised but tolerated by the Israeli state – have sprung up on neighbouring hills and have plagued the villagers for the past four years. Masked men would come into the village at night, on horseback, stealing animals, breaking windows and beating up those men who dared to try and stop them.

Recently they even broke the generator, depriving the village of all electricity and burst the three large water tanks. One by one, people were forced to quit the village, leaving just six indomitable families – but the attacks intensified to such a degree that the wives threatened to leave their husbands if they continued to insist on staying.

"I know the village chief, Abdelatif Sobih", Rabbi Milgrom tells me. "He was the last to leave. He was crying as he loaded his few possessions on to a van to go and stay temporarily with some cousins; after that he didn't know where he would go ... His family had always lived in the village and he said to me that now he had become a refugee, there was nothing left for him but death. You know, if a farmer is cut off from his roots, imprisoned in four concrete walls in some wretched camp without a single tree or bit of grass, without that vital connection to nature and to Mother Earth, which he cultivates and to the sky which gives him its precious rain – away from a life that is hard but of which he is his own master – he loses his reason to live."

We are interrupted by the arrival of a young farmer who announces that everyone is there and that it is time to leave. A small group of around four hundred people is moving off, men in front, Palestinian and international sympathisers mixed together, the women behind, displaying their beautiful traditional robes like flags. An atmosphere of joyous excitement, tinged with apprehension, reigns. The Israeli pacifists have obtained the assurance of the civil and military authorities that the soldiers will be there to protect them against the settlers, but you never know ...

No sooner do they catch sight of the orchards than our fine procession breaks up and everyone runs to their field: they have been prevented from coming here for such a long time. They hurtle down the slopes with open arms, as though welcoming a long-lost child.

Suddenly, shots ring out. At the bottom of the valley, settlers are waiting. Around fifteen of them are screaming and shooting in all directions. Terrified, the farmers nearest them try to hide behind trees, while the others turn back towards us. Rabbi Milgrom tries to reassure them.

"Don't be frightened – they are just trying to scare you. They're shooting in the air!"

How does he know? Hasn't he just told me that people are sometimes killed?

A small group of villagers regroups around the peace campaigners and continues to advance towards the settlers, now wild with rage at this unexpected resistance. "We'll kill you!" they shout, pointing their weapons at the group.

Calmly, the Israeli pacifists try to talk to them.

"Don't be stupid: we are unarmed and you don't have the right to stop the harvest."

These words serve only to fan the flames of their fury. A stocky man, red with anger, chokes out, "You, Jews, have come with these Arab murderers to assassinate us!" while his companions assume even more threatening poses.

A young French pacifist tries to push aside a gun pointed at his stomach and the settler who is aiming it at him spits out, "Don't touch me, you fag. Don't touch my gun or I'll kill you!"

Insults rain down – charming epithets that make up with profusion for their lack of originality. Finally, three soldiers come to help. It is not very many to protect everyone but is perhaps enough to make the settlers see reason. To our astonishment, however, they turn on us.

"The foreigners have no place here", they declare. "They must leave immediately." Obviously, no one moves. The internationals know very well that their presence affords protection to the Palestinians because the army does not want witnesses to violence.

The three soldiers are soon joined by a dozen others, evidently friends of the settlers. They shake each other's hands, slap each other on the back and exchange pleasantries. Their connivance seems total. One of them wags his finger amicably at a settler who has started shooting again.

"No, no, you mustn't do that!"

But he says nothing to those who are taking aim at groups of villagers. To an activist who shouts at him, "Arrest them, for heaven's sake!" he responds with magisterial assurance: "They have the right to take aim as long as they don't shoot!"

Outraged, an elderly Israeli pacifist decides to transform himself into a human shield and stands between the villagers and the settlers. Others follow his example. They know that if the settlers are capable of shooting at an unarmed Palestinian they have not – or not yet – gone so far as to shoot at other Israelis.[2]

More reinforcements arrive. The villagers meanwhile sit down on the ground in silence, their expressions radiating an impressive determination. These several hundred men and women have decided this time that they will not be moved, come what may.

---

2. This is no longer true. On the 16th March 2003, Rachel Corrie, a 23-year-old American Jew, was mown down by a bulldozer in Rafah, as she tried to prevent the destruction of a Palestinian house.

The Israeli commander takes the pacifists aside and tells them that they have to leave because the area is in a military zone. At these words, Rabbi Milgrom – until now the embodiment of calm – flushes scarlet with anger.

"That's not true! As you well know. Aren't you ashamed of lying like that? We are staying and we will bring in this harvest, no matter what you do!"

The dumbfounded officer does not respond. He knows that this time he is not going to have the upper hand. Grumbling, he returns to the settlers. "Return home!" he orders them, and prepares to leave with his men. But the Rabbi has not finished.

"Not so fast! That's too easy! As soon as you've turned your backs, they'll come back. You have a duty to make them return to the settlement!"

The officer reluctantly goes to explain to the settlers that they are behaving illegally and must leave. But they don't want to hear of it and, outraged, turn on the officer himself, who takes them to one side. The discussion goes on at length. How is he going to persuade them? What assurances will he give?

Finally, however, they all leave together, the soldiers leading away those furious recalcitrants who shake their fists at the Palestinians, swearing that they will come back and avenge themselves. Their departure is greeted by an explosion of joy. It is the first time for years that the villagers have scored a victory over the arbitrary power that rules their daily lives. Hardly believing what has happened, they kiss each other, kiss the activists, their eyes shining. They are no longer impotent victims. This success, however partial and temporary, has given them hope again.

For the rest of the day they busily gather their olives – they need to hurry because tomorrow the settlers could come back – and even the children join in. They work without tiring, the women singing, the men joking. They have not been so happy for a long time.

By nightfall, the harvest has been gathered. It is time to take a breath and, above all, to reflect on this incredible day. Sitting around, drinking glasses of tea, the village elders and the pacifists make plans which, for once, do not seem like idle dreams. First, they want to tell all the villages in the West Bank about this experience to encourage them. Then, they want to send regular groups of activists to protect them. They also want to call on the internationals to bear witness: external testimonies are indispensable in countering the propaganda of the Israeli authorities. Everyone chips in his ideas and recounts his experience and the conversation draws on late into the night.

LEA TSEMEL, DEFENDER OF PALESTINIANS

She sounds delightful on the phone. "Yes, let's meet! When? Tomorrow ... Or rather the day after ... phone me again ..."

After several days, I realise it is impossible to get a meeting with Lea Tsemel. This Israeli lawyer, who has for 32 years dedicated herself to defending Palestinians, both in the occupied territories and in Israel, is snowed under with work. From Jerusalem to Haifa, Nazareth and Tel Aviv, in military and civil courts, she never stops – there is no lack of cases and she is almost alone, with her older colleague Felicia Langer, in taking on this impossible role.

I finally track her down in the law courts where she spends her mornings. I had first gone to the main court, in Moscobyia, where the attendants and lawyers were very helpful in trying to find what court she might be in; finally, someone exclaimed, "Lea Tsemel? But she looks after Arabs – she's in east Jerusalem!" At which, these previously obliging people edged away from me as though I had the plague. With ill grace, the guard at the door consented to give me directions to the court in Salaheddin Street.

At the court in east Jerusalem, I am shown into a very small trial room. The two dark young defendants sitting on the wooden benches, Nasser Assawi and Imaoui, are accused of having taken part in the murder of Rehavam Ze'evi, known as 'Gandhi' because, when he was a crack commando fighter in the Haganah, he wore a white sheet. At the end of the 1960s this famous Minister for Tourism, a great friend of Sharon's, organised helicopter 'safaris' to track down Palestinian fighters trying to cross the river Jordan. He was, above all, a man of the extreme right who publicly advocated the transfer of Palestinians.

The defendants sit there with astonishing calm, as if it were not their lives at stake or as if they had already sacrificed themselves – which is effectively what they did the moment they volunteered to assassinate the minister. Every so often, an interpreter explains what is being said about them in Hebrew.

On the same bench, separated only by a policeman, sit two blonde women dressed in black: the wife and daughter of the assassinated minister. Pale, their lips pressed tightly together, they look straight ahead. The atmosphere should be explosive but is instead bizarrely relaxed. On the bench just behind are huddled the families of the accused – a dozen adults and children. There is even a baby.

The three judges enter, dressed in black robes, the chief judge, a woman with very short white hair in the middle. Flanked by her two assistants, she sits with pride underneath the symbol of Judaism, the seven-branched candlestick.

Lea stands before her, a tiny figure in her black gown, with a thin, pale face framed by gleaming brown hair; most striking, however, are her huge green eyes, whose black irises seem to pierce one's very soul.

Today is only a preliminary hearing to decide whether or not the defendants will testify and whether they were implicated in the crime or had simply helped the murderers escape, which would incur a lesser penalty. They are not there to discuss the murder itself. The facts have been established.

Standing opposite Lea, the prosecutor, a pretty red-haired woman, tries to explain to the tribunal why they have not yet agreed how to proceed. Each lawyer gives their reasons. The chief judge reacts with annoyance, while one of her assistants seems to nod in agreement with Lea's arguments. I am surprised; I thought that this woman was a black sheep among her profession, daring as she does to defend the assassins of Jews – in this case, a minister who was no less than a great friend of Sharon! Lea's colleagues subsequently explain that for years, that was the case but her courage and professionalism have finally won everyone's respect.

After a quarter of an hour, the judge decides to end the hearing. All at once, the accused are surrounded by their families; they kiss and place the baby in the arms of the youngest man who, overcome with delight, bounces him up and down and covers him with kisses – all in front of the furious gaze of the minister's family, who leave, their heads held high, without a glance at the treacherous lawyer ...

"I'm starving; come on, we'll talk over lunch."

Lea takes me warmly by the arm and, with her two trainee assistants, a tall dark-haired man and a small blond one – an Arab and a Jew – she leads us to her usual restaurant, halfway between the court and her office. It is, of course, an Arab restaurant, in an area of the city to which Jews used to like to come to dine or to shop; since the intifada, they don't risk it any more.

On entering, the lawyer is greeted by a tremendous wave of respect and affection. Apart from obvious homicide cases like today's, Lea is the last resort and the final hope that justice will be done in all cases of expulsion, confiscation, house demolition and arrest on mere suspicion – everything, in short, that makes up the daily life of Palestinians in Israel and the occupied territories.

I have been hearing about Lea Tsemel for a long time. I had imagined a tall, imposing dark-haired woman, a star of the legal profession, who would be a little distant with journalists who waste her time with their repetitive questions. But I am sitting with a small woman with a quicksilver energy, whose manner and gestures speak of directness and a natural warmth.

"How did I come to be the Palestinians' lawyer?" she smiles. "Perhaps because I am neither blind nor deaf to what is going on around me ... I was born in Israel, in Haifa, in a very Zionist middle-class family. My parents came from Russia and Poland. All the rest of the family were victims of the Shoah. They often spoke about it at home and I would listen, horrified, unable to understand how people could act in such a diabolical way. In Haifa, our neighbours and friends were all Jews; there were Arabs around, but one never saw them. It was as if they didn't exist.

"When I went to university, I chose law because people told me I was a very good speaker. I met Arabs and got on well with them, for the simple reason that I wasn't racist and was just a nice girl who was not at all politicised. I knew about apartheid in South Africa and like my friends I denounced it, without for one second thinking that the situation here was identical.

"At the time of the 1967 war, I was 22 years old. I volunteered for army service. I had the rock solid belief that Israel wanted peace but that we were forced into fighting the Arabs because they wanted to drive us into the sea. But when I saw the way in which all these people, including elderly people, women and children, were forced out of their homes, terrorised and mistreated, with the obvious aim of making them flee to Jordan, I understood that Israel was not seeking peace. The Arabs had so little with which to protect themselves and Israel clearly had the means of imposing peace but did not want to do so, finding pretexts to annexe the territories.

"I found the violence and humiliation that we inflicted on the Palestinians intolerable. For me as a Jew, witnessing these abuses evoked the collective memory of the trauma that our people had endured. I still knew nothing about the Palestinian refugees of 1948, but seeing those people driven into Jordan in 1967 and witnessing the destruction of so many villages made me terribly uncomfortable. I wanted above all to get out of my safe little shell and understand!

"So, I tried to meet groups of liberal students and ask them questions: what had happened to those four hundred or so Arab villages that were marked on old maps but which no longer existed? Why were there all these refugees in the camps? And all those beautiful Arab houses – what had happened to their owners? I was horrified to discover the truth, bit by bit, that the Palestinians had not abandoned their houses and fields voluntarily, as we had been made to believe.

"I was beginning to realise that Israel was neither more nor less than a colonialist state. The only difference was that instead of dominating the indigenous population, it had driven them out. I understood that I had been deceived and that we were not the great democracy of which I had been so proud. The slogan on which we had built our country, 'A people without land for a land without people', was nothing but a lie.

"That was when I began to fight as a lawyer. I was full of enthusiasm and I thought that if I just spoke out against injustice, I would change everything."

She laughed, half-mocking, half-tender, at the thought of her naivety.

"I still think that I can be useful but I am no longer at all sure that I can really help change our society ...

"My new way of thinking obviously scandalised people and a deep divide formed in my life from then on. My new political friends and my family's friends had diametrically opposed viewpoints; they could not see eye to eye, even though for a while I thought I could convince them. Despite the emotional pressures, I stayed loyal to my convictions. I could not deny what I had discovered. However, for most of my old friends I had become a traitor and they cut off all contact with my family and me."

"And how did your family react?"

"They continued to behave affectionately towards me, but it caused enormous problems for them in terms of their relationship with the outside world – it seriously affected my brother's career as an engineer, where the name of Tsemel caused him a lot of damage. As for my children, my daughter, who is now 20, is politically active but my son of 30 is not at all. He was exposed to all sorts of persecution and suffered a lot from other children at school and in our neighbourhood who would say to him, 'Your mother is the Arabs' whore'. He was ashamed of me and did not want to walk next to me in the street."

"Have you yourself been subject to violence?"

"Of course, of all kinds. Since 1970, which is when I really began fighting seriously, there has been something every day. On top of verbal abuse, I have for years been physically attacked. Settlers spit at me ... My office has also been frequently attacked: stones are thrown at windows, rubbish strewn on the staircase, all sorts of abusive words written on the wall, sugar put in the petrol tank of my car, and so on. It is a daily occurrence."

"Have you ever regretted your decision?"

"No. I knew very well from the beginning what I was risking. And then I had the support of the man I married a few years later, Michel Warchawski, who is also a militant. But above all I was encouraged by all those people who so needed someone who would, finally, defend them against the unjust treatment, the violence and the arbitrary arrests. The expressions of those whom I had helped was what enabled me to keep going during those terrible years. It was unthinkable to me that I could let them down.

"My daughter has suffered less from all that than my son. She was born ten years later, at a time when I had begun to be rehabilitated in public opinion. From having been the 'terrorists' lawyer' I became a campaigner for human rights, a known and respected activist. Felicia Langer and I were, in a sense, pioneers. Fortunately, there are today several young lawyers who have taken over the cause of defending Palestinians."

"Tell me about some of the difficult cases you have had."

"Oh, there have been so many in 32 years! Prisoners on hunger strike, the first Palestinians who came from the sea and took hostages and, for some time now, all these kamikaze bombers."

"Yes, these people who want to blow themselves up, killing Israeli civilians with them, but who don't die – how do you manage to defend them?"

"As a lawyer, it is essential to try to explain to the court that if a phenomenon as extreme and as unacceptable as that has become so widespread, there must be reasons for it. Young men and women don't decide to blow themselves up out of the blue, from some aberration. I try to relate their situation, to show the depth and the causes of their despair. It isn't some natural disaster – there are reasons, which it is important to identify.

"And then I try to highlight the differences in individual cases, such as those kamikazes who did not kill – either because their bomb did not explode or because they changed their mind at the last minute. At the moment I am defending a young girl who had doubts just as she was about to press the detonator. I am trying to make an example out of her case because in the end she had an attack of conscience and regretted what she was preparing to do. I want to persuade the court that we should make her regret the central element of the trial."

"Do you believe these young people are indoctrinated, that they are pushed into committing these acts?"

"Absolutely not. With all that they live through and see, most of them have no need to be pushed."

"In the 32 years that you have been defending the Palestinians, what is your opinion of Israeli justice?"

"Most of my trials are judged by military courts which means that everything is biased from the start. The judges are officers and I have very little chance of getting anywhere. I defend very difficult cases in civilian courts, principally those like the one today in which a minister, a friend of Sharon, has been killed. Judges are inevitably influenced by the government's politics. They will not accept that the soldier or the man who conducted the interrogation might have lied or that the security services might be deficient. My job is to find the little chinks through which we can get in, and widen them, so as to highlight different degrees of responsibility.

"In today's case, one of the prisoners is accused of murder and the other of being an accomplice. I am trying to show that that is untrue and that the first man was only an accomplice to murder, while the second helped him escape. I fight for people not to be cast in the same mould and for degrees of guilt to be differentiated.

"And then there are those current cases where, for example, a child is judged for having thrown a stone and gets three months in prison, which is an enormous sentence, but which I have, none the less, to consider a success because he could have got seven months. These are, you see, relative successes ..."

Lea seems suddenly very tired. I feel like taking her hand but content myself with saying:

"But you have also had real victories! Tell me about them!"

"Yes, recently in Jerusalem I had a rather comical case", Lea responds with a renewed smile. "We managed to get a very large compensation payment for a woman whom the police had taken to be a man in disguise. They had shot at her and she had escaped, but they pursued her, still shooting. Her child was wounded. The judge was forced to admit that she was a woman and get the police to withdraw.

"Another important success, which was the fruit of a collective effort, was the ruling on the question of torture cases. We fought until the Supreme Court admitted that the cases were indeed ones of torture and that it was illegal."

"But I thought that torture was legal in Israel?"

"Not really. It was a common practice that the courts refused to denounce clearly. Until, that was, this trial in 1999. They are today trying, by every means, to go back on that decision and we have to fight tooth and nail against those attempts. In fact everything depends on the political climate. A few months ago, I defended a man in his fifties who had endured a very long and particularly brutal interrogation. The military tribunal accused him of belonging to the Popular Front for the Liberation of Palestine and of having conspired to explode a bomb. In fact, the only concrete evidence they had against him was that since 1990 he had, very openly, distributed food to the poor of Jerusalem and that he had received these provisions from an organisation connected to the PFLP. I managed to get his case transferred from a military to a civil tribunal, where I thought he would immediately be released because there was nothing against him. But we lost and he got 11 months – all because of the current climate, in which anyone linked to a party other than Arafat's Fatah has to be severely punished, so as to discourage all political activity.

"On the other hand, I have been able to get two or three people released, one of whom had tried to join Hamas. These seem like tiny successes but we are trying to get new rules created and to attack these unjust laws and practices. We are trying to force the judicial system to treat Arabs as it treats Jews. By bringing to light discriminatory practices, we are trying to convince other lawyers to refuse to accept what is going on."

"Can you give me some examples of this discrimination?"

"If a Jewish child throws stones at Arabs, he will not be subject to any penalty because, contrary to what happens to an Arab child, the psychological and sociological circumstances will be taken into account. Another example is a recent case in which a Jewish settler ran over an Arab child and killed him. He was convicted of involuntary homicide whereas, if he had been an Arab, he would have been convicted of premeditated murder. It is not that the tribunals detest Arabs but when a Jew gives evidence, they understand what he says; when a Jewish mother talks about her son, they are much more moved than when an Arab mother talks about her child, because the Jewish mother could be the judge's mother or wife ... If a Jew is condemned to life in prison for killing an Arab, he will be freed after 12 years, whereas an Arab will stay in prison for the rest of his life.

"Discrimination comes not only from the judge but from the whole judicial system: the prison, the Ministry for Justice and all the various organisations that naturally campaign for Jews and against Arabs. Take the interrogation system, for example. An Arab will be tortured and he will soon end up saying: 'Yes, I placed a bomb because I wanted to kill Jews'. Kill Jews? Life imprisonment! But a Jew will not be tortured by the security services and he will say, 'Yes, I placed a bomb but I didn't really intend to kill anyone'; instead of grilling him, the security service will leave him be."

"In your opinion, have suicide bombings hardened public opinion?"

To my astonishment, Lea draws herself up, her eyes flashing with anger.

"Oh, come on! Not at all! The Israeli government does not want to negotiate and uses that as an excuse. At one time, the excuse was the stones. They said, 'We cannot talk: how can you trust people who throw stones at you?'

"In fact, the impact of the suicide bombings should have been enormous for Israelis. We should have asked ourselves, 'Why are they doing that?' We Jews have also had our heroic suicides, from Samson to Massada. In 1947–48, we had many martyrs in the army and before that in our paramilitary groups, *Stern* and *Irgun*. The Israelis should admire the Palestinians who are sacrificing themselves for their cause, as we ourselves did. Instead of which, we treat them like monsters and fanatics. We don't ask ourselves for a single second what makes these youngsters blow themselves up in the street! People swallow the government's propaganda and their views get harder and harder."

"But aren't they in the end going to demand that the government changes their policies, since the present one is obviously failing to protect their security?"

"I am astonished that that hasn't already happened. But I fear that a change would only be for the worse. Most Israelis now favour even tougher measures. They expect quick and easy solutions, which obviously don't exist. They don't want to question themselves, change their way of life or share even a little.

"The Palestinians do not understand that they should attack Israel's economic interests. Waging the campaign on the moral level and trying to make people understand the injustice to which the Palestinians are subject just doesn't work! The Israelis are persuaded that that they are above all moral criticism. You can see their reaction if the United Nations or any government dares say something to them: 'Who are you to accuse us? We are the victims and don't forget it; you are anti-Semitic – do you want another Holocaust?' And that is how they shut everyone up!"

"So how do you see the future?"

Lea hesitates, lost in her thoughts.

"At any rate, I don't want my children to stay here, if they don't fight. If one doesn't fight, one is participating in the oppression to a certain degree. But they refuse to leave the country, even though it is morally and physically dangerous.

"As for the future, anything can now happen. The only certainty I have is that if we continue to behave like oppressors, in the long term we won't stay here."

"The long term could be one or two centuries?"

"I don't think so. We were given a chance with the Oslo process and we failed. We had the opportunity to be accepted in the region and to integrate into the Middle East, but we lost it. Until the last few months, the great majority of Palestinians were very moderate and very understanding. I don't think that is the case with the new generation. Children who have seen so much violence will never forget it. And I don't think they should forget ...Before, the Palestinians did not know how to hate but now they are learning. We are good teachers!"

Her hoarse voices seems to break a bit more.

"I am starting to ask myself questions: is my presence here and my work for the rights of Palestinians – a work that I do as much for them as for my people, so that we can one day live together – just? Until now, it has been and people like me embodied a future promise and proof that it is possible to live together. But perhaps now, to be here doing what I do, playing the 'good Jew' gives the Palestinians the illusion that future cohabitation is possible when already it isn't ..."

"Don't tell me that – not you, Lea!"

She shakes her head. She seems exhausted.

"I don't know any more. I am telling you the thoughts that revolve in my head. My work here, what I am allowing Palestinians to hope, is an illusion ... Perhaps it would be better to leave them to face Jews of the extreme right, against whom they would be forced to fight to save their skin ...

"Today, many Palestinians continue not to hate Jews, but on the Jewish side, things are hardening. While we are far and away the greatest military power in the region, with the United States behind us, we are still haunted by the myth that we are a minority threatened with extermination. It is so hard to fight all these myths ...

"Sometimes I don't know what I am doing here, but at the same time I don't want to leave, not yet. I am fascinated; I have no idea what is going to happen."

She laughs like a little girl.

"I want to know the end of the story, if there is an end ..."

"So, I will still find you here in 30 years!"

"Probably ... because, despite everything I said, I am an unshakeable optimist. And then" – a soft light emanates from her green eyes – "I love the climate of this country, its landscapes and people. I want to be able to go on living here without betraying my commitment. No, I won't give up. I am not at all ready to give up."

Epilogue

THE ETHICS OF REVENGE

A speech made by Yitzhak Frankenthal, chairman of the Families Forum, at a rally in Jerusalem on Saturday, 27 July, 2002, outside the Prime Minister's residence:

"My beloved son Arik, my own flesh and blood, was murdered by Palestinians. My tall, blue-eyed, golden-haired son, who was always smiling with the innocence of a child and the understanding of an adult. My son. If, to strike his killers, innocent Palestinian children and other civilians would have to be killed, I would ask the security forces to wait for another opportunity. If the security forces were to kill innocent Palestinians as well, I would tell them they were no better than my son's killers.

"My beloved son Arik was murdered by a Palestinian. Should the security forces have information of this murderer's whereabouts and should it turn out that he was surrounded by innocent children and other Palestinian civilians, then – even if the security forces knew that the killer was planning another murderous attack that was to be launched within hours and they now had the choice of curbing a terror attack that would kill innocent Israeli civilians but at the cost of hitting innocent Palestinians – I would tell the security forces not to seek revenge but to try to avoid and prevent the death of innocent civilians, be they Israelis or Palestinians.

"I would rather have the finger that pushes the trigger or the button that drops the bomb tremble before it kills my son's murderer, than for innocent civilians to be killed. I would say to the security forces: do not kill the killer. Rather, bring him before an Israeli court. You are not the judiciary. Your motivation should not be vengeance, but the prevention of any injury to innocent civilians.

"Ethics are not black and white – they are all white. Ethics have to be free of vengefulness and rashness. Every act must be carefully weighed before a decision is made to see whether it meets strict ethical criteria. Ethics cannot be left to the discretion of anyone who is frivolous or trigger-happy. Our ethics are hanging by a thread, at the mercy of every soldier and politician. I am not at all sure that I am willing to delegate my ethics to them.

"It is unethical to kill innocent Israeli or Palestinian women and children. It is also unethical to control another nation and to lead it to lose its humanity. It is patently unethical to drop a bomb that kills innocent Palestinians. It is blatantly unethical to wreak vengeance upon innocent bystanders. It is, on the other hand, supremely ethical to prevent the death of any human being. But if such prevention causes the futile death of others, the ethical foundation for such prevention is lost.

A nation that cannot draw the line is doomed eventually to apply unethical measures against its own people. The worst in my mind is not what has already happened but what I am sure one day will. And it will – because ethics are now being twisted and the political and military leadership does not even have the most basic integrity to say: 'we are sorry'.

"We lost sight of our ethics long before the suicide bombings. The breaking point was when we started to control another nation.

"My son Arik was born into a democracy with a chance for a decent, settled life. Arik's killer was born into an appalling occupation, into an ethical chaos. Had my son been born in his stead, he may have ended up doing the same. Had I myself been born into the political and ethical chaos that is the Palestinians' daily reality, I would certainly have tried to kill and hurt the occupier; had I not, I would have betrayed my essence as a free man. Let all the self-righteous who speak of ruthless Palestinian murderers take a hard look in the mirror and ask themselves what they would have done had they been the ones living under occupation. I can say for myself that I, Yitzhak Frankenthal, would have undoubtedly become a freedom fighter and would have killed as many on the other side as I possibly could. It is this depraved hypocrisy that pushes the Palestinians to fight us relentlessly. Our double standard that allows us to boast the highest military ethics, while the same military slays innocent children. This lack of ethics is bound to corrupt us.

"My son Arik was murdered when he was a soldier, by Palestinian fighters who believed in the ethical basis of their struggle against the occupation. My son Arik was not murdered because he was Jewish but because he is part of one nation that occupies the territory of another.

"I know these are concepts that are unpalatable, but I must voice them loud and clear, because they come from my heart – the heart of a father whose son did not get to live because his people were blinded with power. As much as I would like to do so, I cannot say that the Palestinians are to blame for my son's death. That would be the easy way out, but it is we, Israelis, who are to blame, because of the occupation. Anyone who refuses to heed this awful truth will eventually lead to our destruction.

"The Palestinians cannot drive us away – they have long acknowledged our existence. They have been ready to make peace with us; it is we who are unwilling to make peace with them. It is we who insist on maintaining our control over them; it is we who escalate the situation in the region and feed the cycle of bloodshed. I regret to say it, but the blame is entirely ours.

"I do not mean to absolve the Palestinians and by no means to justify attacks against Israeli civilians. No attack against civilians can be condoned. But as an occupation force it is we who trample over human dignity, it is we who crush the liberty of Palestinians and it is we who push an entire nation to crazy acts of despair.

"Finally, I call on my brothers and sisters in the settlements – see what we have come to."

CHRONOLOGY

November 1917 Lord Balfour, British Foreign Minister, announces that his government would undertake to 'facilitate the establishment of a Jewish National Home in Palestine'.

1920 Riots in Jerusalem against Jewish immigration. Foundation of the *Haganah*, an organisation of Jewish militia that will later become the Israeli Army.

1922 League of Nations confers the mandate of Palestine, formerly a part of the Ottoman empire, on Great Britain.

1929 Riots throughout Palestine against the increase in Jewish immigration and the purchase of land by the Jewish national fund.

1936–1939 The 'great Palestinian revolt' against the acceleration of Jewish immigration and the British proposal to divide Palestine into two states, one Jewish and one Arab. For the first time, Zionist groups use the weapon of terrorism. *Irgun*, led by Menahem Begin, explodes bombs in public places, killing dozens of people.

May 1939 On the eve of war, London proposes the creation in Palestine of a unified state in which Jews and Arabs would share power – a proposal immediately rejected by both Palestinian and Jewish leaders. To obtain Arab support against the Nazi regime, London decides to limit Jewish immigration as well as the purchase of land by Zionists.

Spring 1942 the World Zionist Organisation no longer officially demands a Jewish national home in Palestine but the creation of a Jewish state in the whole of Palestine and unrestricted immigration.

July 1946 *Irgun* attack in the King David Hotel, the British headquarters, kills 91 people.

29 November 1947 Moved by the fate of Holocaust survivors, the Assembly General of the United Nations adopts Resolution 181 calling for the partition of Palestine into a Jewish state (55 per cent), an Arab state and a zone around Jerusalem that will be under international authority. Protests by the Palestinians, who have accepted tens of thousands of refugees throughout the war but who refuse to have their country partitioned.

Spring 1948 Jewish militia terrorise Palestinians and drive them out of their villages.

9–10 April 1948 The massacre by Jewish militia of around a hundred Palestinian villagers in Deir Yassin causes tens of thousands of civilians to flee. Throughout spring and summer 1948, the Jewish militia attack villages: 370 are destroyed.

14 May 1948 Arab armies, refusing the partition proposal, enter Palestine. They are defeated and around 800,000 Palestinians become refugees.

11 December 1948 Resolution 194 of the United Nations proclaims the right of refugees to return home or to compensation.

1949 An armistice between Israel and Arab states is signed. The land mass of Israel is now composed of 78 per cent of Palestine, an increase of 23 per cent compared with what was granted under the United Nations' resolution.

May 1964 Creation in Jerusalem of the Palestine Liberation Organisation, with Fatah as its armed wing.

1st January 1965 Fatah's first military action in Israel.

June 1967 The Six-Day War, as a result of which Israel occupies the whole of the rest of Palestine (the West Bank, the Gaza Strip and east Jerusalem), as well as the Egyptian Sinai and Syrian Golan Heights.

22nd November 1967 The United Nations adopts Resolution 242 which, while reaffirming Israel's right of existence and security, demands the 'withdrawal of the armed forces from the occupied territories'. This is the principle of peace in exchange for the territories.

February 1969 Yasser Arafat becomes president of the executive committee of the PLO.

October 1973 Yom Kippur War.

March 1977 The National Council of the PLO accepts for the first time the idea of an independent Palestinian state created from only part of Palestine.

September 1978 Signing of the Camp David agreement between Egypt and Israel.

June 1982 Israeli invasion of Lebanon. In September, around 2000 Palestinian civilians are massacred in the refugee camps of Sabra and Shatila.

December 1987 The first intifada, or 'war of stones', begins in Gaza and then the West Bank.

November 1988 The PLO proclaims the State of Palestine, recognises United Nations Resolutions 181 and 242 and reaffirms its condemnation of terrorism.

9–10 September 1993 Israel and the PLO recognise each other.

13th September 1993 Oslo Accords. At the White House, Rabin and Arafat sign a declaration of principle on interim arrangements for autonomy of the Palestinian Territories, a process which is to finish in April 1999.

25th February 1994 Baruch Goldstein assassinates 29 Palestinians praying in the Hebron mosque. The Palestinian organisation *Hamas* announces that it will henceforth include civilians in its attacks.

24th April 1994 The Palestinian National Council erases from its charter all articles denying Israel's right to exist.

4th May 1994 Signature in Cairo of the agreement on the autonomy of the Gaza Strip and the town of Jericho.

1st July 1994 Triumphal return of Yasser Arafat to Gaza.

28th September 1995 After several months of peace, Arafat and Rabin sign the Oslo 2 Accords in Washington, on the extension of Palestinian autonomy in the West Bank.

4th November 1995 Rabin is assassinated by an Israeli student from the religious extreme right.

December 1995 Israel withdraws from the six large towns of the occupied territories, except Hebron.

20th January 1996 Arafat is elected president of the Palestinian Authority.

February–March 1996 After a period of peace, the Israeli Secret Service assassinates Ayache, the weapons expert for *Hamas*, the extremist Palestinian group that had agreed to stop the attacks. The terrorist actions begin again, resulting in over a hundred deaths and destabilising the Peres government, which had taken over after Rabin's assassination.

29th May 1996 Netanyahu and his right-wing and extreme right-wing coalition gain victory in the Israeli elections.

27th September 1996 The opening of a tunnel under the Esplanade of the Mosques provokes the worst violence in the occupied territories since the end of the intifada in 1993.

September 1997 Arafat orders the Palestinian police to close 16 offices and associations linked to *Hamas*.

4th May 1999 End of the interim period of Palestinian autonomy set out in the agreement of 13th September 1993. The PLO agrees to postpone the declaration of an independent Palestinian state until after the Israeli elections.

17th May 1999 Election of the Labour candidate Ehud Barak.

4th January 2000 Israel transfers 6.1 per cent of the West Bank to the Palestinians. The Palestinian Authority now has total control of 17.1 per cent of the West Bank and partial control of 23.9 per cent. Israel keeps total control of 59 per cent of the West Bank and 30 per cent of Gaza.

11–24 July 2000 Ariel Sharon visits the Esplanade of the Mosques in Jerusalem, accompanied by a large police escort.

29th September 2000 Violent confrontations on the Esplanade of the Mosques. The police respond to the throwing of stones with rubber bullets and real bullets. Seven Palestinians are killed. The second intifada begins.

30th September 2000 In the Palestinian territories, Israeli soldiers respond to stones with real bullets. Fourteen people are killed and hundreds wounded in the West Bank and in Gaza, a boy of 12, Muhammed al-Durra, is filmed dying in his father's arms, becoming the symbol of the intifada.

October 2000 In Israel, peaceful demonstrations by Israeli Arabs against the events on the Esplanade of the Mosques are suppressed by the Army, killing 13 people and wounding hundreds of others.

1st and 2nd October 2000 In the West Bank and Gaza, armoured vehicles and fighter helicopters shoot young people armed with stones and incendiary bottles. Around 30 Palestinian deaths, including a baby, and hundreds of wounded. The Security Council condemns the excessive use of force by the Israeli army.

2nd October 2000 First Israeli civilian death in the occupied territories.

12th October 2000 Two Israeli soldiers are lynched in Ramallah. In retaliation, there are air raids against Palestinian towns, and blockades.

According to the Israeli human rights organisation, *B'T Selem*, between the 29th September and the 12th October, two Israeli civilians and five soldiers were killed in the occupied territories, but there are no victims in Israel itself, while 55 Palestinian civilians and 14 members of the security forces were killed in the occupied territories.

2nd November 2000 First attack on civilians in Israel: two dead and ten wounded in Jerusalem.

21–27 January 2001 Talks at Taba between Israelis and Palestinians allow a solution finally to be envisaged, but Ehud Barak decides to suspend the negotiations.

6th February 2001 Sharon is elected Prime Minister with 62.5 per cent of the vote. Opposed to the Oslo agreements signed by Rabin, he undertakes a policy of severe repression.

THE OSLO ACCORDS AND ZONES A, B, C, D

13 September 1993–28 September 1995

The Oslo accords, signed in Washington on the 13th September 1993 by Yasser Arafat and the Israeli Prime Minister Yitzhak Rabin, set out an agenda of negotiations to end in April 1999 with the conclusion of the 'final status' of the Palestinian territories occupied by Israel in 1967.

The Oslo 1 accord, titled 'Gaza and Jericho First', sanctioned, on the 13th April 1994, the withdrawal of Israeli forces from the Gaza Strip (except the 30 per cent reserved for the settlements) and from the town of Jericho.

The Oslo 2 accord, signed in Washington on the 28th September 1995, dealt with the extension of Palestinian autonomy in the West Bank.

Under this agreement, the West Bank and the Gaza Strip were divided into three zones:

Zone A comprising 3 per cent of the West Bank and around two-thirds of the Gaza Strip: in this zone the Palestinian National Authority (PNA) was to be responsible for civil and security matters.

Zone B 24 per cent of the West Bank, a mainly rural zone that included numerous villages in which the PNA was to be responsible for civil matters, the Israeli Army keeping control of security.

Zone C 73 per cent of the West Bank, comprising Jewish settlements, Israeli military bases and state land, which was to remain under Israeli sovereignty.

Zone D consisting of borders, main roads and places where the security forces for the Jewish settlements were stationed, all under Israeli control.

However, Israeli governments did not respect the time frame for the different stages. In April 1999, when the West Bank and Gaza should have been awarded final status, the Palestinian Authority had total control of only 7 per cent of the West Bank, including the big cities and two thirds of the tiny Gaza Strip.

Elected Prime Minister in May 1999, Ehud Barak favoured the Syrian issue over that of Palestine. When he finally turned his attention to it, in spring 2000, his majority had decreased and Palestinian distrust increased. The Palestinians still had control of only 17.1 per cent of the West Bank and the civil administration of 23.9 per cent.

Barak then decided to hold a summit meeting to deal with all the unresolved issues at once. Yasser Arafat objected that it was an unrealistic aim but ended by agreeing to it, at the insistence of President Clinton.

This meeting was the negotiations of Camp David 2.

CAMP DAVID 2

11–25 July 2000

Because of the numerous discrepancies between the Israeli and Palestinian points of view, the negotiations failed. The blame was attributed to Yasser Arafat, for refusing the 'generous proposals' of the Israelis, such as the creation of a Palestinian state on 95 per cent of the West Bank and the whole of the Gaza Strip, with east Jerusalem as capital. Also, according to this interpretation, the insistence of the President of the Palestinian Authority on the right of return of the millions of Palestinian refugees buried any possibility of what would have been a historic peace.

However, several dissenting voices have shed a different light on what happened at Camp David, confirming the account of one of the Palestinian negotiators, Akram Haniyye: Robert Malley, President Clinton's special adviser on Arab–Israeli affairs, the three Israeli negotiators Oded Eran, Amnon Lipkin-Shahak and Ami Ayalon and Charles Enderlin, whose book *Shattered Dreams* is based on interviews with the negotiators.

In fact, the Palestinian state proposed by Ehud Barak would have had only a limited sovereignty; Israel would have annexed 9 per cent of the

West Bank for its settlements, in exchange for 1 per cent of Israeli territory. Israel would also have had a 'long-term lease' on around 10 per cent of land along the Jordan River, that separates Palestine from Jordan. The new Palestinian state, which is already made up of only 22 per cent of the original Palestine (78 per cent having been lost to Israel in 1948, the Palestinians demanded only the 22 per cent occupied after the 1967 war), would therefore have had another 19 per cent amputated.

In addition, the two large settlement blocks attached to Israel, containing 8 per cent of the settlers, would have cut the West Bank into three pieces, preventing the territorial continuity that is the indispensable basis of a state.

Barak had taken an historic step by conceding a degree of sovereignty over East Jerusalem (the Arab part of the city) to the Palestinians. But this was only in regard to outlying districts (such as Shuafat and Beit Hanina); the central districts such as Sheikh Jarah, Silwan and Ras al Amoud would have only an administrative autonomy, with Israeli sovereignty remaining.

The Palestinians would also be given mere custodianship of the Esplanade of the Mosques, the Israelis keeping sovereignty over it. Finally, Israel would have kept control of Palestine's external borders, positioning forces on the eastern border with Jordan and the southern border with Egypt.

As to the central question of the fate of refugees, nothing specific was discussed, the Israeli delegation having merely referred to a 'satisfactory solution'.

THE TABA NEGOTIATIONS

21–27 January 2001

Despite the failure of Camp David 2, negotiations continued and the delegations met in the last week of January at Taba, Egypt.

In their final communiqué of 27 January 2001, the parties declared that they had never been so close to an agreement. The documents drafted on the four principal issues (territory, Jerusalem, security, refugees) confirmed that assessment:

- The Israeli delegation offered to return ninety-four per cent of the West Bank and, in exchange for the annexed six per cent (in which most settlers currently live), to give the equivalent of three per cent of Israeli territory, in addition to the three per cent of the 'safe passage' linking the West Bank and Gaza. They also agreed to settlers leaving the centre of Hebron and to the dismantling of the few settlements remaining in Palestinian territory. Finally, in response to a demand formulated at Camp David 2, Israel would give up the Jordan valley.

- For its part, the Palestinian delegation agreed to give up two per cent of the West Bank (comprising around sixty-five per cent of the settlements), in exchange for an equivalent amount of territory (the Israelis offered the sand dunes at Halutza in the Negev desert, bordering the Gaza Strip), the evacuation to take place shortly afterwards – three years according to the Israelis, eighteen months according to the Palestinians.

- The two positions also got closer on the issue of the shared sovereignty of Jerusalem. The Israelis accepted that the city of Jerusalem should be the capital of the two states, Yerushalam (west Jerusalem), the capital of Israel and Al Quds (east Jerusalem), the capital of Palestine. The Arab quarters of east Jerusalem would be incorporated into the Palestinian state and the Palestinians agreed to give Israel those areas annexed in 1967.

- On the holy sites, the Palestinians demanded sovereignty of Haram Al-Sharif (the Esplanade of the Mosques) and the Israelis the whole of the western wall (sovereignty of the holy sites would be entrusted for a limited period to the five members of the Security Council and Morocco).

- Views also converged on the issue of security. The Palestinians conceded a limit on their national armament and the establishment, under certain conditions, of three Israeli water gauging stations. The presence of an international force on the borders was accepted.

There were also the beginnings of a solution to the question of the 3.7 million Palestinian refugees scattered throughout Jordan, Syria, the Lebanon and the autonomous territories.

Although these negotiations had reached an advanced stage, they were interrupted at Ehud Barak's request so that an election campaign could be held. By deciding to resign from office at the beginning of December 2000, Ehud Barak provoked an early election, fixed for the 6th February 2001.

In order that the gains of the previous months would not be lost, the two delegations nonetheless charged Miguel Angel Moratinos, the European Union special envoy, present at Taba – the United States, in the midst of a presidential transition, sent no delegate – with drawing up a statement of conclusions. This would never be put into operation. Once in power, Ariel Sharon refused all negotiations and instead undertook intensified repression of the intifada.

The Taba negotiations were the last official dealings between the Israelis and the Palestinians. That the two parties came very close to a solution underlines the importance of these talks.

The breakdown in communication was followed by international interventions such as 'The Road Map' – proposed by the Quartet, composed of the UN, USA, European Union and Russia – and private initiatives such as the Geneva Talks, but no official meetings between the two countries concerned.

THE RIGHT OF RETURN

At first glance, the question of the right of return seems completely insoluble and Israeli governments have made it one of the principal reasons why agreement can never be reached with the Palestinians.

In fact, there are around 3,700,000 Palestinian refugees, scattered over Syria, Jordan, Lebanon and the autonomous territories. They are the descendants of the diaspora of 1948, when, according to UNWRA, around 800,000 fled their villages, a third into the West Bank, a third into Gaza and the remaining third into Jordan, Syria and the rest of the world. After the 1967 war, another wave of refugees, around 300,000, fled into Jordan.

Resolution 194 of the United Nations of December 1948 stipulates that 'those refugees who wish to return home and live in peace with their neighbour should have the right to do so as soon as possible'. Israel rejected this, arguing that that would alter the balance of the Zionist state, a nation created for Jews.

Along with the status of Jerusalem, this question is one of the principal stumbling blocks in the peace negotiations.

But at the Taba negotiations in September 2001, the negotiators managed to make considerable strides. The Palestinian delegation effectively established a difference between the 'right of return', on which they cannot compromise, and its application, ground on which there can be many compromises. The Israeli delegation accepted this notion and made a two-tier proposal, one of principle and the other of practice.

For the first time, Israel recognised its responsibility in the refugee tragedy, agreed to contribute directly to a solution and affirmed that this should lead to the application of resolution 194.

Refugees would be offered five possibilities:

- Return to Israel
- Return to the Israeli territories ceded by Israel to Palestine
- Return to the Palestinian state
- Settlement in their place of residence (Jordan, Syria, etc.)
- Departure to another country (several states, including Canada, having already signalled a willingness to accept large numbers of Palestinians).

Israel would consent to a return to its territory over a period of 15 years, with 25,000 refugees returning in the first three years. The Palestinians have not offered figures, but say that anything below 100,000 would be insufficient, while affirming that they do not wish to alter the Jewish character of the State of Israel.

An international commission and fund would rapidly be set up to compensate the refugees.